Understanding China

The series will provide you with in-depth information on China's social, cultural and economic aspects. It covers a broad variety of topics, from economics and history to law, philosophy, cultural geography and regional politics, and offers a wealth of materials for researchers, doctoral students, and experienced practitioners.

Xiaobo Dong • Meng Zhang

Chinese Rule of Law Discourse System

Theoretical Basis, Innovative Pathways, and Global Governance

Springer

Xiaobo Dong
School of Foreign Languages and Cultures
Nanjing Normal University
Nanjing, Jiangsu, China

Meng Zhang
School of Foreign Languages and Cultures
Nanjing Normal University
Nanjing, Jiangsu, China

ISSN 2196-3134 ISSN 2196-3142 (electronic)
Understanding China
ISBN 978-981-95-6259-6 ISBN 978-981-95-6260-2 (eBook)
https://doi.org/10.1007/978-981-95-6260-2

This Springer imprint is published by the registered company Springer Nature Singapore Pte Ltd.
The registered company address is: 152 Beach Road, #21-01/04 Gateway East, Singapore 189721, Singapore

Preface

Today, amidst the surging tide of globalization and profound transformations in the international landscape, China stands firm on the world stage with a more confident and open attitude. The remarkable achievements and rich experiences in its rule of law construction have not only become an important cornerstone for national development but also increasingly attracted extensive attention and in-depth exploration from the international community. Against this backdrop, the book "Chinese Rule of Law Discourse System: Theoretical Basis, Innovative Pathways, and Global Governance" has emerged. It aims to systematically sort out, conduct in-depth analyses, and innovate and develop Chinese rule of law discourse system, contributing Chinese wisdom and Chinese solutions to the progress of global rule of law civilization.

At the beginning of this book, a multi-dimensional and in-depth framework for understanding the rule of law discourse is established. It clarifies the concept and core role of the rule of law discourse, laying a theoretical foundation for subsequent analyses. Subsequently, the book delves deeply into the rich connotations, development history of Chinese rule of law discourse, and the central position of the "Chinese characteristics." When tracing the origin of the rule of law ideology, the book points out that Chinese rule of law ideology not only absorbs the essence of Western ideas but is also deeply rooted in the outstanding traditional Chinese political thought, forming a unique rule of law theory which builds an important platform for the exchange and mutual learning of global rule of law civilizations. Furthermore, the book elaborately analyzes the basic components of Chinese rule of law discourse system, especially the fundamental discourse and the cornerstone discourse, revealing the internal logic and practical path of Chinese rule of law construction. In the face of the challenges of the new era, from three aspects of significance, dilemmas, and missions, the book systematically proposes an innovative path for Chinese rule of law discourse, emphasizing the importance of constructing Chinese rule of law discourse system in enhancing the country's soft power and participating in global governance. To this end, it puts forward basic principles and the crucial role of translation in the international communication of the rule of law discourse, providing comprehensive guidance for enhancing the international communication ability of Chinese rule of law discourse.

This book not only comprehensively reviews and innovatively develops Chinese rule of law discourse system but also demonstrates a sense of responsibility for the progress of global rule of law civilization. We hope that through the elaboration in this book, the international community will gain a better understanding of and show greater recognition for Chinese rule of law. Together, we can promote the building of a community with a shared future for mankind and contribute to the prosperity of global rule of law civilization.

Nanjing, China Xiaobo Dong
Nanjing, China Meng Zhang

Competing Interests The authors have no competing interests to declare that are relevant to the content of this manuscript.

Contents

About the Authors

Xiaobo Dong is a Distinguished Professor of Jilin International Studies University and a Professor at School of Foreign Languages and Cultures of Nanjing Normal University, Deputy Director of the Belt and Road Rule of Law Research Center at Academy of China's Modernization of Rule of Law and Researcher at Jiangsu Academy of Talent Development Strategy. He is a renowned contemporary Chinese jurist and legal linguist in China. He is also the Director and Chief Expert of Jiangsu International Rule of Law Research Center, as well as the Chief Expert on major projects of the National Social Science Fund of China. His research interests include history of Sino-west civilization exchanges, legal linguistics, legal translation, language strategy and planning, and cross-cultural communication. In recent years, he has published over 250 interdisciplinary academic papers in prominent journals and more than 80 books, including academic monographs, edited volumes, and translations. He has authored multiple English academic monographs published by internationally leading publishing groups and has dozens of research papers published in high-level journals such as Nature. He enjoys a distinguished academic reputation internationally.

Meng Zhang is Ph.D. candidate at the School of Foreign Languages and Cultures at Nanjing Normal University, and a lecturer at the School of English at Jilin International Studies University. Her research interests include legal linguistics, legal translation, and language policy and planning.

Chapter 1
Concept Definition and Differentiation of Chinese Rule of Law Discourse

1.1 Introduction

Discourse refers to phrases and brief sentences used to express certain beliefs and stances. It declares value pursuits, highlights ideology, and achieves ritualistic communication that influences people's thoughts, behaviors, and even the entire society (Liu, 2018). In terms of its general definition, the rule of law discourse is a language symbol system created through the application of rule of law thinking, with the basic function of highlighting the spirit of the rule of law and promoting the ideal of the rule of law. Generally speaking, as a symbolic representation of ideology, the rule of law discourse not only functions as an internal symbolic discourse but also has the functions of ideological expression and cultural education. The rule of law discourse is a product of the rule of law's development to a certain stage. In a sense, the rule of law discourse is a rational expression. The emergence of the rule of law discourse is a manifestation of human civilization's progress, and its spreading is conducive to the advancement of the rule of law civilization. Only in a society where the rule of law is realized can there be a systematic and complete expression of the rule of law discourse.

Due to variations in rule of law contexts, the rule of law discourse inevitably presents different specific forms. As a rule of law cultural phenomenon, the rule of law discourse is the result of the application of the rule of law theory of a certain period to social practice, and it has practicality and a sense of the times. Differences in time, region, and culture lead to disparities in people's understanding of the rule of law in different historical periods and different countries, thus giving rise to a variety of different rule of law discourses. The rule of law discourse condenses the essence and wisdom of human rule of law thoughts and is the product of mutual reference and exchange among countries. However, it must also be based on the national conditions of each country, making it close to the country's actual situation, local life, and local people, so that it can be mastered and used by the people. Therefore, where there is a country's rule of law, there is a

X. Dong, M. Zhang, *Chinese Rule of Law Discourse System*, Understanding China, https://doi.org/10.1007/978-981-95-6260-2_1

country's rule of law discourse, and a country's rule of law discourse must reflect the country's special national conditions.

A specific rule of law discourse is closely related to a specific rule of law culture. A country's rule of law discourse is rooted in its rule of law culture and is an external and specific manifestation of the rule of law culture. The rule of law culture provides continuous nourishment for the rule of law discourse, and the rule of law discourse presents the rich connotations of the rule of law culture through systematic expression. The rule of law discourse has the rational characteristics of modern civilization. Its rational nature requires it to express ideological demands fairly, express rule of law theories and experiences in accurate and concise language, and conduct objective analyses of the contradictions and problems arising in society in a rigorous and logical manner. In essence, the rule of law discourse is a concentrated expression of rule of law thinking and a language symbol system that embodies the spirit, concepts, and principles of the rule of law. In practice, the rule of law discourse is an indispensable form of expression and application method for demonstrating the status of rule of law culture construction, the path and direction of rule of law development, and the problems and contradictions existing in the rule of law society.

The rule of law discourse has a certain internal structure. From the perspective of the internal structure of discourse, "Discourse consists of two interdependent parts. One part is the content of the discourse, that is, the ideological content expressed by the speaker; the other part is the form of the discourse, that is, the form through which the speaker expresses thoughts, and this form is language" (Fan, 1994). Similarly, the rule of law discourse also consists of content and form. Among them, the content of the rule of law discourse mainly refers to rule of law concepts and rule of law beliefs. The former is the rational sum of knowledge, emotion, will, belief, and other ideological concepts and value judgments about the rule of law; the latter is a sense of identity, conversion, and sacred experience naturally generated by social subjects on the basis of a rational understanding of rule of law phenomena after summarizing the experiences of governing the country and society in accordance with the law. It is the mainstream ideology for adjusting social relations and arranging social order (Ji, 2015). When rule of law practice conveys rule of law concepts to every citizen through a certain form of language and forms rule of law beliefs in the citizens' hearts, it will further cultivate the rule of law culture of the whole people. If there is an ideological and cultural foundation, the rule of law will have a soft binding force, and the cause of the rule of law will obtain a strong and lasting driving force. The form of the rule of law discourse refers to the language used to express the content of the rule of law discourse, such as rule of law-related concepts and judgments, that is, specific words and sentences.

1.2 Concept Definition

The development process of Chinese rule of law discourse has been magnificent, and its conceptual connotations are rich and profound. These two aspects are closely intertwined, jointly depicting a unique picture of Chinese rule of law construction.

From the perspective of evolution, the rule of law discourse in China has undergone a long and continuous transformation. It germinated during the ideological debates in ancient times, then underwent a transformation in the "rule of law" discourse during the modern social changes. After the founding of the People's Republic of China, it has been constantly innovated with national construction.

The exploration of the socialist market economy opened a new chapter in rule of law practice. Reform promoted the transformation from "rule by man" to "rule by law", and social transformation continuously enriched its connotations. New concepts such as the "concept of socialist rule of law" emerged one after another. After the 18th National Congress of the Communist Party of China, it achieved a systematic leap. This process is not only the growth of the rule of law discourse itself but also a vivid manifestation of the interaction between social development and rule of law construction, reflecting the needs and directions of national governance in different historical periods.

Chinese rule of law discourse is an important support for rule of law construction. Domestically, it fosters consensus and resolves conflicts; internationally, it showcases the country's image and safeguards its rights and interests. Centered around the rule of law thinking, it guides people to act in accordance with the law and shapes the concept of the rule of law. It comprehensively embodies the spirit of the rule of law, permeates all aspects of national governance, and highlights the people's principal status and traditional governance wisdom. It is a high-level abstraction of the rule of law theory and model, reflecting the goals and pursuits of the socialist rule of law with Chinese characteristics.

It can be said that the evolution of the rule of law discourse provides a practical foundation for the formation and development of its concept, while an in-depth analysis of its concept more clearly demonstrates the important position and role of the rule of law discourse in Chinese rule of law construction. They complement each other, jointly promoting the continuous progress of Chinese rule of law cause and laying a solid foundation for further exploration of the rule of law discourse planning.

1.2.1 The Evolution of Contemporary Chinese Rule of Law Discourse

The emergence and change of the rule of law discourse in China is a continuous development process. From "Contention of a Hundred Schools of Thought" and the "Age of Confucian Classics Studies" to the modern transformation of the "rule of law" discourse, the discourses of different periods reflect corresponding implications. After the founding of the People's Republic of China, the development of the rule of law discourse entered a new era.

The earliest policy-level establishment of "rule by law" in China can be traced back to 1992. Since the decision to comprehensively build a socialist market economy, China has started to explore the rule of law practice within the framework of the socialist market economy, replacing the governance relying on policies and administrative orders with laws and rules (Yu & Luo, 2023, p. 28). The Third Plenary Session of the 11th Central Committee of the Communist Party of China put forward the main guiding principles of "emancipating the mind and reform and opening up", which provided objective conditions for the development of the rule of law discourse. With the deepening of reform, the rule of law discourse was justified in the logical transformation from "rule by man" to "rule by law" and from "legal system" to "rule by law". These discussions foreshadowed the restart of the exploration process of the rule of law discourse.

Since the 1990s, the legal circle has continuously delved into the "rule of law" domain, with the discussion focus concentrated on the connotations, values, components, standards, and realization of the rule of law. The change of the rule of law discourse takes social transformation as the "context". With China's accession to the World Trade Organization in the early twenty-first century, the economy grew rapidly, interests were clearly differentiated, and society changed drastically. In 2006, the Central Committee of the Communist Party of China officially put forward the concept of the "concept of socialist rule of law" based on the value foundation and governance concept of Chinese rule of law. Subsequently, at the 17th National Congress of the Communist Party of China, the "concept of socialist rule of law" was written into the plenary session report, integrating "socialism" and "rule by law", representing a new development trend of Chinese rule of law discourse. Since the twenty-first century, the rule of law discourse has shown more obvious concrete characteristics, clarifying that "having laws to go by" is the foundation for realizing the rule of law blueprint, and "constructing a legal system" has become the core category in the rule of law discourse system. It was judged that "the socialist legal system with Chinese characteristics has been formed". Since the 18th National Congress of the Communist Party of China, contemporary China has entered a deepening period and a new stage of the construction of the socialist rule of law with Chinese characteristics. The scope of the rule of law discourse has become more comprehensive. The Fourth Plenary Session of the 18th Central Committee of the Communist Party of China promoted the systematic leap of the rule of law discourse with expressions such as the "rule of law system" and the "rule of law China" (Fu & Chi, 2020).

Chinese rule of law is a summary of practical experience and a path choice that embodies national consciousness and people's consciousness. When facing the rule of law discourse that embodies the wisdom and experience of the rule of law, it is also necessary to clearly recognize the national consciousness, people's consciousness, and rule of law consciousness it bears. It is clear that both rule of law construction and the rule of law discourse are integrated into the changes of national governance. Reviewing the changes of the rule of law discourse is to sort out the interactive development process between social development and rule of law construction and also serves as the "historical context" for further exploration of the rule of law discourse planning.

1.2.2 Clarification of the Concept of Chinese Rule of Law Discourse

Chinese rule of law discourse is an aggregate that comprehensively elaborates on the thoughts, theories, cultures, and languages of Chinese rule of law construction practice. It embodies the rule of law thinking and spirit based on Chinese rule of law path. It forms a complete system and has the following characteristics.

Firstly, Chinese rule of law discourse is an important support for rule of law construction. The improvement of Chinese rule of law system must be accompanied by corresponding construction of rule of law discourse. Under the conditions of the socialist market economy, with the multiplicity of ideas and values, interests are prone to confrontation and conflicts. As a result, Chinese rule of law construction faces numerous obstacles in terms of ideas and values. Meanwhile, in the international community, due to differences in political systems, China's socialist rule of law with Chinese characteristics has been facing varying degrees of suspicion, hostility, and even resistance, making it difficult to accurately convey Chinese rule of law voice. Culture serves as the bond and adhesive of society, and values are the spiritual pillar and guiding force for social actions. Therefore, the rule of law discourse, which carries rule of law culture and values, is an effective way to address the differences in ideas and the confrontation of interests at home and abroad in the process of rule of law construction. On the one hand, the rule of law discourse is conducive to rallying forces for domestic rule of law construction. A systematic and complete rule of law discourse can effectively unify complex and diverse ideas and expressions, and resolve issues of value differences and ideological conflicts. By advocating and leading the rule of law concept through systematic rule of law discourse, and through the continuous adaptation of the rule of law concept, people can reach a high-level consensus on the direction of rule of law development, thereby resolving potential conflicts. On the other hand, a systematic rule of law discourse system can effectively tell the story of Chinese rule of law, convey Chinese rule of law ideas, and showcase the achievements of Chinese rule of law construction in international rule of law exchanges. With Chinese rule of law wisdom and spirit, it can correctly present a trustworthy, respectable, and friendly image of China, safeguard national security, and gain the right to define and interpret Chinese rule of law in the international community. Therefore, for the rule of law to truly take root in people's hearts, the rule of law discourse must be coordinated with the legal system. The law can not only maintain social order but also nourish people's hearts.

Secondly, the core of Chinese rule of law discourse is the rule of law thinking. The rule of law discourse can directly reflect the thinking mode of the people in managing social, economic, cultural affairs in accordance with the law, namely the rule of law thinking. The thinking choice of the ruling party largely determines the thinking of a country. In the new historical period, the Communist Party of China has made the momentous historical choices of establishing the rule of law as the basic strategy for the Party to lead the people in governing the country and the rule of law in governance as the basic mode of the Party's governance. At the same time, it has vigorously promoted the rule of law thinking, which have all influenced Chinese rule of law process and shaped the thinking mode of the Chinese people. The report of the 18th National Congress of the Communist Party of China explicitly put forward the concept of "rule of law thinking", and major decisions of the Party's Central Committee have elaborated on it, providing the core of rule of law thinking for the formation of a complete rule of law discourse system with Chinese characteristics. In essence, the rule of law thinking requires taking the law as the criterion for judging right and wrong, using the law as the code of conduct for people, and then advocating the rule of law, respecting the law, and being good at using legal means to solve problems and promote work. The proposal and increasing emphasis on the rule of law thinking also make it necessary to conduct systematic research on the rule of law discourse. It can be seen that the rule of law discourse takes the rule of law thinking as its core and content, and the two are closely related.

Thirdly, Chinese rule of law discourse comprehensively reflects the spirit of the rule of law. The essence of the rule of law lies in the implementation of "governance". Chinese rule of law discourse demands that the spirit of the rule of law permeate all aspects of the Party's governance, national governance, and military governance. Primarily, it requires the ruling Party to govern the country in accordance with the law. The inner-Party regulations are a means to manage the Party and ensure its discipline through the rule of law approach. Only when the ruling Party applies the rule of law approach in its self-governance can it better govern the country in accordance with the law. This is the best manifestation of the spirit of the rule of law. Chinese rule of law discourse adheres to the spirit of the rule of law that places the people at the center and values the family and society. On the one hand, the socialist rule of law with Chinese characteristics shares the same values of freedom, equality, and justice as Western rule of law systems. On the other hand, it is deeply rooted in the long-standing traditional Chinese political and legal culture, fully inheriting the millennia-old experience of national governance and the governance concept of pursuing good laws and good governance. Undoubtedly, Chinese rule of law discourse should embody the socialist spirit of the rule of law, which takes socialism as its goal, draws on Western rule of law experiences, and is based on outstanding traditional Chinese culture.

Fourthly, Chinese rule of law discourse is a high-level condensation of the rule of law theory and the rule of law model. The socialist rule of law model with Chinese characteristics reflected in Chinese rule of law discourse must embody the goal-orientation of "deepening reform, promoting development, resolving conflicts, and maintaining stability". It requires a profound understanding and application of the rule of law approach from the strategic height of national governance. Meanwhile, it should also reflect the principles of the supremacy of the constitution and laws, respect for and protection of human rights, advocate the legitimate exercise of state-organ powers and the effective protection of citizens' rights, and pursue procedural fairness and substantial justice. In the context of comprehensively deepening reform, the construction of Chinese rule of law discourse system necessitates a comprehensive and in-depth understanding of China's reform process and experiences. It is essential to distill iconic rule of law discourses to promote the construction of the rule of law in China. Chinese rule of law discourse system is composed of discourses formed in the practice of the Communist Party of China leading the Chinese people in national governance under the rule of law. This system emerged from the long-term application of the basic principles of Marxism in the practice of building the rule of law in China. It is refined from the practice of building and developing socialism with Chinese characteristics. Moreover, this rule of law discourse system is a result of systematic analysis, summary, and repeated refinement during the implementation of the socialist rule of law theory with Chinese characteristics and the construction of the rule of law discourse. It is also an innovative discourse system developed in the process of promoting the socialist rule of law culture with Chinese characteristics.

In general, Chinese rule of law discourse system supports the construction of the rule of law, takes the rule of law thinking as its core, and comprehensively reflects the spirit of the rule of law. It is formed in the historical process of building the path, system, theory, and culture of the socialist rule of law with Chinese characteristics. It directly reflects the essence, fundamental features, and fundamental orientation of the socialist rule of law path with Chinese characteristics. In essence, it is the Chinese expression of the socialist rule of law model and an important part of the Marxist rule of law discourse system.

1.3 Concept Analysis

As a compound concept, the rule of law discourse is formed by the combination of the concepts of "rule of law" and "discourse". It is intricately connected with adjacent concepts such as rule of law language, rule of law concepts, and rule of law culture. Therefore, when studying Chinese rule of law discourse system, it is necessary to analyze it in comparison with these adjacent concepts.

1.3.1 Rule of Law Discourse and Rule of Law Language

The concept of "discourse" originates from linguistics, yet discourse is not equivalent to language. Discourse consists of two parts: content and form, and the form of discourse is language (Fan, 1994). Discourse is an extension of language. It is the language conveyed by people through various means, including body language and verbal expression. Discourse is social in nature and is presented and utilized in the process of interpersonal interaction. "Discourse is a more abundant and complex specific social form formed by the combination of language and parole, referring to the specific speech mode intertwined with social power relations" (Foucault, 2016, p. 49). According to this view, the rule of law discourse is formed by the combination of the language and parole mode of the rule of law. It showcases complex and rich social systems such as economy, politics, and culture, and is closely related to the power formed by specific political ideologies. Since discourse is used for external communication and expressing certain ideas, the rule of law discourse is a tool for conducting external rule of law dialogues and exchanges, which emerges in a specific social context, namely the rule of law society, to maintain specific power relations.

The rule of law language is the external manifestation of the rule of law path and theory. The rule of law discourse is a vivid expression of the rule of law approach relied on by a rule of law country in governance. It can be said that it is not only the subjective manifestation of the ideology of a rule of law country, but also the basic expression of the rule of law spirit, and a description of the development process of the rule of law culture in a rule of law country. Rule of law culture cannot be separated from social customs and habits. As the verbal carrier of rule of law culture, the rule of law discourse has a specific target group and should reflect the deep-seated national cultural characteristics such as specific thinking habits, values, and beliefs. The way of expressing the rule of law discourse is influenced by traditional concepts, the development model, and the path of the rule of law. Meanwhile, the change of the rule of law discourse is often due to the change of the governance concept of the state and the government, and sometimes it is also a response to the international mainstream rule of law discourse.

The rule of law discourse is a written expression that demonstrates the rule of law spirit and promotes the rule of law ideal through language. As the direct expression of rule of law activities, the rule of law language has the following characteristics: First, it has the same rigor, unity, and standardization as the law; second, it has a certain degree of flexibility and adaptability, being able to keep pace with the development of rule of law practice; third, it has a wide influence. The law is generally applicable to all social members and is the basic code of conduct that all social members must abide by. Therefore, the rule of law language needs to be unified and standardized. To make it better accepted and spread by social members, the rule of law language must be concise. As a civilized discourse in a civilized society, the rule of law discourse has ideological, serious, scientific, and humanistic characteristics. The rule of law discourse continuously obtains new development in the dynamic process of continuous dialogue and interaction, and is gradually accepted and recognized by the public, thus gaining lasting vitality.

The differences between the rule of law discourse and the rule of law language can be summarized as follows: First, the rule of law discourse is a specific discourse mode in the specific political ideological context of a rule of law country and society. It is not limited to written text but also includes various ways of representing the rule of law spirit, such as behavior. In contrast, the rule of law language is only in the form of single language characters. Second, the carriers of the rule of law discourse are diverse, including not only the language symbols in basic rule of law activities but also the language symbols that promote the rule of law spirit in news reports, literary and artistic works, and the slogans of social groups. The rule of law language only exists in the specific written symbols in rule of law activities, such as the fixed written symbols in judicial activities. Third, as an extension and expansion of the rule of law language, the rule of law discourse covers both rule of law activities and areas outside rule of law activities, including the rule of law language and rule of law behavior. The rule of law language is only a component of the rule of law discourse. Fourth, the rule of law discourse focuses more on the representation of the rule of law spirit, rule of law thinking, rule of law concepts, and democratic rule of law ideas in the discourse, while the rule of law language only stays at the fixed structure and meaning of the language itself. Therefore, the rule of law discourse is a dynamic existence, while the rule of law language is a relatively static one.

1.3.2 Rule of Law Discourse and Rule of Law Concepts

A concept is a systematic collection of a subject's subjective and objective understandings of things. Rule of law concepts guide rule of law practices, prompting people to abide by the law, revere the law, and have faith in the rule of law. In turn, rule of law practices further consolidate rule of law concepts. Rule of law concepts are the spiritual qualities and conceptual elements of people regarding the rule of law, which means that people regard the law as the basic norm of social life, recognize the rule of law, submit to the authority of the law, and have faith in the law (Zhou & Zhu, 2010, p. 399). Rule of law concepts are formed through people's understanding of the rule of law in legal practices. On the one hand, rule of law concepts reflect the objective essence of the rule of law; on the other hand, they are people's subjective understanding of the rule of law. The so-called "concept" involves "observing". Only through long-term observation can one form a "notion", that is, an inner belief.

Firstly, people form an initial inner belief by implementing and coming into contact with the rule of law, and gradually transform it into trust and faith in the rule of law approach in their actions. This process of gradually understanding the rule of law is the "observation" and also the process by which the rule of law concept takes root in people's hearts. The end-point of this process is the "notion", and the insights gained from rule of law practices ultimately form legal concepts. Secondly, rule of law concepts are people's views on the ideology expressed by the rule of law thoughts they encounter. Rule of law concepts are derived from rule of law thoughts. Consciousness is only a basic condition for the formation of concepts. The formation of rule of law concepts comes from the thinking and judgment of the rule of law model. The rule of law has inherent stability and regularity, and the rule of law concepts formed by people are correspondingly stable. Once rule of law concepts are formed in people's hearts, their stability will gradually transform the concepts into a habit. Finally, rule of law concepts are reflected in people's value concepts, that is, the respect, admiration, and recognition of the rule of law. When the rule of law is transformed into people's daily behavior patterns and life concepts, it reaches a high-level and high-realm of legal culture.

The construction of a law-based country, a law-based government, and a law-based society hinges on relatively mature rule of law concepts among all citizens.

As ordinary citizens, they should have a clear understanding of their rights and a conscious awareness of abiding by their obligations. As leading cadres, on the basis of basic concepts of rights and obligations, they should not only have a power concept in line with the spirit of the rule of law, but also be models of law-abiding citizens, and have the sense of responsibility to safeguard the authority of the constitution and the law. Rule of law concepts are the foundation of rule of law culture, which are reflected in people's thoughts, behaviors, and attitudes towards the legal system. The acceptance, respect, and faith in the law and legal systems constitute the foundation of rule of law concepts, which support the law-based society and promote the rule of law process. The law-based society provides the soil for the germination, development, and maturity of citizens' rule of law concepts, and the continuous growth of rule of law concepts supports the continuous development of the law-based society.

Rule of law discourse, as the direct expression of rule of law concepts, reveals the profound meaning of rule of law concepts in many fields such as politics, economy, and culture. The core of discourse is the content expressed by concepts, and concepts are spread in the form of language, which is discourse. As an interactive discourse among the state, the government, and the public, rule of law discourse is also the product of communication and interaction among subjects. Therefore, through the process of interactive communication, rule of law discourse gradually spreads and permeates rule of law concepts into society. The criterion for evaluating whether one has the right to speak lies in whether one can effectively convey rule of law concepts. In the process of presenting rule of law concepts, rule of law discourse can not only clearly express the rule of law culture and rule of law ideals contained in rule of law concepts, but also reflect the public's rule of law faith. Rule of law concepts dominate the content of rule of law discourse, and in turn, are consolidated through the expression of rule of law discourse. Rule of law discourse and rule of law concepts are complementary to each other. One of the functions of rule of law discourse is to serve as a tool for external communication and interaction. If the rule of law concepts conveyed by rule of law discourse have world-wide significance and value, then this set of rule of law discourse is an advanced discourse with a leading and forward-looking position. In other words, advanced rule of law concepts are a prerequisite for obtaining international rule of law discourse power. The continuous innovation of rule of law concepts is one of the necessary conditions for maintaining international rule of law discourse power.

The differences between Western and Chinese concepts of the rule of law have given rise to disparities in their rule of law discourses. In Western countries, people's awareness of the rule of law was awakened relatively early, and the concept of the rule of law has become deeply ingrained. They have established a liberal rule of law discourse system centered around liberalism, safeguarded by "constitutionalism", and characterized by the separation of powers, judicial independence, and human-rights protection. In contrast, in traditional Chinese society, which is rooted in Confucian culture, the primary aim was to maintain the hierarchical ethics. Although there were various regulations and systems for national governance, the governance was more characterized by the rule of man. It was not until modern times, with the spread and penetration of Western civilization, that Chinese civilization gradually became aware of the drawbacks of the prevalence of the rule of man and the lack of the rule of law. The concept of the rule of law introduced from the West began to take root in China. After the reform and opening up, China gradually established the basic strategy of governing the country by law, and the rule of law has received unprecedented attention. Although China's concept of the rule of law was influenced by the West, and its legal theories and systems were imported from the West, in the process of solving China's own problems, it has also critically inherited traditional Chinese legal culture. It can be said that China's local concept of the rule of law has emerged from the inheritance of traditional Chinese concepts, the acceptance of modern Western concepts, and their integration in China's own legal practice. There are fundamental differences between Chinese and Western rule of law concepts in terms of background and culture. Since ancient times, traditional Chinese civilization has advocated concepts such as "benevolent governance", "rule by virtue", and "rites", and has explored strategies for national governance based on these concepts. These concepts are bound to have a certain impact on contemporary Chinese people's concept of the rule of law. China's concept of the rule of law is still in the process of modernization. It not only requires the discrimination, screening, and appropriate transformation of traditional Chinese concepts but also the selective and reasonable reference of Western rule of law concepts. Finally, both local and Western rule of law concepts need to be integrated into the practice of the rule of law under socialism with Chinese characteristics to form a new concept of the rule of law that suits China's national conditions.

1.3.3 Rule of Law Discourse and Rule of Law Culture

Rule of law culture is a subset of culture. Culture encompasses the material and spiritual wealth created by humanity over an extended historical period, including history, geography, customs, lifestyles, religious beliefs, literature and art, norms, institutions, ways of thinking, and values. The rule of law, discovered by humanity during the governance process, not only constitutes a culture integrating norms, institutions, ways of thinking, values, and spiritual beliefs but also represents a successful governance model summarized after numerous failed attempts in human history. Therefore, it bears historical significance and inheritability. Rule of law culture functions at multiple levels and in various scopes: Firstly, integrative function. Rule of law culture enables social members to reach a common understanding within the scope of the rule of law and engage in effective interactive communication. Secondly, directive function. It helps social members identify the boundaries and bottom lines of behavior, recognizing that the law serves as the yardstick for actions and that the rule of law is an endeavor of governing by rules.Thirdly, order-maintaining Function. Once established, rule of law culture allows the rule of law to maintain social order. With the absolute authority of the law, the inner recognition and reverence of social members for the rule of law sustain this value, thereby ensuring a more stable social order.The rule of law has a cultural attribute and is one of the ways in which culture exists and manifests. Rule of law culture is a culture that regards the law as the supreme authority. It encompasses value pursuits such as equality, freedom, democracy, and fairness, as well as legal systems, legal concepts, and practical and behavioral patterns of consciously enforcing, abiding by, and applying the law. More precisely, rule of law culture is centered around the establishment of the rule of law concept and mindset. Under the support of the rule of law concept, corresponding institutions are established, organizational structures are operated, and it forms a cultural form and social lifestyle in the process of building a law-based society. Although rule of law cultures vary among different countries under the rule of law, the persistent pursuit of fairness and justice, the respect for the law, the use of the law as the standard for measuring people's behavior, and the pursuit of rule by rules are consistent.

Rule of law discourse and rule of law culture mirror each other. The rule of law thinking, concepts, and spirits represented by the rule of law discourse ultimately originate from rule of law culture. Without rule of law culture, rule of law discourse would lack a foundation. Rule of law culture requires rule of law discourse as an external expression to showcase its profound connotations. Generally, rule of law discourse expresses and demonstrates rule of law culture through four levels: the spirit and concept of the rule of law; legal systems and the management mechanisms of a law-based society; behavioral rules and legal norms; and legal practice methods and behavioral habits. A country's rule of law discourse serves as a bridge for communication and interaction, facilitating the exchange and integration of different rule of law cultures. Advanced rule of law culture is one of the necessary conditions for mastering the rule of law discourse power. Only when a country's rule of law culture looks towards the world and the future can its rule of law discourse gain the initiative on the world stage. In the era of globalization, on the one hand, it is necessary to recognize the national characteristics of rule of law culture. On the other hand, it is essential to attempt to integrate a country's specific discourse with the international general discourse, enabling the global community to recognize the country's rule of law discourse power. This requires standing at a global perspective, eliminating cultural barriers and conflicts through the essential identity of rule of law culture, thus overcoming the obstacles in the communication and interaction of rule of law discourse. The traditional Chinese cultural concept of "harmony without uniformity" aims to achieve this goal. An open and inclusive rule of law culture naturally gives rise to an open and inclusive rule of law discourse. The characteristics of Chinese rule of law culture determine the unique development direction of its rule of law discourse. However, although the development of rule of law cultures in countries around the world has its own characteristics, there are also many commonalities. Therefore, in the process of promoting the exchange of rule of law cultures among countries and the construction of international rule of law, the country that masters the rule of law discourse power has the possibility of influencing other countries and the international community with its rule of law culture, laying a foundation for enhancing the soft power of rule of law culture.

1.3.4 Rule of Law Discourse and Rule of Law Ideal

An ideal represents a beautiful vision and expectation for the future, as well as the pursuit of a perfect state for a certain thing. The ideal of the rule of law refers to the perfect goals, aims, and states expected to be achieved through the implementation of the rule of law (Zhou & Zhu, 2010, p. 403). The ideal of the rule of law is a lofty goal explored by human society in the practice of governance. A democratic and law-based country is the ideal blueprint of all humanity for the future society. Achieving this grand goal requires long-term and collective efforts from humanity. The ideal of the rule of law is formulated on the basis of summarizing current social contradictions and problems. It uses the law as the main means to solve these problems and guides our planning for a better future life. The ideal of the rule of law is an inexhaustible driving force for creating a law-based society. It has both objective necessity and social reality. The rule of law is the mainstream mode of governance in countries around the world and an irreversible trend in the contemporary world. Since a law-based society conforms to the laws of human social development, global rule of law is also a foreseeable reality. Meanwhile, the realization of the rule of law goal is restricted by objective factors such as the current economy, politics, and culture. Therefore, the ideal of the rule of law must be based on the reality of the rule of law.

"One must set a long-term goal from the start". China's founding ideal is embedded in the ideal of the rule of law. For China at the present stage, the ideal of the rule of law is to build the country into a socialist law-based country, create a fair and just law-based society, practice the spirit of democracy, the rule of law, and human rights, and contribute to the global cause of the rule of law. When the rule of law prospers, the country prospers; when the rule of law is strong, the country is strong. Achieving national prosperity through the rule of law is an integral and crucial part of the Chinese Dream. The goal of the socialist ideal of the rule of law is to build a law-based country relying on the rule of law and ultimately achieve socialist modernization in an all-round way.

If the ideal of the rule of law is the desirable state that a country hopes to achieve in governance, then rule of law discourse is the narration of the ideal of the rule of law and its implementation methods. Different countries have different ideals of the rule of law, thus giving rise to different rule of law discourses. The ultimate pursuit of the socialist ideal of the rule of law is social harmony and stability, long-term national peace and order, and the well-being and tranquility of the people. Socialist of law discourse expresses the socialist ideal of the rule of law. While expressing rule of law concepts and spirits, rule of law discourse conveys the ideal of the rule of law to the world, so as to gradually translate the ideal into practical actions. Conversely, the ideal of the rule of law determines the development direction of rule of law discourse and provides continuous impetus for the formation and improvement of rule of law discourse.

1.4 Conclusion

This chapter conducts an in-depth analysis of the conceptual definition and analysis of Chinese rule of law discourse, constructing a multidimensional and in-depth framework for understanding rule of law discourse.

Rule of law discourse, as a language symbol system expressing rule of law beliefs, stances, and value pursuits, is not only a concentrated manifestation of rule of law thinking and rule of law spirit but also an important tool for promoting the progress of rule of law civilization and influencing social thoughts and behaviors. Its core lies in using rule of law thinking, expressing the ideals and pursuits of the rule of law through concise and accurate language, achieving objective analysis of social contradictions, and widespread spreading of rule of law theories.

The development process of Chinese rule of law discourse is a vivid portrayal of the interaction between rule of law construction and social development. From the budding of the rule of law in the ideological debates of ancient times, to the transformation of the "rule of law" discourse prompted by modern social changes, and then to the new chapter of rule of law practice opened after the founding of the People's Republic of China, especially since the exploration of the socialist market economy. In this process, rule of law discourse not only records every step of rule of law construction but also reflects the needs and directions of national governance in different historical periods. From the logical transformation from "rule by man" to "rule of law", to the proposal of the "socialist concept of the rule of law", and then to the systematic leap of concepts such as the "rule of law system" and "rule of law in China", Chinese rule of law discourse shows strong vitality and a sense of the times in continuous enrichment and improvement.

The conceptual connotation of Chinese rule of law discourse is rich and profound. It is not only an important support for rule of law construction but also an effective way to build social consensus and resolve interest conflicts. Under the conditions of the socialist market economy, in the face of the challenges of diverse concepts and values, rule of law discourse unifies complex and diverse concepts through systematic and complete expressions, resolves value differences and conceptual conflicts, and promotes the formation of rule of law consensus. At the same time, on the international stage, Chinese rule of law discourse, as an important tool for telling Chinese rule of law stories and conveying Chinese rule of law thoughts, demonstrates the achievements of China's socialist rule of law construction, establishes a trustworthy, respectable, and friendly image of China, and safeguards national security and international discourse power.

The core of Chinese rule of law discourse is rule of law thinking, which directly reflects the thinking mode of the people in managing social, economic, cultural affairs according to law. The thinking choice of the ruling party has a decisive impact on a country's rule of law process. The decision to make the rule of law the basic strategy for the Party to lead the people in governing the country and law-based governance the basic way for the Party to govern the country is a major historical choice of the Communist Party of China in the new era. The proposal and increasing emphasis on rule of law thinking not only shape the thinking mode of the people but also provide the necessary core for the systematic study of rule of law discourse. It requires taking the law as the criterion for judging right and wrong, using the law as the code of conduct, advocating the rule of law, respecting the law, and being good at using legal means to solve problems. The popularization and deepening of this thinking mode will undoubtedly greatly promote the process of Chinese rule of law construction.

Chinese rule of law discourse also centrally embodies the rule of law spirit, which is the soul of rule of law discourse. The rule of law spirit covers all aspects of governing the Party, the country, and the military. It requires the ruling party to adhere to law-based governance and use rule of law means to manage the Party. Only when the ruling party uses rule of law in its own governance can it better use rule of law in national governance, showing the best effect of the rule of law spirit. Chinese rule of law discourse adheres to the rule of law spirit that puts the people in the principal position, takes the family and society as the foundation, and centers around the people. It not only upholds the value pursuits of freedom, equality, and justice but also takes deep root in excellent traditional Chinese culture, reflecting the uniqueness and inclusiveness of socialist rule of law. As a high-level summary of rule of law theories and rule of law models, Chinese rule of law discourse reflects the goals and pursuits of China's socialist rule of law. It not only reflects the goal orientation of "deepening reform, promoting development, resolving contradictions, and maintaining stability" but also highlights the principles of the supremacy of the constitution and laws and the respect and protection of human rights.

In the context of comprehensively deepening the reforms, constructing Chinese rule of law discourse system necessitates a profound understanding the process and experience of China's reform, extracting symbolic rule of law discourses to promote the construction of the rule of law in China. This discourse system was formed by the Communist Party of China leading the Chinese people in rule of law practice. It reflects the close combination of the basic principles of Marxism and Chinese rule of law construction practice and is an important part of China's socialist rule of law culture.

In the part of conceptual analysis, this chapter details the differences and connections between rule of law discourse and rule of law language, rule of law concepts, rule of law culture, and rule of law ideals. Although rule of law discourse is related to rule of law language, rule of law discourse is an extension and expansion of rule of law language in a specific social context, with stronger sociality and interactivity. Rule of law discourse and rule of law concepts are complementary. Rule of law discourse is a direct expression of rule of law concepts, and rule of law concepts guide the content and development direction of rule of law discourse. Rule of law discourse and rule of law culture mirror each other. Rule of law discourse is the external expression of rule of law culture, and rule of law culture provides rich nourishment for rule of law discourse. Rule of law discourse and rule of law ideals have a relationship of narration and being narrated. Rule of law discourse expresses the goals and pursuits of rule of law ideals, and rule of law ideals provide motivation and direction for rule of law discourse.

In conclusion, through a comprehensive and in-depth analysis, this chapter presents the conceptual connotation, development process, core features of Chinese rule of law discourse, and its differences and connections with related concepts. As an important support for rule of law construction, Chinese rule of law discourse not only build rule of law consensus and resolves interest conflicts at home but also demonstrates Chinese rule of law image and achievements abroad.

References

Fan, X. (1994). Language, parole, and discourse. *Chinese Language Learning*, 2.

Foucault, M. (2016). *The order of things: An archaeology of the human sciences* (W. Mo, Trans.). Shanghai Joint Publishing Company.

Ji, J. (2015). An interpretation of the significance of the rule of law belief. *Jinling Law Review*, (01), 89–98.

Liu, J. (2018). The flashiness of discourse research and the reconstruction of discourse theory. *Journalism Lover*, (09), 4–9.

Yu, S., & Luo, W. (2023). A study on the planning of the contemporary Chinese rule of law discourse. *Foreign Languages and Literature, 39*(02), 27–36.

Zhou, W., & Zhu, S. (2010). *Encyclopedia of Peking University school of law: Jurisprudence, legislation, and legal sociology*. Peking University Press.

Chapter 2
Fundamental Orientations of Chinese Rule of Law Discourse

2.1 Introduction

The contemporary world is a world of diverse coexistence. Nations, ethnic groups, cultures, and societies inevitably face the collision of diverse values. The traditional ways of expressing thoughts, cultures, and values are gradually being "deconstructed" and showing diverse characteristics. Against the backdrop of China's Belt and Road Initiative, it is imperative to clarify the basic connotations, orientations, and characteristics of Chinese rule of law discourse system. The rule of law discourse system largely reflects the basic outlook and trends of contemporary rule of law. Different rule of law discourse systems not only communicate and learn from each other but also follow their own historical development logic and unique creation and individuality. Etymologically, the term "Chinese rule of law discourse" encompasses two words with rich connotation: "Chinese characteristics" and "rule of law discourse". The meaning of each word is profound and requires interpretation in combination with multiple factors such as history, politics, culture, and society.

2.2 "Chinese Characteristics" in Chinese Rule of Law Discourse

When promoting the dissemination of Chinese rule of law and constructing Chinese rule of law discourse system under the Belt and Road Initiative, it is necessary to first clarify the accurate connotation of "Chinese characteristics". The rule of law is a common governance method for humanity, but the specific rule of law paths adapted to the lifestyles of different countries vary greatly. In China, what is advocated is the socialist rule of law with Chinese characteristics. It is neither an abstract

X. Dong, M. Zhang, *Chinese Rule of Law Discourse System*, Understanding China, https://doi.org/10.1007/978-981-95-6260-2_2

rule of law nor the Western rule of law. Instead, it is rooted in China's reality, addresses China's problems, stems from China's history, contains Chinese elements, and is presented in a unique Chinese way of expression. In the study of the rule-of-law discourse system, "China" is a concept that requires our in-depth research. "We need to understand both China in the sense of traditional culture and China guided by practical issues and the realization of rule of law goals" (Chen, 2016a). Firstly, "Chinese characteristics" indicate the spatial coordinates of the rule of law, referring to China in the geographical sense. Geographical China defines cultural China. The people living on this land called China have achieved glorious feats and created a magnificent and world-renowned culture. Therefore, it is a China that has inherited a five-thousand-year-old civilization, with a long history, a splendid culture, and a glorious revolutionary tradition. "Tradition by no means implies decay and conservatism; nor does nationality imply inferiority complex. Tradition is the accumulation of history and culture. It can only be renewed, not eradicated. Losing tradition means losing the characteristics of national culture and the historical and cultural foundation for progress" (Zhang, 2005, p. 2). Thus, the rule of law discourse of socialism with Chinese characteristics is the rule of law discourse of China with historical inheritance and must be oriented towards geographical and cultural China. China is not only an ancient civilized country that has long led the world in politics, economy, and culture but also an ancient country with a developed legal civilization. The Chinese legal system, with a history of more than three thousand years, has been passed down and continued, forming a unique Chinese legal tradition. It has had a wide-ranging and profound influence on neighboring countries and promoted the progress of the ancient world's legal system. Modern China shows distinct "Chinese characteristics" precisely because it has fully absorbed the rich materials and valuable experiences left by the Chinese legal tradition. This is the root cause of the obvious difference between Chinese rule of law and that of other countries. The Chinese legal system is based on traditional Confucian thought and incorporates the essence of Legalist, Taoist, and Yin-Yang School theories, presenting diverse forms and spiritual characteristics. The social existence of the combination of agricultural production, patriarchal family, and centralized political system in ancient Chinese society determined the dual-element pattern in the value foundation governing legal practice, the multi-layer structure within legal norms, and the complementary implementation channels of legal and non-legal norms (Wu, 2013). As early as the twenty-first century BC, customary laws emerged in China. During the Spring and Autumn and Warring States periods, China began to formulate written laws. In the Tang Dynasty, a relatively complete feudal code was formed and was passed down and developed by subsequent feudal dynasties. In the long river of history, the Chinese legal system stands out among the world's major legal systems. The ancient Chinese traditional legal culture has made important contributions to human legal civilization and still has certain reference significance for the rule of law in contemporary countries. The traditional customs in Chinese society have played a significant role in maintaining social order and regulating the relationships between social organizations or members. The Chinese legal tradition can be summarized as follows: (1) Incorporating rituals into the law and combining rituals with the law; (2) Respecting natural principles and considering human feelings in law enforcement; (3) upholding fairness in laws and recognizing hierarchical rights; (4) Laws originating from the monarch, with power being more respected than the law; (5) Family-centered and ethical rule of law; (6) Governing officials by law and clearly defining their duties; (7) Seeking no litigation and resolving disputes through mediation (Zhang, 2005, pp. 2–4). This contains many governance experience summaries based on China's local experience and in line with the characteristics of the Chinese nation, as well as some reasonable propositions that emphasize legal systems and pursue fairness and justice. The profound cultural foundation of the Chinese rule-of-law system nourishes contemporary Chinese rule of law construction. Since the 18th National Congress of the Communist Party of China, the Party Central Committee has clearly proposed to combine the rule of law with the rule of virtue. The parts of the traditional Chinese legal system that are beneficial to contemporary rule of law construction have been emphasized, and useful experiences have been inherited. Concise and profound legal proverbs and aphorisms have gradually become well-known to people. The images of local officials, law-enforcers, and judges in ancient China who were law-abiding, honest, upright, and fearless of power have also become more deeply rooted in people's hearts. In particular, integrating the combination of the rule of law and the rule of virtue, a gem of Chinese political civilization, into contemporary socialist rule of law construction is not only an inheritance of the essence of traditional legal culture but also a promotion of Chinese legal culture.

Secondly, "Chinese characteristics" indicates the temporal coordinate of the rule of law, referring to contemporary China. It refers to China in the historical context of building a moderately prosperous society in all respects, comprehensively deepening reform, comprehensively advancing law-based governance, and comprehensively strengthening Party self-governance, and a China standing firm in the wave of globalization. "China" here is a modern country under the rule of law that is integrated into the international wave of globalization and stands on the world stage, which is different from the former China that was self-isolated, arrogant, closed-minded, and blindly exclusive. In the era of globalization, when building the socialist rule of law with Chinese characteristics, it is crucial to adopt a more open attitude to absorb the outstanding achievements of Western rule of law civilization. The 19th National Congress of the Communist Party of China put forward that "We must continue to promote the building of a community with a shared future for mankind. The Chinese people's dream is closely connected with the dreams of people in other countries. To realize the Chinese Dream, we must have a peaceful international environment and a stable international order." It also states that "China will remain committed to the path of peaceful development and pursue a mutually beneficial strategy of opening up. We will follow the right approach to justice and interests, and foster a new vision of common, comprehensive, cooperative, and sustainable security. We will pursue development through opening-up and innovation, and seek inclusive and reciprocal development prospects. We will promote cultural exchanges that emphasize harmony amidst diversity and inclusiveness," and that "China will always be a builder of world peace, a contributor to global development, and a defender of the international order" (Xi, 2017, p. 5). The cause of socialist rule of law with Chinese characteristics has distinct contemporary features: Firstly, socialism with Chinese characteristics is open and actively integrates into the international environment. Secondly, the socialist rule of law with Chinese characteristics is inclusive and eclectic, modestly learning from the outstanding achievements of the world's rule of law civilization. Thirdly, the cause of socialist rule of law with Chinese characteristics inherits from the past and ushers in the future, keeps pace with the times, and shoulders weighty missions. It is necessary to accelerate the pace of the rule-of-law construction, continuously adjust its own development strategy according to the changing requirements of the times, and resolutely advance the establishment of a socialist rule of law system and a country governed by law in accordance with Chinese characteristics.

Thirdly, "Chinese characteristics" indicates that the subject of the rule of law construction is the Chinese people as a specific political entity. As stated in the Preamble of the *Constitution of the People's Republic of China*, "The Chinese people of all ethnic groups will continue, under the leadership of the Communist Party of China, ... to build China into a great modern socialist country that is prosperous, strong, democratic, culturally advanced, harmonious, and beautiful, and achieve the great rejuvenation of the Chinese nation." This dictates that the construction of socialist rule of law with Chinese characteristics cannot be divorced from the leadership of the Communist Party of China (CPC). The international discourse system of Chinese rule of law is precisely oriented towards China under the leadership of the CPC. Here,"China" refers to the socialist China led by the CPC. The leadership of the CPC is the most essential feature of socialism with Chinese characteristics and the greatest strength of the socialist system with Chinese characteristics. This determines that in Chinese rule of law construction, it is imperative to adhere to the leadership of the Party, uphold the people's democratic dictatorship, follow the socialist path, and maintain Marxist guidance. Violating the "Four Cardinal Principles" equates to a denial of Chinese characteristics. To adhere to the Chinese characteristics of the rule of law, it is imperative to firmly grasp the requirements in these four aspects, continuously strengthen the Party's leadership, continuously safeguard the people's status as masters of the country, continuously improve various socialist systems, develop the socialist market economy, advance socialist democracy, and enhance the socialist rule of law. The term "China" in Chinese rule of law discourse encompasses all aspects of the economy, politics, culture, society, ecological civilization, and Party building, which together form a coordinated and systematic China. The construction of the rule of law in China is closely related to and inseparable from each aspect within this system. Only by deeply understanding the context of the rule of law in China and realizing the organic combination of the rule of law with the economy, politics, culture, society, ecological civilization, and Party building can ultimately be realized the goal of building a free, democratic, equal, and just China under the rule of law.

2.3 "Socialism" in Chinese Rule of Law Discourse

The rule of law is unified with socialism. The rule of law is not only a strategic choice for perfecting socialism but also an inevitable path for the development of socialism. As the goal and path of a law-based China, socialism, on the one hand, determines the socialist nature of Chinese rule of law path, and on the other hand, points out the direction for Chinese rule of law progress. Socialism has a significant impact on many important aspects such as the theoretical construction of the rule of law. "Socialism" is not only a political ideology but also an idea and theory rooted in and acting on national and social governance (Chen, 2016b). The reason why the rule of law of socialism with Chinese characteristics is socialist rule of law is manifested in the following aspects.

Firstly, the socialist system serves as the foundation for Chinese rule of law construction. Article 1 of the Chinese Constitution clearly stipulates that "the socialist system is the fundamental system of the People's Republic of China". The socialist system is the sum total of China's economic, political, cultural and other systems. To develop the rule of law of socialism with Chinese characteristics, it is necessary to adhere to China's socialist economic, political and cultural systems; the construction of the rule of law discourse of socialism with Chinese characteristics must also be firmly based on China's economic, political and cultural systems. Adhering to the socialist system, in the economic sphere, it is necessary to adhere to the basic economic system of taking public ownership as the mainstay and allowing diverse forms of ownership to develop together at the primary stage of socialism; politically, China implements the system of people's congresses as its political system, and adheres to and improves the system of multi-party cooperation and political consultation under the leadership of the Communist Party of China, the system of regional ethnic autonomy and the system of community level self-governance; culturally, it adheres to Marxism-Leninism, Mao Zedong Thought, Deng Xiaoping Theory, the important thought of "Three Represents", the Scientific Outlook on Development and Xi Jinping Thought on Socialism with Chinese Characteristics for a New Era as the guiding ideology, implements the education, science and culture systems with Chinese characteristics, and vigorously strengthens the construction of socialist spiritual civilization. General Secretary Xi Jinping emphasized in the article "Accelerating the Building of a Socialist Country under the Rule of Law" that "China's socialist system guarantees the principal position of the people as masters of the country and also guarantees the principal position of the people in comprehensively advancing the rule of law. This is our institutional advantage and also the fundamental difference between the rule of law of socialism with Chinese characteristics and the rule of law of capitalism" (Xi, 2015).

Secondly, the leadership of the Communist Party of China is the most fundamental guarantee for the rule of law of socialism with Chinese characteristics. The path of the rule of law with Chinese characteristics demonstrates the essential attribute of socialism in the construction of a law-based China, and also indicates that the construction of a law-based China is essentially a socialist construction. General

Secretary Xi Jinping pointed out that "the leadership of the Communist Party of China is the most essential feature of socialism with Chinese characteristics and the most fundamental guarantee for socialist rule of law. To adhere to the path of socialist rule of law with Chinese characteristics, the most fundamental thing is to uphold the leadership of the Communist Party of China" (Xi, 2015). Adhering to the Party's leadership is not in contradiction with the rule of law, because it is not an empty slogan but a series of principled requirements, which are specifically reflected in the Party leading legislation, ensuring law enforcement, supporting judicial work, and taking the lead in abiding by the law. Principles can be compatible with each other. As long as we clearly adhere to the people's democratic dictatorship as the state system, uphold the Party's leadership in the people's construction of socialist rule of law, and ensure that the Party itself operates within the scope of the constitution and laws, we can achieve the organic unity of the Party's leadership and the rule of law. Denying the Party's leadership means denying the most reliable supporting force for Chinese rule of law construction; without the socialist path of people's democracy, the rule of law construction will lose its direction. These have been proven by the historical experience of Chinese rule of law construction since the founding of the People's Republic of China. The Party's leadership, as the fundamental requirement of socialist rule of law, is the fundamental guarantee that can greatly promote Chinese rule of law construction.

Thirdly, the core socialist values are the soul of Chinese rule of law construction. The path of socialist rule of law with Chinese characteristics encompasses the common value pursuits of humanity and at the same time fully promotes the core socialist values. The core socialist values not only highlight the essence of China's socialist cause but also express the key characteristics of China's socialist path. Meanwhile, they also put forward practical goals and testing standards for the construction of the rule of law path with Chinese characteristics. One of the goals of socialist rule of law construction is to implement one by one the visions expressed by the core socialist values. Therefore, the rule of law of socialism with Chinese characteristics is a rule of law that promotes concepts such as the core socialist values, and is a rule of law that aims to achieve prosperity, democracy, civility, harmony, and beauty. Moreover, the rule of law itself is one of the core socialist values and is interdependent with other values such as democracy, equality, freedom, and justice.

Fourthly, socialist rule of law places greater emphasis on substantive rule of law. Socialist rule of law attaches more importance to equality and adheres to the principle of equality before the law. Equality is a fundamental attribute of socialist law and a basic requirement of socialist rule of law. Upholding equality before the law must be reflected in every aspect of legislation, law-enforcement, judicature, and law-abidance. Socialist rule of law adheres to the principal position of the people, and it is for the people, relies on the people, benefits the people, and protects the people. The report to the 19th National Congress of the Communist Party of China pointed out that "as socialism with Chinese characteristics has entered a new era, the principal contradiction in Chinese society has evolved. What we now face is the contradiction between unbalanced and inadequate development and the people's ever- growing needs for a better life". Meanwhile, "the people have ever-growing needs for a better life. Not only do they have higher demands for material and cultural life, but their expectations for democracy, the rule of law, fairness, justice, security, and the environment are also growing" (Xi, 2017, p. 11). The essence of socialist rule of law determines that we must implement the requirements of reflecting the people's interests, wishes, safeguarding their rights and interests, and enhancing their well-being throughout the whole process of governing the country by law, so that the law and its implementation fully embody the will of the people.

2.4 "Rule of Law Discourse" in Chinese Rule of Law Discourse

Rule of law discourse is a system of linguistic symbols created through the application of rule of law thinking, with the basic functions of highlighting the spirit of the rule of law and promoting the ideals of the rule of law. Then, what kind of "rule of law discourse" does China aim to construct? There are many aspects worthy of exploration here. Firstly, Chinese rule of law discourse is a local expression of China's own rule of law practice. Rooted in China's national conditions, it adheres to the general principles of the rule of law, fully learns from and draws on the essence of Western rule of law concepts. Meanwhile, it firmly bases itself on China's national conditions, starting from the country's fundamental institutions and actual situation, and absorbs nutrients from traditional legal culture. The rule of law discourse should be both "national" and "global", and as the saying goes, "Only what is national can be global." Although the socialist rule of law with Chinese characteristics is "Chinese" and "socialist", as a form of the rule of law, it must possess the general characteristics of the rule of law and cannot deviate from the basic laws and characteristics of the rule of law. The construction of the rule of law discourse must also seek common ground and highlight its own features in the communication and dialogue with the rule of law discourses of other countries, so as to achieve exchanges and mutual learning.

In today's world, countries face basically the same problems, such as safeguarding sovereignty, social governance, and sustainable development. The rule of law is the main approach and means to address these common issues. As the central discourse for countries around the world in governance, rule of law discourse has full potential and necessity for communication. At the same time, exploring the basic value concepts that are commonly pursued in the expression of the global rule of law discourse system and can reflect modern political civilization will enable Chinese rule of law discourse system to be established on the basis of respecting general laws. This can prevent the development of the rule of law discourse system into an absolutely isolated self-expression in terms of ideology, culture, and values. On the other hand, researching and exploring the national characteristics of the rule of law discourse system, delving into the historical logic of the rule of law discourse system in the process of national development, and focusing on the rule of law practice and the rule of law discourse system formed on this basis will fully uncover the national characteristics of the rule of law discourse system. In summary, by studying the global and national characteristics of the rule of law discourse system conceptually, Chinese rule of law discourse not only demonstrates respect for the general laws of the rule of law but also fully reflects the exploration and utilization of national and local resources, thus achieving the unity of the global and national aspects in Chinese rule of law discourse system.

Secondly, the innovation of the rule of law discourse system is the key to the maturity of the rule of law theoretical system. First of all, the rule of law discourse system and the rule of law theoretical system are in a relationship of phenomenon and essence. Any thing in the world is a unity of phenomenon and essence. Phenomenon and essence are a pair of philosophical categories that reveal the internal and external connections and interrelationships of objective things. The rule of law discourse system is the manifestation of the rule of law theoretical system, and the rule of law theoretical system is the basic connotation of the rule of law discourse system. As Marx said, if the form of appearance of things and the essence of things directly coincide, all science would be superfluous. The rule of law discourse system and the rule of law theoretical system must have their own independent research spaces and values, and neither can be neglected. The unity of phenomenon and essence illustrates the feasibility of researching the rule of law discourse system and the rule of law theoretical system, enabling them to have the characteristic of interconnection on the basis of their independent research values. Secondly, a mature rule of law discourse system is an important symbol of a mature rule of law theoretical system. A mature rule of law theoretical system needs to be expressed through a mature rule of law discourse system. Without the support of a certain rule of law discourse system, it is difficult for the rule of law theoretical system to be accurately and authoritatively expressed. The logic and self-consistency of the rule of law theory itself will be affected. It may either fail to be articulated or fail to be disseminated. Thirdly, a mature rule of law theoretical system requires continuous innovation of the rule of law discourse system. The maturity of the theoretical system needs to be achieved through continuous innovation of the discourse system. Only by innovating the rule of law discourse system and improving its maturity can the maturity of the rule of law theoretical system be correctly reflected.

Thirdly, the formation of the rule of law discourse system is a long-term process with different stages of development. Chinese rule of law construction has been greatly influenced by Western rule of law theories, which is manifested in the long-standing subordination to the Western rule of law discourse system in the field of the rule of law discourse. It is true that the Western rule of law discourse system contains elements that reflect modern civilization, and these elements share a certain degree of commonality. Just as many achievements of Western civilization can be shared by all mankind, the elements developed in the West that embody the commonalities of modern civilization can also be learned from and used for reference by us. This endows the rule of law discourse system reflecting these modern-civilization elements with global characteristics. However, with the continuous development of the multi-polar world, the traditional concepts of single rationality, will, and truth have been gradually deconstructed. The ideological field of the rule of law has become increasingly complex, with a heightened emphasis on autonomy in legal construction and a gradual emergence of distinct local characteristics. A one-sided and simplistic rule of law discourse system can no longer accurately reflect different ideas, cultures, and values. The rule of law discourse system is gradually evolving from a universal standard to local knowledge, and thus is increasingly taking on distinct national characteristics. Given the distinct global and national characteristics of the rule of law discourse system, innovation in Chinese rule of law discourse system necessitates a conceptual clarification that highlights its uniqueness. It requires a focus on the historical and logical underpinnings of Chinese rule of law development. It is necessary to break away from the rigid Western rule of law discourse system and avoid being restricted by the Western liberal rule of law discourse, so as to refrain from introducing concepts and grafting systems in a way that is ill-fitting and neglects the essence. Since Chinese rule of law construction shows obvious phased characteristics, the development process of the rule of law discourse can accordingly be divided into different stages.

Fourthly, the rule of law discourse is ultimately a "weapon of criticism," and it must be fully utilized to become a "criticism by weapons." The well-known idea that "the weapon of criticism cannot, of course, replace criticism by weapons" was put forward by Marx in the Introduction to *A Critique of Hegel's Philosophy of Right*. This enlightens us that the research on the rule of law discourse ultimately serves its application, namely, the dissemination and function of the discourse, which means explaining the reality of Chinese rule of law, guiding the development of Chinese rule of law, and building confidence in Chinese rule of law. Currently, Chinese rule of law discourse system is constrained by the evaluation criteria of the Western rule of law discourse system. As a result, the theory and practice of the rule of law under socialism with Chinese characteristics often fail to receive accurate evaluations and are even frequently distorted and attacked. Consequently, it is difficult for China to build confidence in its own rule of law path, theory, and system during the process of socialist construction. Promoting the innovation of Chinese rule of law discourse system is the key way to break free from the constraints of the Western rule of law discourse system. Through exploring Chinese rule of law discourse system, the distinctive concepts pertaining to the path, theory, and system of socialist rule of law with Chinese characteristics can be refined. This exploration enables the formulation of new expressions and categories within the rule of law discourse system that accurately convey China's specific rule of law thoughts, principles, culture, knowledge, and thinking patterns. Establishing evaluation criteria for the construction of socialist rule of law with Chinese characteristics holds immense significance for enhancing confidence in this endeavor. This is of great significance for enhancing confidence in socialist rule of law with Chinese characteristics. In summary, research on innovation in the rule of law discourse system can, on the one hand, help break free from the dominance of the Western rule of law discourse system and establish evaluation criteria that highlight China's unique national characteristics in a multi-polar world. On the other hand, it enables an accurate representation of the specific conditions of socialist rule of law construction with Chinese characteristics, thereby enhancing people's recognition of China's path, theory, system, and culture, and truly fostering confidence in the path, theory, system, and culture of socialist rule of law with Chinese characteristics.

2.5 Conclusion

In today's world of diverse coexistence, the collisions of diverse values among countries, ethnic groups, cultures, and societies are becoming increasingly intense. The traditional ways of expressing thoughts, cultures, and values are continuously being deconstructed and reconstructed, presenting unprecedented diversity and complexity. Against this backdrop, the construction of Chinese rule of law discourse system is of particular importance. It is not only an important part of Chinese rule of law construction but also a crucial tool for China to voice and communicate in the global rule of law arena.

Firstly, it is imperative to clarify the core position of "Chinese characteristics" in Chinese rule of law discourse system. Chinese characteristics are not only reflected in geographical and cultural uniqueness but also in the specific paths and practical approaches of rule of law construction. The socialist rule of law with Chinese characteristics is rooted in China's reality and aims to solve China's problems. It integrates multiple elements of China's history, culture, and society and presents itself to the world in a unique way of expression. This rule of law respects the general principles of the rule of law while fully considering China's national conditions and traditional culture, achieving an organic combination of historical inheritance and contemporary innovation. Chinese characteristics are also manifested in the time coordinate of rule of law construction. Contemporary China is at the historical intersection of building a moderately prosperous society in all respects, comprehensively deepening reform, comprehensively advancing the rule of law, and comprehensively strengthening Party self- governance, necessitating accelerated rule of law construction to meet the demands of the times.

Secondly, the rule of law of socialism with Chinese characteristics is distinctively featured. The socialist system serves as the cornerstone of the rule of law construction. The Constitution clearly defines its fundamental status, and adhering to this system guarantees the principal position of the people. The leadership of the Communist Party of China is the most fundamental guarantee for the rule of law. It is complementary to the rule of law and is manifested in every aspect where the Party leads legislation, law-enforcement, judicature, and law-abidance. Denying the Party's leadership would shake the foundation of the rule of law. The core socialist values are the soul of the rule of law construction. They provide practical goals and testing standards for the rule of law, and the rule of law itself is an important part of these values. Socialist rule of law emphasizes substantive fairness and adheres to the principle of equality, which runs through the entire process of legislation, law-enforcement, judicature, and law-abidance. It takes the people as the principal, and the people's interests are integrated throughout the process of governing the country by law.

In the construction of the rule of law discourse system, "rule of law discourse" is the indigenous expression of Chinese rule of law practice. Starting from China's national conditions, it not only draws on the essence of Western rule of law concepts but also bases itself on the country's actual situation and draws nutrients from traditional legal culture. The construction of the rule of law discourse needs to reflect the unity of universality and nationality. It should not only engage in exchanges and mutual learning with the rule of law discourses of other countries but also highlight its own characteristics to form a rule of law discourse system with Chinese characteristics. This discourse system should not only accurately express Chinese rule of law thoughts, legal principles, and rule of law culture but also serve Chinese rule of law practice and guide the development of Chinese rule of law.

The innovation of the rule of law discourse system is an important symbol of the maturity of the rule of law theoretical system. The rule of law discourse system and the rule of law theoretical system are in a relationship of phenomenon and essence, depending on and promoting each other. An innovative rule of law discourse system can more accurately express the connotation of the rule of law theoretical system and promote the maturity and improvement of the rule of law theoretical system. Meanwhile, with the development of the multi-polar world, the rule of law discourse system is increasingly characterized by distinct national features. Therefore, the innovation of Chinese rule of law discourse system must clarify the concepts, highlight individuality, pay attention to historical and real-world logic, and break free from the constraints of Western rule of law discourse system.

The rule of law discourse is not only the result of theoretical research but also a guide for practice. Ultimately, it should serve the reality of Chinese rule of law, explain Chinese rule of law practice, and guide the development of Chinese rule of law. Currently, Chinese rule of law discourse system is constrained by the evaluation criteria of the Western rule of law discourse system, resulting in inaccurate evaluations of the theory and practice of the socialist rule of law with Chinese characteristics. Therefore, promoting the innovation of Chinese rule of law discourse system and getting rid of the dominant influence of the Western rule of law discourse system are of great significance for enhancing confidence in the socialist rule of law with Chinese characteristics. By constructing a rule of law discourse system with Chinese characteristics, we can more accurately express the specific situation of Chinese rule of law construction and enhance China's voice and influence in the global rule of law arena.

In conclusion, the construction of Chinese rule of law discourse system is a complex and long-term process that requires fully exploring and utilizing national and local resources while respecting the general laws of the rule of law, and continuously innovating the discourse system to achieve the unity of universality and nationality. Only through such efforts can a unique image of Chinese rule of law be established on the global stage, offering robust discourse support for the construction of socialist rule of law with Chinese characteristics. Simultaneously, innovation in the rule of law discourse system enables a more accurate explanation of Chinese rule of law realities, guides its rule of law development, and nurtures confidence in its rule of law, thereby laying a solid rule of law guarantees for the realization of the Chinese Dream of national rejuvenation.

References

Chen, J. (2016a). The Chinese theoretical system of socialist rule of law: China, *Journal of Yangzhou University (Humanities and Social Sciences Edition)*, 1.

Chen, J. (2016b). "Socialism" in the theoretical system of socialist rule of law in China. *Jianghan Tribune*, 6.

Wu, S. (2013). On the pluralistic characteristics and contemporary significance of the Chinese legal system. *Academic Frontiers of People's Tribune*, 9.

Xi, J. (2015). Accelerating the construction of a socialist country under the rule of law. *Qiushi*, 1.

Xi, J. (2017). *Secure a decisive victory in building a moderately prosperous society in all respects and strive for the great success of socialism with Chinese characteristics for a new era-report at the 19th National Congress of the Communist Party of China* (p. 25). People's Publishing House.

Zhang, J. (2005). *Tradition and modern transformation of Chinese law* (pp. 2–4). Law Press.

Chapter 3
The Ideological Resources of Chinese Rule of Law Discourse

3.1 Introduction

To innovate Chinese rule of law discourse system, it is necessary to adhere to the unity of nationality and inheritance. Nationality requires that innovation must be in line with the path of socialist rule of law with Chinese characteristics, be based on Chinese rule of law reality, reflect China's unique local rule of law resources, and condense theoretical, practical, national, and cultural characteristics, so as to provide theoretical support for Chinese rule of law construction. Inheritance requires that innovation must be based on the critical inheritance of excellent legal cultures, drawing on the past to serve the present and integrating foreign elements with Chinese realities. Considering China's actual national conditions, for Chinese rule of law discourse system to achieve innovation through inheritance, it must draw on Western liberal rule of law ideology and traditional Chinese political ideology.

3.2 Ideological Reference: Western Liberal Rule of Law Ideology

Western liberal rule of law is regarded as a model of human rule of law and has contributed important elements to human rule of law civilization. Since modern times, the rule of law has continuously developed in Western countries, giving rise to the liberal rule of law model. Liberal rule of law not only summarizes the core essence of the rule of law and the general laws of Western rule of law construction but also makes the rule of law a common understanding among humanity. Western liberal rule of law ideology provides important ideological reference for China's socialist rule of law construction.

X. Dong, M. Zhang, *Chinese Rule of Law Discourse System*, Understanding China, https://doi.org/10.1007/978-981-95-6260-2_3

3.2.1 The Rule of Law as a Significant Achievement of Human Civilization

The rule of law is considered the best way of governing a country so far. The theory of the rule of law originated in the West and is a summary of the experience of Western countries in governing their countries by law over the past few hundred years. Established capitalist countries such as the UK, the US, France, and Germany have relatively complete rule of law theories, mature legal systems, and rich rule of law practices, serving as exemplars for other nations. The rule of law theories of Western capitalist countries have spread to many Asian, African, and Latin American countries during the process of colonial expansion and globalization. In the 1950s, socialist countries also had discussions about the rule of law. In the 1980s, the Communist Party of the Soviet Union put forward the idea of a socialist rule of law country, which influenced other socialist countries (Wang & Cheng, 2014, p. 458). With the spread of political modernization across the globe, democratic politics has become a general trend, and the rule of law, along with democracy, has become a common pursuit worldwide. The rule of law has gradually been accepted by newly-emerging nationalist countries and socialist countries and has become a consensus in human society. The rule of law is no longer exclusive to Western countries but has gradually become a common achievement of human civilization. Marx and his contemporaries, when summarizing and criticizing capitalist rule of law, also recognized the achievements of capitalism in the rule of law as the precursor to socialism, believing that liberal rule of law represents a significant progress in human civilization. General Secretary Xi Jinping emphasized that "the rule of law is one of the important achievements of human civilization. The essence and gist of the rule of law have universal significance for the governance of countries and societies around the world. We should learn from the world's excellent rule of law civilization achievements" (Xi, 2015). Although Western liberal rule of law theory has its unique aspects, it objectively reflects, to a certain extent, the basic laws of rule of law construction, which are worthy of in-depth exploration and reference. Therefore, Western liberal rule of law ideology can serve as an important ideological reference for the innovation of Chinese rule of law discourse system.

3.2.2 Core Views of Western Liberal Rule of Law Ideology

Liberal rule of law thought is a form of the rule of law aimed at safeguarding freedom. Generally speaking, the core views of liberal rule of law can be summarized as follows: the purpose of the rule of law is to protect individual freedom; state power poses the greatest threat to freedom, necessitating the establishment of a limited government and the separation of powers to prevent its abuse. Specifically, liberal rule of law mainly includes the following aspects.

The Connoation of the Rule of Law

The connoation of the rule of law is uncertain. Even in the context of liberalism, the rule of law has multiple meanings. Liberal nations' understanding of the rule of law has evolved over time, yet consistently centered on the protection of individual freedom, giving rise to its intrinsic attributes, namely, opposition to the rule of man, the institutional guarantee of the rule of law, i.e., "constitutional" rule of law, and the external form and essential connotation of the rule of law have been developed.

The rule of law originated from the Latin "imperiumlegum", and its original meaning was "the rule of law" rather than the rule of man. Aristotle was the first to propose that "the rule of law should be superior to the rule of one man." Therefore, the rule of law was initially conceived as the opposite of rule by man. Modern rule of law and liberalism share the same pursuit in opposing rule by man. In the process of opposing feudal autocracy, liberalism relies on the rule of law to combat rule by man, restrict monarchical power, and protect individual rights.

There is a close connection between the rule of law and freedom. In the view of liberals, freedom does not mean "doing whatever one wants". They advocate freedom under the rule of law and believe that freedom is only possible under the rule of law. Hobbes defined freedom as "the state in which there are no external obstacles". "In all actions not prohibited by law, individuals have the liberty to do what their reason deems most beneficial to themselves". Locke even believed that "where there is no law, there is no freedom". Montesquieu held that "liberty is the right to do whatever the laws permit". It can be seen that the most distinctive contribution of liberal rule of law is to connect freedom with the rule of law: freedom is the purpose of the rule of law, and the rule of law is the guarantee of freedom, and the rule of law greatly embodies the spirit of freedom. The closer connection between the rule of law and freedom is also manifested in the relationship between formal rule of law and the laissez-faire market economy. Locke believed that the purpose of the law is to guide people to freely pursue legitimate interests. Since Adam Smith, liberal economists have strongly advocated a laissez-faire market economy, believing that the less government intervention, the better, and the government should play the role of a "night-watchman". The rule of law's guarantee for the laissez-faire market economy makes the market economy clear, secure, and highly efficient. Therefore, the formal rule of law has greatly promoted the development of the capitalist economy. The rule of law aimed at protecting freedom gives legitimacy to the government's rule by law. Liberals believe that the government poses the greatest threat to freedom, but it is also a "necessary evil". To confer legitimacy upon this evil and justify governmental rule, reliance must be placed on the rule of law. Based on the theory of the state of nature and the social contract, Locke put forward his theory of consent, arguing that the legitimate foundation of the government lies in the legitimate transfer of individual rights, and rule should be carried out based on the consent of the governed. This coincides with the requirements of the rule of law, which embodies the requirement of the legitimacy of rule. The government's intervention in individual rights must be based on the law, and the law must reflect the will of the people. Therefore, it requires that state power, especially administrative power, must be exercised in accordance with the law.

"Constitutional" Rule of Law

Liberals contend that the optimal mechanism for safeguarding the rule of law is undoubtedly "constitutionalism". Since "constitutionalism" means "restricting the government", in their view, the mechanism of using the constitution to limit government power is highly stable and reliable. Thomas Paine attached particular importance to the significance of the constitution. "A constitution is something antecedent to a government, and a government is only the creature of a constitution" (Paine, 1776/1982). Government power is constrained by the constitution. Paine provided a paradigm of "constitutional" rule of law for the United States. Under the "constitutional" rule of law, fundamental human rights are guaranteed by the constitution, government powers are restricted and independent of each other, and sovereignty always remains in the hands of the people. Specifically, the "constitutional" rule of law encompasses requirements such as human rights, separation of powers, and a republican system. Liberal rule of law holds that the primary purpose of the law, especially the constitution, is to safeguard human rights. The concept of natural law has a long-standing history in the West. The early liberal theory of the rule of law was based on the theory of the state of nature, the social contract theory, and especially the theory of natural rights. It is believed that people are born with inalienable and non-transferable natural rights such as the right to life, health, liberty, and property. Liberalism regards the protection of human rights as the primary goal of the rule of law, thus establishing the human rights principle of modern legalism. John Locke emphasized the protection of individual liberties, especially property rights. Locke developed Thomas Hobbes' theory of the state of nature and adhered to the social contract theory. He believed that the primary purpose of establishing a political society was to protect property (Locke, 1689/1996, p. 53). Paine also proposed that the purpose of establishing a state was to safeguard human rights. "Man did not enter into society to become worse than he was before, nor to have fewer rights than he had before, but to have those rights better secured" (Paine, 1776/1982, p. 142). People establish governments to safeguard human rights. To restrain government power, the first step is to set no-go areas for government power, that is, inviolable human rights.

The rule of law implies that government power is limited and restricted by the law. The power under the rule of law is a limited power. A government that strictly adheres to the law in administration must be a limited government. Montesquieu believed that "no unlimited power can be legitimate" (de Montesquieu, 1721/1958, p. 178). To prevent the abuse of power, the government should "check power with power". To further safeguard individual rights, government power must be further divided. Therefore, Montesquieu put forward the theory of the "separation of powers". The theory of the "separation of powers" advocates the separation of legislative, executive, and judicial powers. Each power operates in accordance with the law rather than being subject to the will of individual rulers. Thomas Jefferson and others designed the power-separation model of the United States. Vertically, it demarcates the boundaries of power between the federal government and state governments; horizontally, it demarcates the boundaries among the legislative, executive, and judicial powers, so that the enjoyment and operation of power are all subject to the law.

Liberal rule of law holds that a country under the rule of law should be a republic. In essence, it opposes autocracy and advocates people's participation. James Harrington was the first to propose the idea of a republic under the rule of law. He advocated establishing a state on the basis of common rights or common interests. Through people's participation in legislation, individual freedom is transformed into the freedom of the republic (Harrington, 1656/1981, p. 21). A republic under the rule of law emphasizes citizens' participation in public affairs and legislation through debate and decision—making (Harrington, 1656/1981, p. 25). Harrington's concept of a republic under the rule of law is a state system with freedom as the highest value criterion and the law as the absolute ruler. Jean-Jacques Rousseau believed that the rule of law should be combined with a republican form of government. "Every State that is governed by laws is a Republic" (Rousseau, 1762/1980, p. 57). Rousseau opposed monarchy, arguing that an autocratic monarch "is a man who places himself above the law" (Rousseau, 1762/1980, p. 130). He advocated popular sovereignty. The law should reflect the general will, and the legislative power, which is also the supreme power, belongs to the people. If the government abuses its power, the people as the sovereign can restrict, change, and take back the power entrusted to the government.

Formal Rule of Law

Based on the degree of closeness between the law and morality in the rule of law, there are varying levels of the rule of law. Formal rule of law emphasizes the separation of the law from morality, asserting that laws should possess sound formal characteristics. In contrast, substantive rule of law emphasizes the combination of the law with morality, insisting that the law must conform to justice. Historically, most Western developed countries with the rule of law have generally gone through the process from formal rule of law to substantive rule of law. In 1885, A.V. Dicey published *Introduction to the Study of the Law of the Constitution*. Based on the mainstream liberal ideology in the UK at that time, he summarized three sub-principles of the principle of "the rule of law" in the UK: First, the supremacy of the law and the prohibition of arbitrary power; second, equality before the law, where all people are equally subject to the jurisdiction of the common law; third, the constitution is the result of the courts' enforcement of individual rights (Dicey, 1885/2001, pp. 244–245). Dicey's view of the rule of law is regarded as a model of formal rule of law. Since modern times, the issue of the rule of law has sparked in-depth thinking and extensive discussions among many scholars. For a long time, the view of formal rule of law has gradually become the common understanding of the rule of law (Gao, 2000). Representatives of the Analytical Jurisprudence School and the Contemporary Natural Law School both define the rule of law in terms of the formal standards of the rule of law, emphasizing the importance of abiding by rules without inquiring about the value orientation of the rules. Formal rule of law first requires the supremacy of the law. With the aim of opposing the rule of man, the rule of law first demands the absolute supremacy of the law and the establishment of the absolute authority of the law. The political tradition of "the king is under the law" established by the *Magna Carta* in medieval England has been repeatedly restated by jurists. Chief Justice Coke believed that the king should be under the law and the Magna Carta, and the king's governance of the kingdom should be carried out in accordance with the law and the *Magna Carta* (Li, 2015). The core of John Locke's theory of the rule of law lies in the supremacy of the law, that is, placing political authority under the control of the law (expressed as "the king is under the law" in the UK at that time). Locke argued that "the liberty of men under government is to have a standing rule to live by, common to every one of that society, and made by the legislative power erected in it" (Locke, 1689/1996, p. 16). Jean-Jacques Rousseau held that "rulers are the servants of the laws, and their entire power is based on the laws" (Zhang, 1983, p. 248). Thomas Paine stated that "in an autocratic government the king is the law, and in a free country the law ought to be the king" (Paine, 1776/1982, pp. 35–36). Under the rule of man, obedience is to the will of the personalized ruler, while under the rule of law, obedience is to the impersonal law. The essence of the rule of law lies in the fact that the authority of the law is higher than that of individuals, and power is governed by the law (Zhou, 2016, p. 92).

Formal rule of law emphasizes that the law should be universal in form. John Locke emphasized that the law must be "established and perpetual" (Locke, 1689/1996, p. 85). Jean-Jacques Rousseau believed that the law should embody the general will. Joseph Raz argued that the law should have formal characteristics such as non-retroactivity, publicity, clarity, and relative stability. It is precisely because the law is universal and certain that it can exclude human arbitrariness and reflect the superiority of the rule of law over the rule of man.

Formal rule of law underscores equal application of the law. Although liberalism acknowledges the natural differences among social members, it also adheres to equality before the law. "The law treats the rich and the poor, the noble and the peasant equally, without any discrimination due to special circumstances" (Locke, 1689/1996, p. 88). *The Declaration of the Rights of Man and of the Citizen* in France in 1789 officially confirmed this principle, clearly stating that "all citizens are equal before the law and have the right to equal protection of the law." However, this equality is formal equality and equality of opportunity, rather than substantive equality and equality of results.

Formal rule of law also requires that laws must be operable. Under the rule of man, the law often lacks operability, manifested as non-publicity, uncertainty, self-contradiction, and ultimately being decided by the ruler. One of the most prominent achievements of liberal rule of law in the formal rule of law stage is to greatly enhance the operability of the law. The operability of the law in form required by the rule of law is manifested in the publicity, certainty, and consistency of the law, the standardization of legal terms, and the requirements for continuous improvement of legislative technology and popularization of legal knowledge. The operability of the law aims to separate the implementation of the law from the arbitrariness of legislators or law-enforcers through certain operating procedures.

Universal compliance with the law is the ultimate requirement of formal rule of law. Although liberal rule of law advocates freedom and rejects external constraints, it also realizes that only by abiding by the law can freedom be obtained. Jean-Jacques Rousseau believed that the premise of the rule of law is universal compliance with the law, and "respect for the law is the first and most important law." Moreover, universal compliance with the law inherently requires equality. "No matter what the political system of a country is, if there is one person within its jurisdiction who does not abide by the law, all the others will inevitably be at the mercy of this person" (Rousseau, 1755/1962). Even in liberal rule of law countries, compliance with the law must become a good social morality and form a belief in the rule of law.

Substantive Rule of Law

The modern concept of substantive rule of law owes its origin to the rise of the concept of positive freedom. In the 19th century, with the advent of the Industrial Revolution, the social problems brought about by the rapid social development prompted people to consider the issues of law and justice from the perspective of the overall society. As a result, there was a shift from the laissez-faire market economy view to comprehensive state intervention in the economy. The defects of the formal rule of law based on individualism and the concept of negative freedom became increasingly apparent. The concept of freedom shifted from negative freedom to positive freedom, which led to the transformation from the negative liberal rule of law view to the positive liberal rule of law view. The positive liberal rule of law requires that the rule of law not only protects people's negative freedom from infringement but also endows individuals with more material conditions to develop and realize freedom. Scholars such as Jennings opposed Dicey's laissez-aire rule of law view and advocated a positive freedom rule of law view. The most concentrated manifestation of positive rule of law in policy during this period was the "welfare state" policy. After World War II, Western European countries established welfare-oriented political systems on this basis.

The new liberal rule of law further developed the liberal rule of law and endowed the rule of law with many new connotations. The new liberal rule of law inherits many concepts of the classical liberal rule of law but adheres to the positive freedom view. Influenced by the concept of social fairness based on humanism, the traditional formal rule of law was increasingly unable to guarantee social fairness during the rapid development of capitalism. The substantial social injustice caused by the formal rule of law gradually became prominent, heightening the demand for substantive rule of law. Therefore, the new liberal rule of law endows the rule of law with more substantive connotations and incorporates values such as fairness and social justice into the rule of law. Different from the classical liberal rule of law, which advocates a "minimal government," the new liberal rule of law advocates an "effective government." The new liberal rule of law goes beyond the formal rule of law and emphasizes the substantive connotations of the rule of law, requiring that the principles of the rule of law be implemented and that rights and order be substantially guaranteed. In 1959, the *Delhi Declaration* was issued, which presented the general view of the international community on the "rule of law standards" at that time: First, the function of the legislative body is to create and maintain various conditions for the maintenance of individual dignity and to implement the principles in the *Universal Declaration of Human Rights*. Second, it is necessary to prevent the abuse of administrative power while requiring the government to maintain the legal order. Third, there should be a proper criminal procedure to fully guarantee the defendant's right to defense and the right to a public trial. Fourth, judicial independence and the freedom of lawyers are required (Qin & Zhang, 1999). This declaration is of landmark significance for the development of the substantive rule of law.

The view of the substantive rule of law holds that the term "rule of law" itself should contain moral requirements. In ancient times when the boundaries between law and morality were not clearly defined, the law itself had more moral connotations, and emphasizing the rule of law necessarily meant the substantive rule of law. Aristotle's two-layer meaning of the rule of law included the requirement of good laws (Aristotle, 1983, p. 199). It was only in modern times, with the development of positivist jurisprudence, that law and morality gradually separated, and the liberal rule of law showed increasing characteristics of formal rule of law. The extreme development of this formal rule of law led to atrocities against humanity committed in the name of the rule of law in Nazi Germany. After World War II, jurists such as Radbruch deeply reflected on the formal rule of law and emphasized the morality of the law (Radbruch, 1910/2013, pp. 20–21). Rawls put forward a rule of law proposition containing the value orientation of the substantive rule of law. He adhered to the idea that freedom takes precedence, refused to obey unjust laws, and advocated that freedom should be an equal freedom. Raz put forward eight principles of the rule of law, and Fuller put forward eight principles of the rule of law with more substantive rule of law characteristics on the basis of adhering to the morality of the law. Dworkin clearly challenged the pure formal rule of law. He advocated moral rights, demanded more legal protection for those in a disadvantaged position, and required that the principles of the law must reflect values such as "fairness" and "justice" (Gao, 2000). The rule of law ideas of scholars such as Nonet, Unger, and Habermas also have the characteristics of the new liberal rule of law.

Laws of the Development of the Rule of Law

Liberal rule of law theory has developed a systematic set of rule of law theories. In guiding the practice of the rule of law, some regular understandings about the development of the rule of law have also emerged.

First, the rule of law is a requirement of human nature. Liberal rule of law theory posits that the rule of law is a requirement of human nature. This view is based on the capitalist assumption of human nature. Liberalism adheres to the stance of the inherent evil of human nature, believing that there are irreconcilable contradictions between individuals, and between individuals and society. People have an innate tendency to do evil. Therefore, laws are needed to restrain people. Law, as a universal good, can contain the evil in human nature. Thus, liberal rule of law theory holds that the rule of law precisely emerges from the needs of human nature, using the good in human nature to counterbalance the evil. The rule of law is prominently manifested in using laws to contain the potential evil of public power. Hume argued that when designing any political system, every person in possession of public power should be preassumed as a "rogue". Similarly, "if men were angels, no government would be necessary. If angels were to govern men, neither external nor internal controls on government would be necessary" (Hamilton et al., 1788/1995, p. 264). Precisely because those holding public power may do evil, external control of the government through laws is required.

Second, Constructivist Rationality and Ecological Rationality in the rule of law. The concepts of "Constructivist Rationality" and "Ecological Rationality" were proposed by Hayek. Hayek believed that there are two ways to observe human behavior patterns: constructivist rationalism and ecological rationalism. Constructivist Rationalism holds that "man is endowed with intelligence and moral qualities at birth, which enable him to shape civilization through deliberate thinking" (Hayek, 1960/1997, p. 68). Ecological Rationalism argues that "various free institutions, like all other things created by freedom, are not constructed because people foresee the possible benefits of these institutions in advance" (Hayek, 1960/1997, p. 61). Consequently, there are two different theoretical perspectives on the development of the rule of law: the constructivist rationalist rule of law theory and the ecological rationalist rule of law theory. The constructivist rationalist rule of law theory contends that the history, present, and future of the rule of law can and should be designed and created through human rationality. The ecological rationalist rule of law theory maintains that the history, present, and future of the rule of law are inevitably formed through people's real life experiences and specific practical error-correction processes. However, it is incorrect to oppose and separate the ecological rational rule of law based on British empiricism and the constructivist rational rule of law based on Continental rationalism. In fact, the development of the rule of law in any country is a combination of the two. The construction of the socialist rule of law must rely on both.

Third, there is no fixed model for the rule of law construction, and it must be carried out based on the actual situation of each country. Based on its unique liberal tradition and the actual situation of the monarchy, the United Kingdom developed its own liberal rule of law system. The success of the British rule of law influenced other European and American countries. However, countries such as the United States, France, and Germany did not copy the British model. Instead, they explored rule of law models suitable for their own situations. In the history of the global development of the rule of law, apart from the British "Rule of Law" model, there are also the American "constitutional" rule of law model, the French "Realm of Law" model (Li, X., 2014), and the German "Rechtsstaat" model (Liu, 2014). Many Asian, African, and Latin American countries that copied Western rule of law models not only failed to achieve the rule of law but also encountered various setbacks. All countries with a well-developed rule of law have based their efforts on their national conditions, while Latin American countries that copied other countries' models have all failed. Therefore, no country can succeed in rule of law construction without basing it on its own national conditions. Adapting to national conditions represents a common cause of success in rule of law construction across countries and is a universal law in the development of the rule of law.

Western classical liberal rule of law theory laid the foundation for the rule of law, providing a basic form and a reference for the core spirit of the rule of law for socialist rule of law theory. New liberal rule of law theory endows the rule of law with more substantial connotations, offering a reference for the value orientation of socialist rule of law theory. Moreover, the basic laws of the development of the rule of law revealed by liberal rule of law theory are partially applicable to the development of socialist rule of law.

3.2.3 Socialist Rule of Law as an Inevitable Response to Western Liberal Rule of Law

The transition from Western liberal rule of law to socialist rule of law is an inevitable trend in the development of the rule of law for humanity. Socialist rule of law is a response to the defects of Western liberal rule of law, and it is thus inevitable that it will overcome and surpass Western liberal rule of law.

A Dialectical View of Western Liberal Rule of Law

Socialist rule of law does not reject some viewpoints of liberal rule of law. Marx himself associated law with freedom, emphasizing that "the code is the Bible of the people's freedom" (Marx & Engels, 1995, p. 176). However, the freedom embraced by socialist rule of law is not the freedom of a few in a class society, but the freedom of all. The freedom advocated by the theory of socialist rule of law represents a greater degree of human freedom than that of Western liberalism. Therefore, it should absorb the spirit of freedom in liberal rule of law while transcending the limited understanding of freedom in liberalism. In capitalist society, there is no "true community" where individual freedom can be truly realized. Only in communist society is it "the common condition for the free development of individuals," where "the free development of each is the condition for the free development of all."

The socialist rule of law system with Chinese characteristics is not a closed system, but an open one with inclusiveness and the potential for development. In the process of its formation and development, it inevitably requires learning from Western liberal rule of law systems. Of course, this learning process does not entail indiscriminate acceptance but rather adheres to the principles of prioritizing China's own needs and utilizing external resources for China's benefit, based on the realities of Chinese rule of law. It involves rational reference and absorption.

Limitations of Liberal Rule of Law

Liberal rule of law has inevitable defects. With the Critical Legal Studies movement after World War II and the reflection on the capitalist rule of law, these defects of liberal rule of law began to be gradually exposed. In modern times, the West has witnessed a "crisis of the rule of law" (Berman, 1983/1993, p. 38). Unger pointed out that "Regardless of its effectiveness in preventing direct government oppression of individual freedom, the strategy of the rule of law fails to address these issues in the fundamental relationships of work and daily life" (Unger, 1976/1994, p. 240). In the West, the rule of law has always been regarded as the soul of modern states (Unger, 1976/1994, p. 180). However, after the 20th century, with the development of the welfare state, "in legislation, administration, and adjudication, there has been a rapid expansion of the disintegration of the rule of law in society (modern society)" (Sun, 2002, p. 57). Liberal rule of law has both universality and particularity. The theory of Western liberal rule of law is a summary of Western experiences in the rule of law. It is a summary of the experiences of Western liberal countries in governing their countries through law over the past few hundred years, and to a certain extent, it reveals the general laws of the rule of law. The rule of law has become the mainstream governance model for humanity, thus showing universality. Nevertheless, Western liberal rule of law is based on Western Christian culture, civil society, private ownership, and individualism. Therefore, the rule of law theories summarized from the rule of law practices of Western countries are products of their own experiences, with particularity, and are not applicable to countries without Western religious culture and liberal traditions.

Moreover, liberal rule of law is hypocritical, which is mainly manifested in the following aspects: Firstly, the economic foundation of liberal rule of law is capitalist private ownership. From the very beginning, liberal rule of law served the purpose of safeguarding the private property of the emerging bourgeoisie. Its intention was to use legal rights to protect the wealth accumulated through capital from being wantonly expropriated by feudal autocratic rulers. Liberal rule of law is based on the concept of rights-centeredness, and property rights are regarded as the foundation of freedom (Tamanaha, 2004/2010, p. 63). The liberal rule of law based on private ownership has led to a growing gap between the rich and the poor in capitalist society, and in essence, the rule of law is precisely maintaining this gap. Since the socially vulnerable groups can hardly benefit from it, capitalist rule of law is an unfair game that only benefits a minority. Engels pointed out long ago that in capitalist society, the so-called equality before the law is hypocritical. "Legal equality is equality on the premise of the inequality between the rich and the poor, that is, equality restricted within the scope of the existing major inequalities. In short, it simply calls inequality equality" (Marx & Engels, 1957, p. 648). Secondly, the justice advocated by liberal rule of law is only formal justice, not genuine justice. "Formal justice benefits those who hold economic power", so they "regard the judicature of formal rationality as the 'guarantee' of 'freedom'" (Gao, 2000). Thirdly, liberal rule of law claims that its laws are universal. However, in a class society, laws are merely the manifestation of the will of the ruling class. Fourthly, the requirement of law-abiding under liberal rule of law is not universal. The general law-abiding in capitalist society means that the proletariat is required to submit to the existing exploitation relations. The bourgeoisie, due to their class privileges, can actually be free from the constraints of the law.

Contradictions Among the Principles of Liberal Rule of Law

Among the various principles of liberal rule of law, the contradiction between the rule of law and equality is particularly evident. Conservative liberals believe that the "all men are created equal" advocated by early Enlightenment thinkers is an unattainable hypothetical state, and that inequality is not only universal and inevitable but also reasonable, as it arises from free competition and serves as a necessary means to ensure efficiency. Since the nineteenth century, liberal rule of law has carried a strong conservative color. As a forerunner of conservatism, Burke did not agree with the natural-rights concept of "all men are created equal". He believed that the law only needs to guarantee freedom, not equality, and the inequality in civil society is both natural and reasonable. The contradiction between freedom and democracy runs through the entire development of liberal rule of law. Liberalism emphasizes the uniqueness of the individual, while the rule of law and democracy require the universality of the law. Rousseau, an advocate of radical democracy, advocated popular sovereignty and equality. He believed that the general will was supreme and unrestricted. In contrast to Rousseau, figures like Jefferson advocated for the protection of the rights of the minority. As Jefferson asserted, "While in all cases, the will of the majority ought to prevail, that will must be reasonable to be valid. Moreover, the minority possess equal rights, which must be safeguarded by equal laws. Any infringement upon these rights constitutes oppression." (Jefferson, 2011, p. 318).When the rule of law conflicts with democracy, giving priority to democracy is very likely to lead to what Tocqueville called the "tyranny of the majority". The contradiction between the individual uniqueness inherent in liberalism and the universality of the law runs through the entire development of liberalism. Although liberalism has, to a certain extent, given rise to and promoted the development of the rule of law, with the development of the Enlightenment, the demand for democracy has become the mainstream of the era. When democracy becomes an irresistible trend and turns its spearhead towards freedom, freedom immediately draws a clear line from democracy. Therefore, under liberal rule of law, there is also a contradiction between freedom and democracy.

Under the framework of liberal rule of law, achieving unity between formal rule of law and substantive rule of law proves to be a formidable challenge. The formal rule of law pursued by liberalist rule of law safeguards the freedom of capital privilege rather than substantive justice. To ensure substantive justice, it is inevitable to negate, to a certain extent, the formal rule of law advocated by liberalism. Traditional formal rule of law places greater emphasis on protecting the private domain from unlawful state intervention, whereas substantive rule of law implies that state power must encroach upon those private domains that were once individual and concurrently forge new domains that do not belong to individuals; the state must more fully exercise its functions to guarantee the realization of individual freedom. The conflict between negative freedom and positive freedom is transformed into the conflict between formal rule of law and substantive rule of law. This contradiction is insurmountable within the capitalist system, rendering the unification of capitalist formal rule of law and substantive rule of law unachievable.

In summary, the liberalist rule of law system constitutes a complex and contradictory synthesis. Only by possessing a clear understanding of the particularity, limitations, hypocrisy, and inherent contradictions of Western liberalist rule of law can we avoid detours on our path to building the rule of law.

The Superiority of Socialist Rule of Law Based on Public Ownership

Compared with the rule of law developed on the basis of capitalist private ownership, socialist rule of law always adheres to the rule of law based on public ownership and emphasizes the universality of law more. The biggest difference between the socialist rule of law theory as the superstructure and the Western capitalist rule of law theory lies in the difference in the economic system. Under the socialist system, public ownership and the people's principal status put forward higher requirements for the universality of law in socialist rule of law: the law reflects the will of the vast majority of the people, rather than the will of a minority of the propertied class, so it has a more extensive public will foundation. The general observance of law under socialist rule of law further emphasizes that "no organization or individual may enjoy the privilege of overstepping the Constitution and the law." The combination of socialist rule of law and the people being the masters of the country puts forward higher requirements for law-abiding in socialist rule of law, which requires establishing the authority of the Constitution and the law, opposing any form of privilege, and truly realizing equality before the law.

The freedom guaranteed by socialist rule of law is the freedom of the vast majority. The bourgeois ideology of freedom was initially a movement against feudal autocracy and was progressive, which greatly promoted human emancipation. However, the freedom under capitalist private ownership has the following three defects: First, the capitalist system safeguards the freedom of a minority, namely the propertied class. Second, capitalist freedom is essentially limited, confined only to free trade and free employment. Third, capitalist freedom is formal and illusory. The limitations of this illusory freedom have been continuously exposed throughout history, and as a result, Western liberalist rule of law has constantly been challenged by non-rule-of-law factors. The freedom guaranteed by socialist rule of law is not that of a minority but of the vast majority. The concept of freedom advocated by socialist rule of law theory allows for a greater degree of human freedom compared to Western liberalism. It aims to achieve the free and all-around development of all mankind.

Socialist rule of law is the unity of formal rule of law and substantive rule of law, and it is the governance by good laws. From the perspective of the Marxist concept of the rule of law, the substance and form of the rule of law are two inseparable aspects (Wang & Cheng, 2014, p. 112). Without formal rule of law, substantive rule of law has no support and is not operable; without substantive values, the form of the rule of law loses its direction and value orientation. Socialist rule of law is the unity of substance and form. The governance by good laws in socialism is a true substantive rule of law, which surpasses the formalist rule of law in Western liberalism that emphasizes "formal legality" and "procedural justice". "Law is an important instrument for governing the country, and good laws are the prerequisite for good governance." As a modern socialist rule of law, Chinese rule of law should not only be a formal governance by law but also a substantive governance by good laws (Zhang, 2016).

Socialist rule of law adheres to the unity of the people being the masters of the country and governing the country according to law, thus reconciling the conflict between the rule of law and democracy. The people's congress system is the fundamental political system in China. Through this system, the people participate in the country's political life in accordance with the law and jointly manage national affairs. Governing the country according to law is an important foundation for ensuring the implementation of this fundamental political system. In addition, governing the country according to law requires giving full play to the principal position of the people, asking the people to safeguard the authority of the Constitution and the law, and fully reflecting the common will of the people.

Socialist rule of law does not completely negate the Western liberalist theory of the rule of law. Instead, it represents a form of the rule of law that is superior to capitalist rule of law. Hegel pointed out, "To truly overthrow a philosophical system lies in revealing the contradictions contained in the principles of this system and reducing these principles to ideal components within a higher and more concrete form of the idea (Hegel, 1817/1981, p. 200)." Therefore, our understanding of capitalist rule of law should also follow such a logical development process, that is, to uncover the contradictions within the various principles of the capitalist rule of law system and resolve the contradictions among these principles in a way that transcends the limitations of capitalism. Socialist rule of law is not built on a blank slate but represents a further deepening and development based on the existing achievements of human rule of law. Thus, it is necessary to draw on the ideological and theoretical resources of capitalist rule of law. Moreover, the principles that constitute socialist rule of law are fundamentally different from those of capitalist rule of law, which are based on capitalist social practice, because they are combined with socialist practice. Therefore, socialist rule of law responds to the defects exposed during the development of the rule of law to the capitalist stage, propelling the political civilization form of the rule of law to a higher level.

3.3 Ideological Foundation: Chinese Excellent Traditional Political Thought

China is one of the four ancient civilizations in the world, and it is the only one among them with an uninterrupted civilization. The Chinese nation is a great nation with a long-standing history. The profound and extensive Chinese culture has endured for thousands of years without interruption. Chinese civilization is a civilization of rites and music, which emphasizes the implementation of rites and music education and upholds benevolence, righteousness, propriety, wisdom, and trustworthiness. "The ancient legal system in our country contains a wealth of wisdom and resources. The Chinese legal system stands out among the world's major legal systems. We should study the traditional legal system in ancient China, including its successes and failures, excavate and inherit the essence of Chinese legal culture, draw on its nourishment, and select the good for use." (Xi, 2015). Traditional Chinese political thought is an important part of it. In the process of building a socialist country ruled by law with Chinese characteristics in the new era, there is no doubt that nourishment needs to be drawn from China's excellent traditional culture.

3.3.1 Excellent Cultural Genes of Traditional Chinese Political Thought

Throughout Chinese history, there have been many outstanding statesmen and thinkers. They used traditional Chinese political thought to govern the country, achieving peaceful and prosperous eras and enabling the people to live and work in peace and contentment. Therefore, these excellent ideological propositions should be inherited and promoted in contemporary China, thus providing ideological nourishment for the construction of a China under the rule of law.

The People-Oriented Thought in Ancient China

The people-oriented thought is a traditional ideology of Confucianism and an important part of ancient Chinese political thought. The connotation of the people-oriented concept has been continuously developed by statesmen and thinkers of different dynasties as dynasties changed and times evolved. "The people" occupy a central position in ancient Chinese political thought. Fundamentally, the ancient Chinese political process was profoundly influenced by the key concept of "the people are the foundation of the state". On the one hand, the people-oriented thought reflects the political stance of ancient Chinese statesmen, which clearly defines the fundamental position of the people in the country. On the other hand, it is also the starting point of ancient Chinese political philosophy, that is, the people must be regarded as the center of political activities.

In the Shang Dynasty, both the kings and the common people revered Heaven and ancestors, and both were related to the people-oriented thought. Because both the "people" and the "monarch" had to submit to the "Mandate of Heaven" and "ancestors". By the Zhou Dynasty, several generations of kings embraced and upheld the principle of "governing with the people at the core". Meanwhile, they established the "patriarchal system" and the "enfeoffment system", thus achieving a formal unity of the Zhou Dynasty for more than 800 years. "I must draw lessons from the Xia Dynasty and also from the Yin Dynasty. I dare not say that the Xia Dynasty received the Mandate of Heaven and endured for many years; nor dare I say that it would not last longer. It was only because they did not respect virtue that they lost the Mandate of Heaven early. I dare not say that the Yin Dynasty received the Mandate of Heaven and endured for many years; nor dare I say that it would not last longer. It was only because they did not respect virtue that they lost the Mandate of Heaven early" (Xiangtai Yue Family School, (n.d.-a), p. 14). The original intention of Duke Zhou's memorial was to exhort King Cheng to implement benevolent governance to maintain the Mandate of Heaven for a long time. In essence, it also reflected the ruling ideology of the Zhou Dynasty, which was to follow the will of the people and respect the people-oriented principle. During the Spring and Autumn and Warring States periods, the rise of the "shi" (scholar-official) class changed the scope of the "people". Guan Zhong, the famous Chancellor of the State of Qi in the Spring and Autumn period, was the first to clearly put forward the concept of "taking the people as the foundation" in ancient Chinese classics. "The foundation of hegemony and kingship lies in taking the people as the foundation. If the foundation is well-managed, the state will be stable; if the foundation is in chaos, the state will be in danger" (Wang, 2012, p. 151). Guan Zhong clearly put forward the basic proposition of "taking the people as the foundation" and its importance to the safety of the state. Confucius had a significant and far-reaching impact on the people-oriented thought in ancient China. After Confucius put forward the idea of "The practice of benevolenceoriginates from within oneself", there was a feasible way to emphasize the importance of "people". Confucius attached great importance to education and advocated "education without discrimination; moral cultivation of all people". Xunzi systematically inherited the people-oriented thought of Confucius and Mencius and made appropriate innovations and expansions on this basis. Xunzi's people-oriented thought was mainly manifested as: taking the economy as a prerequisite, the royal power as a necessary means, and combining ritual and law as a reinforcement, and finally aiming at "benefiting the people". His comprehensive proposal of the people-oriented thought marked the formation of the traditional

Chinese people-oriented thought (Zhang & Xu, 2014). The traditional people-oriented thought indicates that the ruling class recognized the fundamental and decisive role of the people in promoting the political and historical process. It also holds that rulers must always keep in mind the fundamental goal of benefiting the people, and it also implies a restriction on the monarch's power. However, it must be admitted that in fact, the status of the "people" was restricted far more than the "people" could restrict the royal power.

The "people-centered" ideology can be summarized as follows:

Firstly, emphasizing the importance of the people, with the view that the people are more important than the monarch and the monarch is established for the people. "Revering Heaven and protecting the people" was a warning for the Zhou Dynasty rulers to remind themselves to revere the Mandate of Heaven and understand the people's conditions. The Duke of Zhou interpreted the "Mandate of Heaven" as an understandable object through the idea that "the people's conditions are observable", which, to a certain extent, determined the humanistic trend of traditional Chinese political thought. The Duke of Zhou's view of understanding the Mandate of Heaven from the people's conditions shows that he highly valued the influence of the people, which was the precursor of the later ideology of valuing the people (Lan, 2012, pp. 42–44). The ideas of "the people are more important than the monarch" and "the monarch is established for the people" more straightforwardly indicate that the people are more significant to the country than the monarch. The people are the foundation, and the monarch only exists to serve the people. The statement "When a state is destined to prosper, it heeds the people; when it is doomed to perish, it heeds divine will" (Zuo, 2004, p. 170) shows that the people are the decisive force in a country's rise and fall. "Those who share the people's joys will have the people share their joys; those who share the people's sorrows will have the people share their sorrows. One who shares the world's joys and sorrows but fails to become a true king has never existed" (Mencius, 2007, p. 29). This is an inspiration from Mencius to rulers from the perspective of the people, suggesting that those who share weal and woe with the people can win the people's hearts and rule the country. "A ruler who loves the people secures stability; one who values the worthy gains glory; lacking both, the state perishes" (Wang, 2012, p. 232), which reflects Xunzi's view that the people are the foundation of political stability. Xunzi believed that "Heaven gave birth to the people not for the sake of the monarch; Heaven established the monarch for the people. Therefore, in ancient times, dividing land and establishing states was not just to honor the nobles; setting up official positions and differentiating ranks and salaries was not just to respect the officials" (Wang, 2012, p. 487).

In the early Han Dynasty, Jia Yi (a prominent statesman, writer, and thinker in the early Han Dynasty. His insightful essays deeply analyzed and summarized the historical lessons from the rapid fall of the Qin Dynasty, offering crucial advice for the Han Dynasty's governance) deeply summarized the historical lessons of the fall of the Qin Dynasty. He proposed that the people should have a stable living environment and a space for development. Thus, he developed the traditional Chinese people-centered ideology under the historical conditions of the early Han Dynasty and put forward a people-centered ideology with the core of "the people are the foundation of governance". In the early Tang Dynasty, Emperor Taizong realized the crucial role of the people and advocated that "the state depends on the people". Wei Zheng (Chancellor under Emperor Taizong, celebrated for his candid counsel and advocacy of benevolent governance rooted in Confucian ideals) also said, "Regard the people as if they were injured, pity their toil, and love them as one's own children" (Wang, 2013, p. 621). During the Song, Yuan, Ming, and Qing dynasties, a turbulent historical period when feudal autocracy was becoming increasingly corrupt and capitalism was gradually emerging, the people-centered ideologies put forward by Wang Fuzhi and Tang Zhen clearly combined with anti-autocratic ideas and reflected democratic factors of the budding capitalism. Wang Fuzhi's idea of "not making the world the private property of one person" and Tang Zhen's statement of "all emperors are thieves" clearly show this tendency.

Secondly, ensuring the well-being of the people. The people are like water, and the ruler is like a boat. The people are the foundation of the state. According to the *Book of Documents*, Yu, the founder of the Xia Dynasty, once said, "To understand people is wisdom and enables one to appoint officials. To bring peace to the people is benevolence, and the common people will cherish it." (Xiangtai Yue's Family School (n.d.-b), p. 6). The Duke of Zhou also said, "Nurture and protect the humble people; extend benevolence to the destitute" (Xiangtai Yue's Family School (n.d.-c), p. 9). After Confucianism became the official ideology, this concept was further developed and deeply rooted in people's hearts. "The ruler is like a boat, and the common people are like water. Water can carry the boat, and water can also capsize it" (Wang, 2012, p. 151). This statement has become a topic for thinkers advocating people-centered governance since the Han and Tang Dynasties. In the early Tang Dynasty, Wei Zheng and Emperor Taizong Li Shimin clearly put forward the theory of the people being water and the ruler being a boat, clearly indicating the extreme importance of water to the boat. It was precisely because the Tang Dynasty took the fall of the Sui Dynasty as a warning that it was able to create the prosperous "Reign of Zhenguan (golden era of stable governance, economic growth, and cultural achievement under Emperor Taizong's Confucian leadership)". "In governance, the people are the foundation of everything. The state takes the people as its foundation, the ruler takes the people as his foundation, and officials take the people as their foundation. Therefore, the safety and danger of the state depend on the people, the prestige and disgrace of the ruler depend on the people, and the honor and disgrace of officials depend on the people. This is what it means that the people are the foundation of everything" (Jia, 2011, p. 101). This shows Jia Yi's recognition of the fundamental status of the people. "In governance, the people are the source of all strength. The state relies on the people for strength, the ruler relies on the people for strength, and officials rely on the people for strength. Therefore, in a war, victory depends on the will of the people; in an attack, success depends on the will of the people; in defense, survival depends on the will of the people. If the people are led into battle but do not desire victory, victory cannot be achieved. When the people support their ruler and are eager to advance in the face of the enemy without restraint, the enemy will surely be terrified, and victory in war can be achieved.

However, if the people are afraid and flee when facing the enemy, defeat in war is inevitable. Thus, disasters and blessings do not solely depend on heaven but also on the people" (Jia, 2011, p. 101). This reflects Jia Yi's clear understanding of the significant influence of the people in major national events and dynastic changes. Social stability is the basis for the peaceful life of the people. Therefore, it is necessary to alleviate the misfortunes of the people caused by social unrest, natural disasters, and other uncertainties, and to provide timely relief and comfort to those who have suffered misfortunes.

Thirdly, it emphasizes benefiting the people. It holds the view that the people are the masters while the monarch is the guest, and the essence of governance lies in nurturing the people. Guanzi was well-aware that it was indispensable for rulers to gain benefits from the people. However, he also recognized that only when rulers implemented policies beneficial to the people and brought them tangible benefits could the rulers themselves reap rewards. "Knowing that giving is a means of taking is the treasure of governance" (Guan, 2009, p. 5). "In general, the way to govern a country must first enrich the people. When the people are wealthy, they are easy to govern; when the people are poor, they are difficult to govern. Wealthy people will love their hometowns and cherish their families. Loving their hometowns and cherishing their families will make them respect the superiors and fear breaking the law. Respecting the superiors and fearing breaking the law will make them easy to govern" (Guan, 2009, p. 256). Confucius' idea of "benefiting the people according to their interests" (Confucious, 2007, p. 306) and Mencius' concept of "governing the people by ensuring permanent livelihoods" (Mencius, 2007, p. 104) precisely elaborate on this proposition. Xunzi once classified the ways in which monarchs treated the people into three types. The first type of monarch was ignorant of benefiting and loving the people, only knowing how to exploit the people's labor and wealth. The second type of monarch, on the basis of benefiting and loving the people, then made use of the people's labor and wealth. The third type of monarch only focused on benefiting and loving the people without demanding any return from them. Xunzi believed that a monarch adopting the first way of governance would lead the country to peril and decline; a monarch adopting the second way could stabilize his regime; while a monarch adopting the third way could bring peace and order to the world. In the Song Dynasty, Zhang Zai, Cheng Hao (prominent philosophers in the Song Dynasty, whose thoughts had a profound influence on the development of Confucianism and Neo-Confucianism, emphasizing moral cultivation, understanding of the universe, and the relationship between man and nature) and others said, "The way of governance should be based on conforming to the people's will, enriching the people's livelihood, and ensuring their peace without harassment." Emperor Chengzu of the Ming Dynasty once said, "I believe that serving Heaven should be based on sincerity and respect, and loving the people should prioritize tangible benefits." Wang Fuzhi (a renowned philosopher in the late Ming and early Qing dynasties, whose profound philosophical thoughts covered multiple aspects such as ontology, epistemology, and history) advocated "hiding wealth among the people." Huang Zongxi (a prominent thinker and historian in the late Ming and early Qing dynasties, criticizing autocratic monarchy), in *Waiting for the Dawn: A Plan for the Prince*, argued that in ancient society, the people were the masters and the monarch was the guest, and the monarch's duty was to serve the people (Huang, 1633/2011, p. 8). Tang Zhen (an outstanding thinker in the early Qing Dynasty, well-known for his critical view on autocratic monarchy) held the same view. Given the historical conditions at that time, the proposal of the concept of civil rights can be regarded as the peak of the ancient people-oriented ideology. Since they could not completely abandon the monarchy, it was a remarkable achievement to be able to criticize the autocratic monarchy.

In conclusion, the view that the state, the monarch, and politics should all be people-oriented is the core idea of ancient Chinese people-oriented ideology. This view has been consolidated and enriched through the profound thinking, continuous self-reflection, and clear-headed awareness of statesmen, philosophers, and thinkers throughout the dynasties (Zhang, 2004, p. 334).

The Thought of Benevolent Governance in Ancient China

The thought of benevolent governance in ancient China was initiated by Confucius and further developed by Mencius. Its core concept is the people-centered ideology. Firstly, Mencius believed that the foundation of benevolent governance is "providing the people with means of livelihood". He emphasized that rulers should love the people, oppose tyranny and excessive taxation, and ensure that the common people have basic living guarantees, which is the cornerstone of political stability. Mencius advocated the theory of innate goodness, urging rulers to implement "benevolent governance" extensively. That is, they should extend their benevolence to others, understand the people's conditions, be aware of the people's sufferings, and improve people's livelihood. Considering the social development level at that time, Mencius' view of attaching importance to the small-scale peasant economy, advocating the solution of people's livelihood issues, and ensuring political stability was a very advanced concept. "Benevolent governance must start with the demarcation of land boundaries" (Mencius, 2007, p. 105). Realizing the dependence of the national economy and people's lives on land, Mencius regarded the land issue as the key to "benevolent governance", which was indeed hitting the nail on the head.

Secondly, Mencius further elaborated on Confucius' proposition of "practice thrift and care for the people", and put forward the idea of loving the people by reducing corvée and taxes. This ensured that the people could carry out agricultural activities in a timely manner during the seasons suitable for crop cultivation, management, and harvest, ultimately guaranteeing the people's livelihood and the country's material foundation. When the people can farm and harvest on time and are not burdened with heavy taxes, they will naturally live in contentment and peace, which is also the ultimate goal of benevolent governance. "If the agricultural seasons are not violated, there will be more grain than can be consumed" (Mencius, 2007, p. 5). "There is fat meat in the kitchen and fat horses in the stable, yet the people wear hungry looks and there are starved corpses in the wilderness. This is leading beasts to devour people" (Mencius, 2007, p. 7). In general, in an agricultural society, it is benevolent governance for rulers to enable the people to work in accordance with the natural seasons and have no worries about their livelihood. Even from a modern perspective, Mencius'view of regarding the quality of people's lives as the benchmark for rulers'governance ability is extremely reasonable and scientific. In addition to the aspect of people's livelihood, Mencius also developed the Confucian view on punishment. His proposal of "reducing punishments" meant reducing and relaxing penalties. He strongly opposed extremely harsh punishments such as "collective punishment", thus reflecting the concept of benevolence.

As for wars that are violent, aggressive, and life-taking, Mencius could not tolerate them at all. He believed that extreme acts like war would only bring about the destruction of lives and irreparable harm to the people. Therefore, he criticized that "A just war was nowhere to be found during the Spring and Autumn Period". "When states fight for land, the killed fill the fields; when they fight for cities, the killed fill the cities. This is what it means to seek land and devour human flesh. Their crimes are too heinous to be atoned for even by death" (Mencius, 2007, p. 159). This is Mencius' merciless condemnation of rulers who launched wars of annexation. "If the king implements benevolent governance for the people, reduces punishments, lightens taxes, encourages deep plowing and weeding, and allows the young men to learn filial piety, fraternal duty, loyalty, and good faith in their leisure time, then at home they can serve their fathers and elder brothers, and outside they can serve their superiors. In this way, they can even use sticks to fight against the strong armors and sharp weapons of the states of Qin and Chu" (Mencius, 2007, p. 9). "In the present era, if a state with ten thousand chariots implements benevolent governance, the people will be as delighted as if they were rescued from a desperate situation" (Mencius, 2007, p. 53). These are all Mencius' earnest exhortations to rulers to implement benevolent governance and his hope that rulers can save the people from misery through benevolent governance.

In Mencius' view, the implementation of the "benevolent governance" requires a multi-pronged and simultaneous approach. In terms of political aspect, the practice of benevolence should gradually extend from oneself to others. Firstly, rulers should embody benevolence and righteousness in their own conduct, setting a good example to inspire the general public. Secondly, benevolence and righteousness should be incorporated into practical policies. As Mencius said, "If a ruler loves benevolence, he will be invincible under heaven" (Mencius, 2007, p. 151). Rulers must respect and promote the worthy. They should "value virtue and respect scholars" (Mencius, 2007, p. 66), select and appoint the virtuous and capable, so that "the worthy hold positions and the capable occupy offices". Then, "all the scholars under heaven will be pleased and willing to serve in his court" (Mencius, 2007, p. 67). Thirdly, the penalties should be mitigated. As for economic aspect, taxes should be reduced, following the principle of "lightening tax burdens". Attention should be paid to agricultural production, with emphasis on "deep plowing and timely weeding". It can be said that Mencius recognized the significance of the economic foundation for the superstructure. Therefore, he stressed that the people must be able to be self-sufficient and free from concerns about their livelihood. In the aspect of education, moral education should be carried out. As Mencius advocated, "The young and strong should use their leisure time to cultivate filial piety, loyalty, and trustworthiness" (Mencius, 2007, p. 9; Zhang, 2012).

The Thought of Rule By Virtue in Ancient China

The thought of rule by virtue can be regarded as the essence of traditional political culture in ancient China. It originated in the Three Dynasties (Xia, Shang, and Zhou), was carried forward by Confucianism, and was adopted by rulers of all dynasties. Generally speaking, the thought of rule by virtue encompasses several levels of requirements: Firstly, it requires rulers to lead by example, pay attention to self-cultivation and diligence in government affairs, and give full play to the moral influence. Secondly, it emphasizes the moral education of the people, advocating "governing the state with virtue". Thirdly, it advocates that virtue should take precedence over punishment. The concepts of "upholding virtue and exercising caution in punishment" in the Zhou Dynasty and "governing the state with virtue" evolved, improved, and innovated from the Western Han Dynasty through the Eastern Han Dynasty, the Wei, Jin, and the Southern and Northern Dynasties, integrating rituals and laws. Eventually, the idea of rule by virtue, which holds that "virtue and rituals are the foundation of governance, while punishment is the means of governance" (Yue (Ed.), 2013, p. 3) was clearly stipulated in the *Tang Code* and continuously inherited and promoted in later generations.

"Virtue" was the foundation and governing strategy for all dynasties in ancient China. Confucianism, represented by Confucius, actively advocated rule by virtue, offering various specific measures of virtuous governance to those in power. Through thinking and practice, a complete strategy of rule by virtue was formulated. As the saying goes, "If one is upright, one needs no orders; if one is not upright, even orders will not be obeyed" (Confucious, 2007, p. 189). This means that both kings and ministers are the practitioners of the Confucian theory of rule by virtue. Only those with noble character who lead by example and win people's hearts through virtue can shoulder the heavy responsibility of governing the country. "Embrace the five excellences and avoid the four evils, and then one can engage in government affairs" (Confucious, 2007, p. 306). Confucius believed that high-moral character was the basic qualification for those in power. Based on this view, politics is essentially a matter of morality. When rulers reach the highest realm of virtue and rituals—"benevolence"—in the process of governing the country, a peaceful and prosperous era will naturally emerge. The saying "He who exercises government by means of his virtue may be compared to the north polar star, which keeps its place and all the stars turn towards it" (Confucious, 2007, p. 12) further emphasizes the crucial role of virtue in national governance.

During the Warring States period, the various schools of thought all had certain understandings of rule by virtue. Mencius and Xunzi inherited and developed Confucius's idea of rule by virtue. Mencius proposed nourishing the people with virtue, educating the people with virtue, and winning over the world with virtue. "Relying on force while feigning benevolence leads to dominance through hegemony, which typically requires a powerful state. However, governing with true virtue and benevolence leads to a just and legitimate rule that is not dependent on the size of the state. Emperor Tang managed to build a respected realm with only seventy li of land, and King Wen of Zhou achieved the same with a mere hundred li" (Mencius, 2007, p. 65). This passage expounds that virtue has the effect of defeating the large with the small and conquering the strong with the gentle, and it is the guarantee of long-lasting achievements. "Propriety is the guiding principle of governance. If governance is not based on propriety, it will not succeed" (Wang, 2012, p. 477). This is Xunzi's further elaboration on rule by virtue. The essence of rule by propriety is actually rule by virtue. Although the Legalists prioritized the "law" as the cornerstone of governing the country, they also attached importance to rule by virtue. In particular, they recognized that "virtue" played an irreplaceable role in maintaining the social ethical order. "Well-defined moral values enable the effective promotion of moral education" was a representative view of Shang Yang, a core figure of the Legalist school. "Those who practice frugality will prosper, while those who indulge in luxury will perish" (Mo, 2016, p. 47). This shows the impact of "virtue" on the rise and fall of a country. The Mohists gave a new meaning to rule by virtue, that is, cultivating virtue through frugality, and the highest virtue lies in extreme simp

After the Qin Dynasty achieved great unification, rule by virtue was highly respected by many statesmen. In the early Western Han Dynasty, there was a trend of valuing military power and despising virtue in society. In response, the Confucians put forward the proposition of rule by virtue again. "In governance, morality takes precedence; in conduct, benevolence and righteousness are the cornerstone. Hence, those in high-ranking positions without virtue shall be ousted, the wealthy lacking in righteousness shall face penalties, the lowly who cherish virtue shall be esteemed, and the poor who adhere to righteousness shall be glorified" (Wang, 1986, p. 159). Lu Jia (an important thinker, diplomat, and writer in the early Han Dynasty, emphasizing the combination of Confucian and Taoist idea) thus expressed his profound insights into rule by virtue—the core spirit of politics is virtue, and virtue, which is supreme benevolence, has a decisive influence on the rise and fall of a country. Dong Zhongshu, the consummate integrator of Han-Dynasty Confucianism, inherited the pre-Qin Confucian proposition of rule by virtue in his political thought: "The fundamental principle of the Heavenly Way is centered around the concepts of yin and yang. Yang corresponds to moral virtue, and yin corresponds to legal penalty. Penalty is associated with the act of killing, while virtue is related to the act of giving life. As such, yang is dominant during the summer season, with the main task of facilitating the birth, development, and nourishment of all things in nature. Yin is dominant during the winter season, remaining in a state of inactivity and non-application. Through this observation, it can be concluded that the Heavenly order emphasizes moral governance rather than the use of penalties" (*Hanshu* (Vol. 8), 1962, p. 2502). In terms of the state-governing strategy, Dong Zhongshu advocated that virtue should take precedence over punishment. The virtue and ability of officials are also related to the survival of the country: "The downfall of a country is due to the corruption of officials. The moral decline of officials is manifested in blatant favoritism and bribery" (Zuo, 2004, p. 52).

3.3.2 *The Significance of Traditional Chinese Political Thought for the Innovation of Chinese Rule of Law Discourse System*

General Secretary Xi Jinping summarized China's excellent traditional culture as "advocating benevolence, valuing the people, adhering to integrity, upholding justice, promoting harmony, and pursuing common ground" (Xi, 2014). This coincides with the core spirit of modern rule of law in many aspects. The rule of law under socialism with Chinese characteristics must draw on the ideological essence of people-orientation, benevolent governance, and rule by virtue. The people-oriented ideology serves as the foundation for benevolent governance and rule by virtue. Benevolent governance and rule by virtue are centered around the people-oriented ideology, and they are closely related, complementing and functioning together. The "people-centered" concept advocated by the theory of socialism with Chinese characteristics is an inheritance and transcendence of the people-oriented ideology. Building a service-oriented government is a development and innovation of the concept of benevolent governance. Adhering to the combination of rule by law and rule by virtue is an inheritance and sublimation of the ideology of rule by virtue. Therefore, the people-oriented, benevolent governance, and rule by virtue ideologies constitute an important source for the innovation of Chinese rule of law discourse system.

Modern Significance of the Traditional People-Oriented Ideology Centered on Respecting, Loving, Benefiting, and Enriching the People

The "people-centered" concept in the Scientific Outlook on Development is a critical inheritance of the traditional people-oriented ideology. The core of the Scientific Outlook on Development is the people-centered approach, which emphasizes that the people should be the masters of the country. The government exists to seek the well-being of the people, and the purpose of the ruling party is to serve the people whole-heartedly. The power of all state organs comes from the people. The essence of the Scientific Outlook on Development is to put the people in the most important position, emphasizing that the starting point and the ultimate goal of the Party's governance are the rights and interests of the people. It is necessary to give play to the people's initiative, safeguard the people's various rights and interests, pursue common prosperity, and promote the all-around development of the people. The "people-centered" concept adheres to the historical materialism that the people are the creators of history, implements the Party's mass line, firmly establishes the firm belief of "establish the Party for the public interest and govern for the people", and serves the people whole-heartedly. It takes the people as the supporting force, aims to comprehensively improve the people's qualities, measures by the respect for the people, and ultimately safeguards the people's rights and interests, ensuring that development is for the people, by the people, and the fruits of development are shared by the people (Hu, 2007). This is a critical inheritance of the traditional people-oriented ideology, and it enriches the connotation and extension of the people-oriented ideology in line with the characteristics and development needs of the era, enabling the people-oriented ideology to have new connotations in the new era and ultimately serving the construction of socialism with Chinese characteristics. General Secretary Xi Jinping emphasized that "the people should be placed in the highest position in the heart…The people-centered approach is the value orientation of the Party's governance. The people are the source of strength for the ruling party, and the people's position is the fundamental political position of the ruling party… To achieve the Two Centenary Goals and the Chinese Dream of the great rejuvenation of the Chinese nation, we must always adhere to the people-centered approach, taking the improvement of people's well-being and the promotion of the all-around development of the people as the starting point and the ultimate goal of promoting economic and social development. The people-centered approach is reflected in the ruling concept, institutional design, and the sharing of development fruits by the people" (Xi, 2016a, pp. 212–226).

General Secretary Xi Jinping clearly pointed out that we should adhere to the people-centered development ideology and practice the new development concepts of innovation, coordination, green development, openness, and sharing (Xi, 2016a, p. 128). The five new development concepts demonstrate the traditional ideology of benevolent governance, answering the questions of the subject, the object, and the ultimate goal of development. The "people-centered" concept was first established at the Fifth Plenary Session of the 18th Central Committee of the Communist Party of China. This is an essential expression of the people as the masters of the country, clarifying the core concept of putting the people first, and it is also the spirit that the five new development concepts should implement throughout. The new development concepts translate the people-centered approach into reality. To fulfill the people's expectations for happiness, efforts are made to create a fair, stable, and harmonious social environment for the people, allowing them to freely pursue a better future.

Consistencies Between the Service-Oriented Government and the Ancient Thoughts of Benevolent Governance and Good Governance

The goal of good governance in the modernization of national governance reflects the concept of benevolent governance in traditional political culture. The rule of law discourse system of socialism with Chinese characteristics pursues good laws and good governance, shaping the goal of good governance in the modernization of national governance with good laws that meet moral requirements. The ultimate goal of good governance is to realize the Chinese Dream of the well-being of all the Chinese people. The goal of good governance inherits the people-centered core of the concept of benevolent governance, requiring those in power to take the well-being of the people as the ultimate goal and establish a service-oriented government. At the same time, the goal of good governance innovates the connotation of benevolent governance according to the requirements of the times. Benevolent governance is a monarchical rule that requires rulers to be benevolent themselves, which sets requirements for a good ruler. In contrast, good governance emphasizes national governance and citizens' participation in management. It requires the government to adhere to the principle of maximizing public interests, return power to the people, implant the concepts of democracy and fairness in the hearts of the people, actively cultivate citizens' awareness, establish the "people-centered" concept of citizens' rights supremacy, multi-dimensionally broaden the channels and opportunities for citizens to participate in public decision-making, guide citizens to actively participate and better cooperate with the government, and jointly carry out socialist modernization. Therefore, the key to good governance lies in the manifestation of the people's dominant position and the people's will. Good governance requires the popularization of democratic and political values of rule of law (Yu, 2014). The prerequisite for good governance is good laws. Only under the premise of governing the country according to the law and good laws can we ensure the practical path for the realization of benevolent governance and promote the modernization of national governance.

The Inheritance and Innovation of the Ideology of Rule by Virtue in Chinese Rule of Law Discourse System

Ancient statesmen have always advocated the importance of virtue in national governance and proposed rule by virtue as a crucial approach to governing the country. In traditional political culture, rule by virtue requires rulers to possess good moral qualities, using virtue to correct themselves, benefit the people, cultivate integrity, and establish a just public image.

Chinese rule of law discourse system inherits and promotes the essence of the rule by virtue ideology that meets the needs of the times. In 2006, Comrade Hu Jintao put forward the Socialist Concept of Honor and Disgrace. Centered on serving the people, it advocates collective honor, patriotism, respect for labor, and the spirit of scientific exploration. It was proposed in response to bad moral trends such as money-worship, hedonism, sacrificing justice for personal gain, embezzling public funds for private use, dishonesty, and fraud. The "Eight Honors and Eight Disgraces" uses traditional moral concepts to shape the modern concept of honor and disgrace, guiding the public to balance the relationships among individuals, collectives, and the nation. It represents the core essence of outstanding traditional Chinese qualities, meets the call of the new era, and is a socialist expression with Chinese characteristics of worldviews, outlooks on life, and values. It provides a guiding beacon for the spiritual cultivation and actions of modern Chinese citizens, elevates the status of morality in national governance, and is a critical inheritance of the traditional ideology of governing the country by virtue.

Since the Fourth Plenary Session of the 18th Central Committee of the Communist Party of China, the Party Central Committee has further emphasized the combination of governing the country by law and governing the country by virtue to promote the modernization of national governance. Governing the country by virtue is a good application of the rule by virtue ideology in traditional Chinese political culture. The core socialist values of "patriotism, dedication, integrity, and friendliness" clearly advocate moral norms for citizens. This is an inheritance and promotion of the outstanding rule by virtue genes in traditional culture, such as patriotism, hard working spirit, honesty, and amicable relations. It integrates a sense of morality into people's production, life, and spiritual world, creating a positive and healthy social atmosphere.

General Secretary Xi Jinping emphasized, "We must adhere to the combination of governing the country by law and governing the country by virtue. Law is written morality, and morality is the law in people's hearts. Both law and morality have the function of regulating social behavior and maintaining social order. When governing the country and society, we must grasp both law -based governance and virtue-based governance. We should attach importance to both the regulatory role of the law and the educational role of morality, so that the law and morality complement each other, and law-based governance and virtue-based governance achieve mutual reinforcement" (Xi, 2015). This passage profoundly explains the relationship between law and morality in the modern national governance strategy, placing rule by virtue on an equal footing with rule by law. "Those who have no sense of shame will do anything." Without the nourishment of morality, the rule of law culture will lack a source of vitality, and the implementation of the law will lack a solid social foundation. In the process of promoting the rule of law, we must vigorously promote the core socialist values and outstanding traditional Chinese virtues, cultivate social morality, professional ethics, family virtues, and personal morality, and improve the ideological and moral level of the entire nation to create a favorable cultural environment for governing the country by law (Xi, 2015). This fully demonstrates that the contemporary Chinese concept of governing the country by law inherits and promotes the rule by virtue ideology in traditional Chinese culture.

The law ensures social stability, while virtue nourishes people's hearts. "The rule of law and the rule of virtue are inseparable and neither should be neglected. National governance requires the coordinated efforts of law and morality…Laws and regulations should set clear moral guidelines and promote virtues and righteous deeds. Legislation, law-enforcement, and judicial work should all reflect the moral requirements of socialism and integrate the core socialist values, so that socialist rule of law can achieve good governance through good laws" (Xi, 2016b). The rule of virtue in socialism, through the critical inheritance of traditional ideas of governing by virtue, has been transformed into contemporary core moral concepts such as the socialist concept of honor and disgrace and the core socialist values. It is organically integrated and unified with the modern concept of governing the country by law. Based on the cultivation of social morality, professional ethics, family virtues, and personal morality, it provides a moral foundation for the rule of law, thereby further consolidating the practical foundation of the rule of law.

3.4 Conclusion

The formation and development of Chinese rule of law ideology represent the inheritance and innovation of China's profound historical and cultural heritage. This ideological system not only absorbs the essence of Western liberal rule of law ideology but also takes root in China's excellent traditional political thoughts, thus forming a rule of law theory with distinct national and contemporary characteristics.

Western liberal rule of law ideology is regarded as a model of human rule of law. Its core concepts include safeguarding individual freedom, restricting state power, implementing the separation of powers, and practicing constitutionalism. These ideas have provided important intellectual references for China's socialist rule of law construction. However, socialist rule of law does not simply copy Western liberal rule of law; instead, it goes beyond it on the basis of reference. Socialist rule of law emphasizes the universality and people-orientation of the law, adheres to the rule of law based on public ownership, and aims to guarantee the freedom of the vast majority of people. At the same time, socialist rule of law also focuses on the unity of formal and substantive rule of law, pursues the governance of good laws, and achieves a dialectical negation and transcendence of Western liberal rule of law.

China's traditional political thoughts contain rich rule of law wisdom, such as the people-centered ideology, the ideology of benevolent governance, and the ideology of rule by virtue. These thoughts provide important nourishment for the innovation of Chinese rule of law discourse system in the new era. The people-centered ideology emphasizes that "the people are the foundation of the state", believing that the people are the foundation and root of the country. This ideology has been critically inherited and developed in modern rule of law construction, forming the development concept of "putting people first". The ideology of benevolent governance advocates that rulers should implement benevolent governance extensively, love and benefit the people, which coincides with the construction concept of a modern service-oriented government.

The ideology of rule by virtue emphasizes the important role of morality in national governance, providing theoretical support for the combination of governing the country by law and by virtue. On the basis of inheriting China's traditional political thoughts, Chinese rule of law ideology has been innovated and developed. For example, the development concept of "putting people first" is integrated into rule of law construction, emphasizing that the rule of law should take safeguarding people's rights and interests as the starting point and foothold; the ideology of benevolent governance is transformed into the practice of building a service-oriented government, emphasizing that the government should provide high-quality and efficient services for the people; the ideology of rule by virtue is integrated into the rule of law system, emphasizing that law and morality complement and promote each other.

The formation and development of the socialist rule of law ideology with Chinese characteristics demonstrate the profound connotation and unique contribution of the global exchange and mutual learning of rule of law civilizations. This ideological system does not exist in isolation. Instead, it draws on the common wisdom of global rule of law, especially the reasonable core of Western liberal rule of law ideology, and is deeply rooted in the historical soil of Eastern civilization, realizing the creative transformation and innovative development of traditional legal culture. It reflects the integration and innovation of rule of law concepts in different legal systems and cultural backgrounds, providing a new paradigm of pluralistic coexistence for global rule of law development.

References

Aristotle. (1983). *Politics* (S. Wu, Trans.). (pp. 167–168, 199). The Commercial Press.

Berman, H. J. (1983/1993). *Law and revolution: The formation of the western legal tradition* (W. He, Trans.). (p. 38). China Encyclopedia Press.

Confucious. (2007). *The Analects* (Y. Zhang, Trans. & Anno.). Zhonghua Book Company.

de Montesquieu, C. L. S. (1721/1958). *Persian Letters* (D. Luo, Trans.). (p. 178). People's Literature Publishing House.

Dicey, A. V. (1885/2001). *An introduction to the study of the law of the constitution* (B. Lei, Trans.). (pp. 244–245). China Legal Publishing House.

Gao, H. (2000). Conflicts and integrations in modern Western rule of law. *Tsinghua Law Review*, 1.

Guan, Z. (2009). *Guanzi* (Li, S., Trans. & Anno.). (pp. 5, 256). Zhonghua Book Company.

Hamilton, A., Jay, J., & Madison, J. (1788/1995). *The federalist papers* (F. Cheng, Trans.). (p. 264). The Commercial Press.

Hanshu (Vol. 8e). (1962). Zhonghua Book Company (p. 2502).

Harrington, J. (1656/1981). *Oceana* (X. He, Trans.). (pp. 21, 25). The Commercial Press.

Hayek, F. A. (1960/1997). *The Constitution of Liberty (Volume I)* (Z. Deng, Trans.). (pp. 61, 68). Sanlian Bookstore.

Hegel, G. W. F. (1817/1981). *The Lesser logic* (L. He, Trans.). (p. 200). The Commercial Press.

Hu, J. (2007, October 25). Hold high the great banner of socialism with Chinese characteristics and strive for new victories in building a moderately prosperous society in all respects: Report at the 17th National Congress of the Communist Party of China. *People's Daily*.

Huang, Z. (1633/2011). *Waiting for the dawn: A plan for the prince* (Z. Duan, Trans. & Anno.). (p. 8). Zhonghua Book Company.

Jefferson, T. (2011). *Selected works of Jefferson* (Z. Zhu, Trans.). Commercial Press.

Jia, Y. (2011). *New writings* (Wang, Z., Trans.). (p. 101). Fenghuang Publishing House.

Lan, Y. (2012). *A history of Chinese political thought* (pp. 42–44). Higher Education Press.

Li, H. (2015). History and myth: The 800-year legend. *Peki University Law Journal*, 6.

Li, L. (2014). From the legal system to the rule of law system: From "constructive rationalism" to "evolutionary rationalism"-Based on the political reports from the 15th to the 4th Plenary Session of the 18th CPC Central Committee. *Journal of Gansu University of Political Science and Law*, 6.

Li, X. (2014). A multi-dimensional investigation of the development of the rule of law in France: The path of the rule of law in the "country of law". *SJTU Law Review*, 4.

Liu, G. (2014). The historical origin of the German "Rechtsstaat". *SJTU Law Review*, 4.

Locke, J. (1689/1996). *Two treatises of government* (Vol. 2, pp. 16, 35–36, 53, 85, 88) (Q. Ye & J. Qu, Trans.). The Commercial Press.

Marx, K., & Engels, F. (1957). *Collected works of Marx and Engels* (Vol. 2, p. 648). People's Publishing House.
Marx, K., & Engels, F. (1995). *Collected works of Marx and Engels* (Vol. 1, p. 176). People's Publishing House.
Mencius. (2007). *The book of Mencius* (L. Wan & X. Lan, Trans. & Anno.). (pp. 5, 7, 9, 29, 53, 65–67, 104-105, 151, 159). Zhonghua Book Company.
Mo, Z. (2016). *Mozi* (X. Li, Trans. & Anno.). (p. 47). Zhonghua Book Company.
Paine, T. (1776/1982). *The selected works of Thomas Paine* (Q. Ma, et al., Trans.). (pp. 35–36, 142, 146). The Commercial Press.
Qin, D., & Zhang, A. (1999). Cultivating the dominant spiritual culture of Chinese society. *Exploration and Free Views*, 2.
Radbruch, G. (1910/2013). *Introduction to Jurisprudence* (J. Mi, Trans.). (pp. 20–21). The Commercial Press.
Rousseau, J. J. (1755/1962). *Discourse on the origin and basis of inequality Among Men* (C. Li, Trans.). (p. 53). The Commercial Press.
Rousseau, J. J. (1762/1980). *The social contract* (Z. He, Trans.). (pp. 57, 130). The Commercial Press.
Sun, G. (2002). *On the socialist rule of law* (p. 57). Law Press.
Tamanaha, B. Z. (2004/2010). *On the rule of law: History, politics, theory* (G. Li, Trans.). (p. 63). Wuhan University Press.
Unger, R. (1976/1994). *Law in modern society* (H. Zhou, Trans.). China University of Political Science and Law Press.
Wang, J. (2013). *Important political principles of the Zhenguan reign* (p. 621). Shanghai Sanlian Bookstore.
Wang, L. (1986). *New discourses (Annotated and Collated)* (p. 159). Zhonghua Book Company.
Wang, R., & Cheng, L. (2014). *On the rule of law* (p. 112, 458). Shandong People's Publishing House.
Wang, X. (2012). *Collected annotations on Xunzi* (p. 151, 232, 477, 487). Zhonghua Book Company.
Xi, J. (2014, July 9). Readings on the Series of Important Speeches by General Secretary Xi Jinping: On Building a Strong Socialist Culture Country. *People's Daily*.
Xi, J. (2015). Accelerating the construction of a socialist country under the rule of law. *Qiushi*, 1.
Xi, J. (2016a). *Readings on the series of important speeches by General Secretary Xi Jinping* (pp. 128, 212–226). Learning Press & People's Publishing House.
Xi, J. (2016b, December 10). *Xi Jinping Emphasizes Combining Law-Based Governance and Governance by Virtue to Advance the Modernization of the National Governance System and Governance Capacity during the 37th Group Study Session of the Political Bureau of the CPC Central Committee*. http://www.xinhuanet.com/politics/2016-12/10/c_1120093133.htm
Xiangtai Yue Family School. (n.d.-a). *Sibu Beiyao: Classics section-book of documents, Volume 2: Institutions of Gao Yao, Chapter 4*. Zhonghua Book Company.
Xiangtai Yue Family School. (n.d.-b). *Sibu Beiyao: Classics section-book of documents, Volume 8: Announcement to Shao*. Zhonghua Book Company.
Xiangtai Yue Family School. (n.d.-c). *Sibu Beiyao: Classics section-book of documents, volume 9: Exhortation against indulgence, Chapter 17*. Zhonghua Book Company.
Yu, K. (2014). Promoting the modernization of the national governance system and governance capacity. *Frontline*, 1.
Yue, C. (Ed.). (2013). *Commentaries on the Tang Code* (p. 3). Shanghai Ancient Books Publishing House.
Zhang, F. (2004). *Chinese imperial concepts: The cultural paradigm of "Respecting the Monarch-Blaming the Monarch" in social general consciousness* (p. 334). Renmin University of China Press.
Zhang, H. (1983). *History of western legal thoughts* (p. 248). Peking University Press.
Zhang, W. (2016). Research on Xi Jinping's thought on the rule of law (Part II)-General theories of Xi Jinping's thought on the rule of law. *Legal and Social Development*, 3.

Zhang, Z. (2012). On Mencius' "benevolent governance" thought centered on the concept of "people-oriented". *Social Sciences*, 5.

Zhang, Z., & Xu, Y. (2014). The development logic of ancient Chinese people-oriented thought from the perspective of historical process. *Journal of Shandong University (Philosophy and Social Sciences)*, 6.

Zhou, Y. (2016). *Constitution*. Higher Education Press.

Zuo, Q. (2004). *Annotations and translations of Zuo Zhuan* (Vol. I, pp. 52, 170) (M. Li, Trans. & Anno.). Shanghai Ancient Books Publishing House.

Chapter 4
The Basic Constituents of Chinese Rule of Law Discourse

4.1 Introduction

In the construction of the socialist rule of law system with Chinese characteristics, this chapter focuses on the core components of Chinese rule of law discourse system: the fundamental rule of law discourse and the cornerstone rule of law discourse. These two are not only the theoretical cornerstones of the rule of law construction but also the guiding principles for practical operations. The rule of law, being the cornerstone of modern national governance, the construction of its discourse system is not only related to the improvement and implementation of legal systems but also profoundly affects the effectiveness of national governance and the realization of social fairness and justice. Against the backdrop of the exchange and mutual learning of global rule of law civilizations, the establishment of Chinese rule of law discourse system is not only a profound summary of its own rule of law practice experience but also an important contribution to the diversity of the world's rule of law civilizations.

The fundamental rule of law discourse, as the soul of Chinese rule of law discourse system, profoundly reflects the essential characteristics and core values of the socialist rule of law with Chinese characteristics. It is based on the fundamental principle of "the organic unity of the Party's leadership, the people being the masters of the country, and law-based governance." This principle of "the three-in-one unity" is not only a high-level condensation of the path of Chinese rule of law construction but also a profound understanding of the essential attributes of the rule of law.

However, the realization of the fundamental rule of law discourse cannot be achieved without the support of the cornerstone rule of law discourse. The cornerstone rule of law discourse, as the specific practical path of China's rule of law discourse system, focuses more on the operational aspects and detailed design of the rule of law construction. It takes "strengthening and improving the Party's

X. Dong, M. Zhang, *Chinese Rule of Law Discourse System*, Understanding China, https://doi.org/10.1007/978-981-95-6260-2_4

leadership over law-based governance" and "building a socialist rule of law system with Chinese characteristics" as its core contents, providing specific practical guidelines and operational specifications for Chinese rule of law construction.

4.2 Fundamental Discourse

Discourse is the product of context, historical conditions, or significant real-world changes (Liu, 2018, p. 9). Discourse must be combined with its specific social environment and social issues. As the social environment and social issues change, so does the discourse. The importance of discourse depends on the significance of the things it describes. When the term "rule of law" is mentioned, people often first think of the Western rule of law. Concepts such as freedom under the rule of law (where the law guarantees freedom), equality before the law, and legal protection of human rights, which are advocated by the Western rule of law, come to mind. These terms have immeasurable significance for the establishment, consolidation, and promotion of the Western rule of law and can be regarded as the fundamental discourses of the Western rule of law discourse system. Then, what are the fundamental discourses of the socialist rule of law discourse system with Chinese characteristics? Why are they fundamental? And what role do they play in the entire rule of law discourse system? These are important questions that must be answered in the construction of Chinese rule of law discourse.

The essence of the path of socialist rule of law with Chinese characteristics lies in the fundamental arrangement of the organic unity of the Party's leadership, the people being the masters of the country, and law-based governance. Given the fundamental significance of this arrangement for the overall rule of law construction, the organic unity of the Party's leadership, the people being the masters of the country, and law-based governance, namely the "three-in-one unity", is the fundamental rule of law discourse of socialism with Chinese characteristics. This fundamental discourse is a high-level condensation of Chinese rule of law discourse. It not only has rich connotations but also a profound historical origin. In terms of the connotation of the fundamental rule of law discourse, its fundamentality is manifested in that it encompasses the core concepts, fundamental values of the rule of law, and the ways of existence and life of people under the rule of law. Regarding its historical origin, it is the product of the combination of the rule of law theories and practices both at home and abroad throughout history. The construction and spreading of China's fundamental rule of law discourse are beneficial domestically as they help people internalize the core concepts of the rule of law, guide their behavior, and maintain social stability. Internationally, they facilitate international audiences to accurately understand the core of Chinese rule of law construction, promote the achievement of a consensus on the rule of law, and enable China to have the right to interpret its rule of law.

4.2.1 *Criteria for Identifying Fundamental Discourse*

In the numerous rule of law discourses, how can we determine which ones are fundamental? What criteria should be employed to make such a determination? The rule of law discourse system is a unified expression of the concept system, value system, and rule system regarding the rule of law. Therefore, to identify fundamental rule of law discourse should also start from three aspects: the concept, value, and rules of the rule of law. There are differences between Chinese and Western rule of law discourses in answering what the rule of law is, why it is necessary, and how to achieve it. This difference is first manifested in the different understandings of the core concepts, fundamental values of the rule of law, and the ways of existence and life of people under the rule of law in China and the West. The Western slogans of freedom, equality, and human rights have fundamentally shaped the form of Western rule of law and determined the way of life of people under the rule of law. These discourses play a fundamental role in the Western rule of law discourse system and constitute the foundation of the rule of law discourse system. Fundamental rule of law discourse can both govern the overall rule of law discourse system and grasp the core of the rule of law discourse. Specifically, its fundamentality is manifested in that it encompasses the core concepts of the rule of law, the fundamental values of the rule of law, and provides basic guidance for people's lifestyles under the rule of law.

Fundamental rule of law discourse must be able to express the core concepts of the rule of law. The rule of law discourse system contains a concept system about the core concepts, general concepts of the rule of law, and their interrelationships. The core concepts of the rule of law are a high-level generalization of the essence and characteristics of the rule of law. There are both consistencies and differences between the core concepts of Chinese and Western rule of law. The consistency indicates that Chinese rule of law still falls within the scope of human rule of law, while the differences fundamentally determine the differences between the Chinese rule of law discourse system and the Western rule of law discourse system. The rule of law is defined as a form of governance that is opposite to the rule of man, and the rule of law is superior to the rule of man. (Aristotle, 1983, pp. 167–168) Therefore, the relative certainty of the concept of the rule of law against the rule of man provides a premise for the consistency between Chinese and Western rule of law. However, the ambiguity of the concept of the rule of law objectively exists, which makes it possible to have completely different understandings of the rule of law. As long as it does not violate the fundamental stipulations of "opposing the rule of man" and "governance by rules", it is entirely possible, reasonable, and necessary for there to be certain differences in the core concepts of the rule of law. The differences in the core concepts of the rule of law require us to start from the core concepts of the rule of law that conform to China's national conditions and the Chinese people's concept of the rule of law to explore fundamental rule of law discourse and then construct the Chinese rule of law discourse system.

Fundamental rule of law discourse must be capable of guiding people's lifestyles. The rule of law discourse system encompasses a set of normative systems regarding people's production, life, thinking, and behavior under the rule of law. Ultimately, the rule of law should return to guiding and safeguarding people's lifestyles. The original intention for people to choose the rule of law is simply to free themselves from the poor governance of the rule of man. The rule of law is not merely an idea and theory but also a practice. Therefore, the ideological and theoretical changes must be applied to practice and used to improve people's lifestyles. Since the Middle Ages, Western countries have gradually formed a set of modern political, economic, and legal beliefs, or a so-called "conceptual system", about how human society should live and exist, which has triggered the modern social transformation in Western countries. (Wei, 2019, p. 5) Then, what kind of rule of law can safeguard survival and guide life? What is good governance? How can good governance be achieved? These are all questions that rule of law discourse needs to answer. In the Chinese context, what kind of rule of law is in line with China's national conditions and can improve people's lives while adapting to the Chinese way of life? Rule of Law discourse is a conceptual guide that conforms to the basic survival and lifestyle of a specific group of people, and prompts them to generate resonance and consensus and then put it into practice. Fundamental rule of law discourse must conform to the basic survival mode, lifestyle, way of thinking, and behavior pattern of a country's population, and play a guiding role in people's survival and life. Due to the differences among different ethnic groups in these aspects, rule of law discourse, especially fundamental rule of law discourse, must vary among countries. Therefore, the study of rule of law discourse must also focus on the guidance of the rule of law on people's lifestyles, especially on the preservation and improvement of the specific lifestyles of one's own country and nation. Only by not blindly following others in concepts and not mimicking others in value choices can one maintain one's own uniqueness in lifestyle. The uniqueness of the rule of law path lies in the uniqueness of the rule of law life based on the uniqueness of rule of law concepts and rule of law values. China's unique core concepts of the rule of law, basic rule of law values, and the way of survival and life under the rule of law determine that we must follow the path of socialist rule of law with Chinese characteristics.

Fundamental rule of law discourse must answer three questions: what are the core concepts of a country's rule of law, the basic values of the rule of law, and the basic lifestyle under the rule of law. The fundamental rule of law discourse of socialism with Chinese characteristics should comprehensively answer the above three aspects of questions. In the theoretical exploration of defining the core concepts of the rule of law and clarifying the basic values of the rule of law, it should be applied to the practice of improving people's survival and lifestyle, making the rule of law a way of life.

4.2.2 *Connotations of Fundamental Discourse*

After the success of the bourgeois revolutions, developed Western countries with an established rule of law system successively adopted the "rule of law" based on the fundamental principles of "separation of powers" and "alternation of political parties in power". In contrast, China has summarized the historical experiences and lessons in governance, and in light of its national conditions, implemented the strategy of "governing the country by law". Through practice, China has identified the fundamental principle of "the unity of the Party's leadership, the people being the masters of the country, and governing the country by law".

The fundamental requirement of Chinese rule of law construction is to adhere to the organic unity of the Party's leadership, the people being the masters of the country, and governing the country by law. The report of the 15th National Congress of the Communist Party of China pointed out that governing the country by law integrates the Party's leadership, the promotion of people's democracy, and strict compliance with the law. The report of the 16th National Congress further emphasized that the Party's leadership is the fundamental guarantee for the people to be the masters of the country and for governing the country by law; the people being the masters of the country is the essential requirement of socialist democratic politics; and governing the country by law is the basic strategy for the Party to lead the people in governing the country. The report of the 19th National Congress put forward that the three aspects are unified in the great practice of China's socialist democratic politics. In the context of the socialist rule of law with Chinese characteristics, the Party's leadership is the fundamental characteristic, the people being the masters of the country is the essential purpose, and governing the country by law is the essential practice. The organic unity of the three is a scientific summary of the experiences in China's socialist democratic rule of law construction (Zhang, 2016, p. 3). This principle was basically formed at the 15th National Congress, formally proposed at the 16th National Congress, and reemphasized at the 17th, 18th, and 19th National Congresses, becoming the hallmark discourse of the socialist rule of law with Chinese characteristics. It should be noted that China's remarkable achievements in various fields are directly related to the establishment of the governance strategy and the corresponding fundamental principles (Li, 2015, p. 5). The formation of the "Three Unities" theory not only has an inherent logical mechanism of historical evolution but also, against the backdrop of the globalization of the rule of law, is a scientific expression that combines Chinese rule of law elements with the rule of law civilizations of other countries based on China's national conditions. It has Chinese characteristics, style, and grandeur, reflects the essential features of China's socialist rule of law construction, and constitutes the fundamental discourse of the socialist rule of law with Chinese characteristics.

Fundamental Discourse and Core Concepts of Chinese Rule of Law

To adhere to the path of socialist rule of law with Chinese characteristics, the most fundamental thing is to uphold the leadership of the Communist Party of China. This fundamental principle is prominently reflected in the Party's guarantee and promotion of the rule of law construction.

The leadership of the Communist Party of China is the fundamental characteristic of the socialist rule of law with Chinese characteristics. Upholding the Party's leadership not only has historical legitimacy and practical justifiability but also is necessary for Chinese rule of law construction. Firstly, the purpose and main content of the Party's leadership is to support the people to be the masters of the country, which is consistent with the fundamental purpose of the socialist rule of law. Secondly, upholding the Party's leadership does not conflict with the rule of law construction. The Party must govern in accordance with the Constitution and laws, and its leadership must be carried out under the premise of safeguarding the rule of law. The Party leads the people in formulating the Constitution and laws and, at the same time, must take the lead in abiding by the Constitution and laws and act within the scope of the Constitution and laws. This in itself implies the compatibility between the Party's leadership and the rule of law.

The socialist rule of law with Chinese characteristics takes the people's congress system, which embodies the people's democratic dictatorship, as its fundamental political system (Wang, 2017, p. 5). The rule of law cannot be separated from politics. There are essential differences in the rule of law based on different political foundations. Different rule of law discourses are formed on the basis of different state systems and political systems. China's adherence to "the people being the masters of the country" as a key component of the fundamental rule of law discourse is an inevitable choice based on China's state system and political system. In the West, the separation of powers, especially the legislative power among the three powers, and the representative system on which the exercise of this power relies, are the institutional carriers of democracy. In China, such an institutional carrier is embodied in the people's congress system. Both are carriers for realizing the value of democracy and are the political-system foundations of the rule of law. The people's congress system is conducive to ensuring that the people are the masters of the country and is an important institutional carrier of China's socialist political civilization. China's state system and political system determine that China cannot copy the rule of law model based on the Western separation of powers and judicial independence. Chinese rule of law must embody the system model of "the people being the masters of the country" that conforms to the national conditions, namely the people's congress system, so as to achieve the ultimate goal and essential requirement of the rule of law, that is, the people being the masters of the country. Therefore, it is inevitable to take "the people being the masters of the country" as a component of China's fundamental rule of law discourse.

The unique rule of law concept formed in Chinese rule of law construction is centrally reflected in the fundamental strategy of governing the country by law. Chinese rule of law adheres to the principle that while realizing individual freedom, equality and justice must also be taken into account, that is, it forms a rule of law concept guided by freedom, equality and justice. The starting point of the socialist rule of law theory is the specific, real individuals in complex social relations. Through the rule of law, individual freedom and political rights are guaranteed, and more emphasis is placed on ensuring equality before the law and social justice through the rule of law so that individuals' economic and social rights can be realized. The socialist rule of law with Chinese characteristics is continuously developing and realizing a social-oriented positive view of freedom. The value orientation of freedom, equality and justice determines that governing the country by law, as the fundamental discourse of the socialist rule of law with Chinese characteristics, is more in line with China's reality, more targeted and practical.

Fundamental Discourse and Core Values of Chinese Rule of Law

The leadership of the Communist Party of China (CPC) embodies freedom under the premise of progress and stability. In the Chinese rule of law discourse, the leadership of the CPC represents a special view of freedom. That is, to pursue freedom under progress and stability, it is essential to uphold the leadership of the CPC. Some international rule of law scholars often claim that the leadership of the CPC conflicts with freedom. They believe that there is an irreconcilable contradiction between the rule of law in China and the leadership of the CPC, or that the rule of law under the leadership of the CPC fundamentally differs from the Western liberal rule of law and thus cannot be regarded as a type of rule of law. These biases stem from a lack of in-depth understanding of the essence of the CPC's leadership, the fundamental differences between Chinese and Western societies, and the modernization processes in China and the West that have led to these differences. The leadership of the CPC does not deny freedom. On the contrary, the CPC aims to achieve the free and all-around development of people. The leadership of the CPC serves as a guarantee for freedom under progress and stability. The freedom that the socialist rule of law with Chinese characteristics seeks to achieve is based on the social orientation. It starts from real individuals, is a relative freedom constrained in interpersonal interactions, and is a freedom that is gradually realized in a limited and conditional way based on the actual level of economic development. Freedom must be premised on achieving progress and maintaining stability. Freedom is not the freedom of individuals in isolation but the freedom of the entire people. It must be realized through unified will, unified action, and coordinated steps. Therefore, the leadership of the CPC is needed to ensure the realization of such freedom.

For a nation-state in the forest of the world's nations and in the fierce international competition, freedom should not include the freedom that leads to national self-destruction, the freedom that causes the regression of civilization and national division, nor the freedom of individuals to act willfully and lawlessly. Instead, it can only be freedom premised on progress and stability. Over the past century, the CPC has demonstrated in its practice of leading the people in revolution, construction, and reform that it has always been an advanced force, representing the direction of the country and the nation's progress. It is the guarantee of stability and the bond of unity, capable of rallying people's hearts for the construction of the rule of law. This is consistent with the freedom pursued by Chinese rule of law. A stable social order is a common goal pursued by human society and a prerequisite for realizing other values. In the Chinese concept, the rule of law is both a means and an end of social governance, ultimately aiming to achieve an ideal social state governed by law. Since modern times, the process of the Chinese nation's pursuit of national rejuvenation has been a process of exploring a social state that moves from "chaos" to "governance". The fundamental pursuit of Chinese society is a harmonious society. In achieving harmony among people, individual freedom must yield to the progress and stability of the entire society. The modern Chinese history of pursuing freedom, democracy, and progress shows that only under the leadership of the CPC can the realization of freedom be guaranteed. Since modern times, the prevalence of the rule of law discourse in China reflects the longing for order (Su, 1998, p. 1). "Governance" is closely related to "chaos". When learning the rule of law from Western liberalism in the late Qing Dynasty, people recognized the importance of freedom as a value of the rule of law. As the national crisis deepened and the salvation movement brought social unrest, it was difficult to establish the concept of the supremacy of the law. Therefore, China embarked on a rule of law path that is fundamentally different from that of the West. The CPC has taken the rule of law as the basic strategy for governing the country, the basic way of exercising governance, and the only way to achieve the well-being of the people. It has led the people to pioneer the path of socialist rule of law with Chinese characteristics.

The people being the masters of the country is a manifestation of true democracy. Western scholars have put forward very rich discussions on the relationship between democracy and the rule of law. Democracy is the foundation of the rule of law, and the rule of law is the guarantee of democracy. In China, these two concepts have long been emphasized in parallel and developed synchronously. Democracy is implemented within the framework of the rule of law, and democracy is institutionalized through the legal system. The people being the masters of the country is a unique expression of the value of democracy in the discourse of the socialist rule of law with Chinese characteristics. Since the introduction of Western learning into China, the discourse of democracy has become prevalent, and the value of democracy has been established in China. However, the way to realize democracy has long remained elusive. Various democratic systems copied from the West, such as the presidential system, the cabinet system, the parliamentary system, and the citizen election system, have failed to function effectively. The system of people's congresses established after the founding of the People's Republic of China has, for the first time in Chinese history, achieved true democracy. Moreover, it is precisely through the system of people's congresses as the form of realizing the people being the masters of the country that the Communist Party of China has led the people to break free from the historical cycle of rise and fall. Only when the people are allowed to supervise the government will the government not slack off. Only when everyone takes responsibility will the state not perish with the passing of leaders. The people being the masters of the country is the essence and core of socialist democratic politics. Democracy under the rule of law means institutionalizing and legalizing democracy, which is an important task in Chinese rule of law construction. Therefore, comprehensively promoting the rule of law must adhere to the principal position of the people.

The institutional carrier for the people to be the masters of the country is the system of people's congresses. Similar to the congressional system in the United States and the parliamentary monarchy in the United Kingdom, they are all ways for different countries to realize the value of democracy in light of their respective national conditions. Objectively speaking, people's understanding and perception of democracy are influenced by many factors such as national conditions, time, and space, and the democratic political systems developed accordingly also vary greatly (Wang, 2015). In China, the system of people's congresses is the fundamental political system arrangement that integrates the leadership of the Party, the people being the masters of the country, and the rule of law. It is based on China's actual national conditions, has been fully tested in practice, and is an effective institutional arrangement that can fully guarantee and realize the people being the masters of the country, which must be adhered to in the long term. Therefore, we must, with a high degree of self-confidence, continuously improve and promote the practice of the system of people's congresses, institutionalize and legalize democracy, and thus continuously improve socialist democracy and the rule of law with Chinese characteristics.

Law-based governance emphasizes social justice. Law is an art of goodness and justice, and the realization of justice is the core pursuit of the construction of the rule of law. The socialist rule of law with Chinese characteristics endows the rule of law with more substantial connotations, integrating values such as fairness and social justice into the rule of law, thus effectively promoting the realization of substantive rule of law. China not only respects and safeguards human rights in legislation, integrating the principles of fairness, justice, and openness throughout the entire legislative process, but also continuously improves the channels and methods of rights relief in the construction of the rule of law, enabling the people to truly feel fairness and justice. Creating a fairer, more harmonious, and more orderly social environment is the goal and guarantee for building a moderately prosperous society in all respects. "If reform fails to bring tangible benefits to the people and create a fairer social environment, or even leads to more unfairness, it will lose its meaning and cannot be sustained" (Xi, 2014, p. 1). This is especially true for the construction of the rule of law. "We should use the promotion of social fairness and justice and the improvement of people's well-being as a mirror" (Xi, 2014, p. 1). Therefore, the 18th National Congress of the Communist Party of China clearly stated: "On the basis of the common struggle of all the people and the development of the economy and society, we should step up the building of institutions that play a major role in safeguarding social fairness and justice, gradually establish a social fairness guarantee system mainly featuring equal rights, equal opportunities, and equal rules, strive to create a fair social environment, and ensure the people's equal right to participate and develop" (*Selected Important Documents Since the 18th National Congress (Volume II)*, 2016, p. 12). The report of the 19th National Congress of the Communist

Party of China proposed: "Improving people's well-being is the fundamental goal of development. It is necessary to strive to deliver more benefits to the people and address more of their concerns, shore up weak links in people's well-being in the course of development, and promote social fairness and justice". (Xi, 2017, p. 23). This is what is meant by the rule of law as the fundamental legal discourse in China.

Law-based governance emphasizes safeguarding social stability through the implementation of laws and creating a safe and harmonious social environment. Ensuring the full and correct implementation of laws is the fundamental way to maintain social harmony and stability, smooth the expression mechanisms of different interests, meet the people's legal demands, resolve social contradictions at the source, and improve the level of social governance. Law-based governance is the fundamental path to realizing social justice. Previous social governance methods, with a strong flavor of "rule by man", were prone to causing social injustice. The proposal of the strategy of law-based governance is a fundamental solution to the previous unjust governance. Attaching great importance to social justice at the national strategic level and exploring reliable ways to achieve social justice from the laws of social governance not only follows the general laws of civilized governance in countries around the world but also inherits the Chinese legal concept of justice, such as "rectifying the crooked and leveling the uneven" since ancient times. In contemporary China, the people are the main body of the rule of law, so it can only safeguard the people's status as the masters of the country; the purpose of law-based governance is to improve people's well-being, and this fundamental purpose can only be achieved through fairness that meets the people's requirements. Law-based governance emphasizes social justice to continuously promote the realization of fairness and justice. It not only aims at equality before the law but also emphasizes using legal means to minimize social injustice as much as possible and create a truly just social life. This is a rule of law in the real sense.

Fundamental Discourse and Basic Ways of Life Under Chinese Rule of Law

The rule of law is not only a means but also an end. As a means, the ultimate goal of the rule of law is to achieve the well-being of the people and the happiness and tranquility of individuals. The well-being of the people is the supreme law. In this sense, the rule of law has an instrumental nature. According to Kant, human beings are ends in themselves, not means. Therefore, the rule of law should also have the instrumental function of safeguarding the subject status of human beings. Although the rule of law serves the ultimate goal of the people's well-being, the rule of law itself should also be regarded as an objective pursued by human society. Because without the rule of law, it is impossible to achieve the well-being of the people. The ultimate goal of the people's well-being, of course, includes the goal of the rule of law. The rule of law has both external and internal values. The so-called external value of the rule of law refers to its efficacy, which can promote the realization of other values. The internal value of the rule of law is that the rule of law is a possible way of life that people yearn for and is worth pursuing. This state itself is valuable and does not rely on the realization of other values. From the perspective of internal value, the rule of law is a way of life oriented towards human well-being and should not be simply regarded as a tool. The report of the 18th National Congress of the Communist Party of China reiterated the purpose of the rule of law from the perspective of national construction, describing the rule of law as an ideal way of life. The Fourth Plenary Session of the 18th Central Committee of the Communist Party of China set the legal system and the country under the rule of law as the overall goal of the rule of law construction and elaborately designed the roadmap for achieving this goal. This marks a qualitative leap in our understanding of the rule of law, from regarding it as a means to an end, and from focusing on its external value to its internal value.

To uphold the purposiveness and internal value of the rule of law, only by regarding the rule of law not only as a feasible governance method but also as a way of life worth pursuing can we continuously advance the socialist rule of law with Chinese characteristics. By adhering to the rule of law as a way of life, we should take whether the rule of law can improve the people's basic living conditions and enhance their well-being as the standard for measuring the success of the rule of law construction. General Secretary Xi Jinping has repeatedly emphasized: "We should promote law-based governance, law-based exercise of state power, and law-based administration of government in a coordinated way, and build a country, government, and society based on the rule of law in an all-around way". This important assertion about the rule of law construction is profound in meaning and is a profound summary of the laws governing Chinese rule of law construction. Among them, the Party leads the people in governing the country according to the law, the Party exercises state power in accordance with the law, and the government administers in accordance with the law. A country under the rule of law refers to the legalization of the public power of the entire country; a government under the rule of law mainly refers to the legalization of the exercise of the state's administrative power; and a society under the rule of law mainly refers to the legalization of the exercise of social public power by political parties and other social communities relative to the state's public power. (Jiang, 2013, p. 6) The "coordinated promotion" of the three and the "all-around construction" of the three indicate that the rule of law has penetrated into all fields and levels, covering all aspects of the country's political life and citizens' personal lives, and has had an all-dimensional and three-dimensional impact on individuals' ways of survival and life.

4.3 Cornerstone Discourse

The cornerstone discourse of Chinese rule of law discourse system serves as the link to the fundamental rule of law discourse and is crucial in unifying and permeating the entire landscape of the rule of law construction. The criterion for identifying cornerstone discourse lies in their ability to support the entire discourse system on the rule of law and connect with the basic discourses. Accordingly, "strengthening and improving the Party's leadership over law-based governance" and "building a socialist rule of law system with Chinese characteristics" have been identified as the two cornerstone discourses. The former emphasizes that the Party's leadership is the fundamental guarantee for the socialist rule of law, the greatest advantage of the socialist system with Chinese characteristics, and the core proposition of Chinese rule of law theory. It is specifically manifested in leading legislation, ensuring law enforcement, and other aspects. The latter, on the other hand, is the cornerstone for comprehensively promoting the rule of law in the country. It encompasses five subsystems, including a complete system of legal norms and an efficient system for the implementation of the rule of law, which reflects the innovation and comprehensiveness of the socialist rule of law with Chinese characteristics. These two discourses jointly act on the rule of law discourse system. They respectively provide solid support and guidance for Chinese rule of law construction from the aspects of the leading force and the institutional framework.

4.3.1 Criteria for Identifying Cornerstone Discourse

Cornerstone rule of law discourse differs from fundamental rule of law discourse. It connects with fundamental rule of law discourse, more specifically describes the distinctive features of Chinese rule of law path, and is also the discourse that governs the overall situation of rule of law construction and runs through all aspects of it.

The term "cornerstone" can be understood at two levels: first, as the foundational stones of a building, it metaphorically represents the fundamental basis or foundation of a system; second, it is a symbol of core strength or pivotal support. Based on this definition, China identifies the discourse that functions as the "cornerstone" or "central pillar" within China's socialist rule of law discourse system.

The Fourth Plenary Session of the 18th Central Committee of the Communist Party of China pointed out that the overall goal of comprehensively promoting law-based governance is to build a socialist rule of law system with Chinese characteristics and a socialist country under the rule of law, and made arrangements for the five sub-systems. Meanwhile, the session indicated that "it is necessary to strengthen and improve the Party's leadership over rule of law work and implement the Party's leadership throughout the process of comprehensively promoting law-based governance", and took "upholding the leadership of the Communist Party of China" as the basic principle that must be adhered to in achieving the overall goal of comprehensively promoting law-based governance. Therefore, China takes "strengthening and improving the Party's leadership over law-based governance" and "building a socialist rule of law system with Chinese characteristics" together as the cornerstone discourse of Chinese rule of law discourse system.

It is necessary to determine the criteria for identify cornerstone rule of law discourse. Different from the comprehensiveness and overall-governing nature of fundamental rule of law discourse, cornerstone rule of law discourse is the cornerstone that supports the entire rule of law discourse system on the basis of fundamental rule of law discourse. It should be able to connect with basic discourses and build the framework of the rule of law discourse system. In terms of the role of "strengthening and improving the Party's leadership over law-based governance" in the rule of law discourse system, the specific ways of the Party's leadership over law-based governance are "leading legislation, ensuring law enforcement, supporting judicial work, and taking the lead in abiding by the law". These four requirements are closely related to the basic rule of law discourses of legislation, law enforcement, judicial work, and law-abiding. "Strengthening and improving the Party's leadership over law-based governance" corresponds to the four major aspects of legislation, law enforcement, judicial work, and law-abiding in the rule of law, and respectively gives rise to discourses such as "the Party leads legislation", "the Party ensures law enforcement", "the Party supports judicial work", and "the Party takes the lead in abiding by the law". This corresponding and derivative relationship reflects the unity of the Party's leadership and law-based governance, which is the fundamental rule of law discourse. At the same time, corresponding to the construction of a country, government, and society under the rule of law, the Party's leadership always runs through the process of the Party governing the country in accordance with the law, the government administering in accordance with the law, and the society being governed in accordance with the law. Expressions such as "the Party exercises state power in accordance with the law", "adhering to the just, prudent, and law-based exercise of power", and "taking leading officials' taking the lead in learning the law and setting an example in abiding by the law as the key to comprehensively promoting law-based governance" demonstrate the leading and exemplary role of the Party's leadership in the construction of a country, government, and society under the rule of law.

In terms of the role of "building a socialist rule of law system with Chinese characteristics" in the rule of law discourse system, the five sub-systems of the rule of law system respectively play roles in the various links of legislation, law enforcement, judicial practice, and law-abiding. The rule of law system itself encompasses the infrastructure for the four major rule of law links: The formation of a complete legal norm system necessarily requires scientific, democratic, and law-based legislation in the legislative process; the establishment of an efficient rule of law implementation system necessarily demands strict law enforcement in the law-enforcement process; the creation of a rigorous rule of law supervision system necessarily calls for strengthening the restriction and supervision of power to prevent power corruption and degeneration, especially the restriction and supervision of law-enforcement and judicial powers; the construction of a powerful rule of law guarantee system primarily requires adhering to the leadership of the Communist Party of China, which serves as a strong political guarantee for comprehensively promoting the rule of law. At the same time, it is necessary to improve the systems for legislation, law enforcement, judicial practice, and law-abiding, cultivate a high-quality rule of law construction team, and foster a fertile ground for the rule of law culture. The reason why the "rule of law system" is regarded as the cornerstone discourse is that "it establishes the cornerstone category and core concept of the contemporary Chinese rule of law theoretical system, and has practical explanatory power, scientific penetration power, and theoretical integration power for Chinese rule of law construction practice" (Zhang, 2019, p. 10). The socialist rule of law system with Chinese characteristics is an overarching concept in jurisprudence. It is not only the overall goal of governing the country by law but also the legal manifestation of the theoretical system of socialism with Chinese characteristics. It vividly reflects the degree of standardization and orderliness of the operations in each link of Chinese rule of law and indicates the harmonious state of Chinese rule of law structure with strict organization and coordinated operation (Li, 2015, p. 5). The discourse of "building a socialist rule of law system with Chinese characteristics" upgrades the "legal system" to the "rule of law system", emphasizing not only "governance by law" but also "governance by good laws and good governance". It centrally demonstrates the innovation of the socialist rule of law theory and path with Chinese characteristics. The addition of the term "socialism with Chinese characteristics" further highlights the Chinese elements of the rule of law.

The leadership of the Communist Party of China is the backbone of Chinese rule of law construction, and the socialist rule of law system with Chinese characteristics is the "cornerstone" for comprehensively promoting the rule of law. Therefore, "strengthening and improving the Party's leadership over law-based governance" and "building a socialist rule of law system with Chinese characteristics" play the role of cornerstone discourse within the discourse system of socialist rule of law with Chinese characteristics.

4.3.2 Connotations of Cornerstone Discourse

"Strengthening and improving the Party's leadership over law-based governance" emphasizes that the Party's leadership is the fundamental guarantee for socialist rule of law, the greatest advantage of the system, and the core proposition of the rule of law theory. It is necessary to continuously enhance the Party's ability and proficiency in leading the implementation of the rule of law. "Building a socialist rule of law system with Chinese characteristics", on the other hand, is a fundamental project for the modernization of national governance. It encompasses five sub-systems: a comprehensive system of legal norms, an efficient system for the implementation of the rule of law, a rigorous system for the supervision of the rule of law, a robust system for guaranteeing the rule of law, and a well-developed system of intra-Party regulations. These two aspects are complementary. The construction of the rule of law system must adhere to the Party's leadership. It requires the coordinated promotion of legislation, law enforcement, judicial work, and law-abiding behavior. Moreover, it should be combined with the system of moral norms to jointly drive the comprehensive advancement of the rule of law in the country.

The Specific Connotations of "Strengthening and Improving the Party's Leadership over Law-Based Governance"

The leadership of the Party is the soul of the socialist rule of law with Chinese characteristics (Wang, 2019, p. 6). The Fourth Plenary Session of the 18th Central Committee of the Communist Party of China pointed out that "the Party's leadership is the most fundamental guarantee for comprehensively promoting the rule of law and accelerating the construction of a socialist country under the rule of law. It is necessary to strengthen and improve the Party's leadership over law-based governance and implement the Party's leadership throughout the whole process of comprehensively promoting the rule of law". When deploying the comprehensive promotion of the rule of law, the plenary session proposed to take "adhering to the leadership of the Communist Party of China" as the basic principle, improve the Party's leadership over law-based governance, and continuously enhance the Party's ability and level to lead the rule of law. It emphasized that the Party should adhere to governing the country by law and exercising power in accordance with the law, and consciously operate within the scope of the Constitution and laws. Leading cadres at all levels should take the lead in abiding by the law and handling affairs in accordance with the law. It is necessary to continuously improve the institutional mechanism for formulating intra-Party regulations, enhance the enforcement of intra-Party regulations, and implement the principle of strictly governing the Party in accordance with regulations. Party members and cadres should improve their rule of law thinking and ability to handle affairs in accordance with the law. The effectiveness of rule of law construction should be regarded as an important part of the performance of leading groups and leading cadres at all levels and included in the performance evaluation index system.

The Party's Leadership is the Most Fundamental Guarantee for Socialist Rule of Law

The relationship between the Party and the law is the core issue in the construction of the rule of law and a concentrated reflection of the relationship between politics and the rule of law. As General Secretary Xi Jinping said, "There is politics in the rule of law, and there is no rule of law divorced from politics. Public law is just a complex form of political discourse, and the disputes in the field of public law are just an extension of political disputes. Behind each form of the rule of law, there is a set of political theories; within each rule of law model, there is a political logic; under each rule of law path, there is a political stance". The Party's leadership is the foundation of the socialist rule of law discourse system with Chinese characteristics. General Secretary Xi Jinping pointed out that the system of multi-party cooperation and political consultation under the leadership of the Communist Party of China, as a basic political system in China, is a great political creation of the Communist Party of China, the Chinese people, all democratic parties, and personages without party affiliation. It is a new-type political party system that has grown out of the Chinese soil (*Xi Jinping: Selected Quotations on Comprehensively Advancing the Rule of Law* 2015, p. 34). It can truly, widely, and persistently represent and realize the fundamental interests of the overwhelming majority of the people and the fundamental interests of all ethnic groups and sectors across the country, effectively avoiding the drawbacks of the old-type political party system that represents a small number of people and a small number of interest groups. It closely unites all political parties and personages without party affiliation to strive for a common goal. Through institutionalized, procedural, and standardized arrangements, it gathers various opinions and suggestions and promotes the scientific and democratic decision-making, effectively avoiding the drawbacks of the old-type political party system that leads to social division due to decision-making and governance based on party interests, class interests, regional and group interests (Xi, 2018). This new-type political party system that conforms to China's national conditions can achieve the unity of centralized leadership and extensive participation, the unity of social progress and national stability, and the unity of vitality and efficiency.

The Party's Leadership is the Greatest Strength of the Socialist System with Chinese Characteristics

China's national system and governance system neither copy the models of Western capitalist countries nor those of other socialist countries. Instead, it is a national system and governance system with Chinese characteristics that is based on China's basic national conditions and is compatible with China's historical heritage, cultural traditions, and economic and social development level. The Party's leadership constitutes the greatest advantage of China's national system and governance system.

First, the Communist Party of China is the designer and improver of China's national system and governance system. Under Mao Zedong's leadership, the Chinese people achieved victory in the New Democratic Revolution, carried out the socialist revolution, and carried out socialist transformation, establishing the basic socialist system, which laid the premise and foundation for all development and progress in contemporary China. Deng Xiaoping pioneered the path of socialism with Chinese characteristics and its theoretical framework. Jiang Zemin and Hu Jintao led the people across the country to forge ahead on this correct path, continuously developing and improving China's national system and governance system. Since the 18th National Congress of the Communist Party of China, the Central Committee with Comrade Xi Jinping as the core has based on China's national conditions, made overall plans, and strengthened top-level design, deeply promoting the practical, theoretical, and institutional innovation of the cause of socialism with Chinese characteristics for a new era and advancing the modernization of the national governance system and governance capacity (Long, 2016, p. 5). At present, China has formed relatively mature and perfect institutional mechanisms in the fields of politics, economy, culture, society, and ecological civilization, jointly building the overall layout of socialism with Chinese characteristics characterized by the "five-sphere integrated plan". It can be said that the Communist Party of China not only firmly believes in the system but also focuses on deepening reforms, adheres to and improves the existing system, and continuously promotes institutional innovation based on practice through theoretical innovation, constantly eliminating the drawbacks of the institutional mechanism, and promoting the formation of a more complete, stable, and effective governance system.

Second, the values and principles of the Communist Party of China are embedded within the socialist system with Chinese characteristics. The Communist Party of China is committed to serving the people wholeheartedly, governing for the public good and in the people's interest, and striving for the goal of building a great modern socialist country that is prosperous, democratic, culturally advanced, harmonious, and beautiful. The nature, purpose, governing philosophy, and aspirations of the Communist Party of China are intrinsically aligned with China's core socialist values. These values, in turn, harmonize with China's national system and governance framework, creating an organic, coordinated, and unified integration. Therefore, only by upholding the Party's leadership can the values and principles within the national system and governance framework be truly realized.

Third, the Communist Party of China can effectively translate the strengths of the socialist system with Chinese characteristics into governance efficacy. The Communist Party of China is composed of Party members with high awareness, discipline, and self-sacrifice spirit, and it is a political party that can truly represent and unite the people. Throughout different historical periods, the Party has demonstrated exceptional organizational and mobilization capabilities, rallying the people and stimulating their enthusiasm, initiative, and creativity. This enables the continuous realization of the overall efficacy of the socialist system with Chinese characteristics, driving China's revolution, construction, and reform to achieve significant breakthroughs and victories.

The Leadership of the Party Constitutes the Core Proposition of Chinese Rule of Law Theory

Behind discourses lies theory.

For new rule of law discourses to be tenable, they need theoretical support as their fundamental core. Theory is manifested in discourses, which are required for communication, promotion, explanation, and clarification to convince people. It is believed that the leadership of the Party constitutes the cornerstone and core issue of the rule of law theory of socialism with Chinese characteristics.

Firstly, the constitutional theory system forms the foundation of the rule of law theory system of socialism with Chinese characteristics. Since the leadership actions of the Party often have constitutional effects and impacts, the theory related to the Party's leadership is inevitably one of the most fundamental and important contents of the constitutional theory of socialism with Chinese characteristics (Chen & Jiang, 2015, p. 3). As some scholars have pointed out: "The legalization of the relationship between the Party and the government and the Party's transformation towards the rule of law have always been the most fundamental issues in China's constitutional science. This is not only because 'the Chinese people, under the leadership of the Communist Party of China' is the foundation of the Chinese Constitution, but also because this leadership mechanism, as an effective executive power, has formed a rich institutional network for the operation of China's Party-government system". (Tian, 2015, p. 3) Therefore, the positioning, nature, and functions of the Communist Party of China, the distinctions and connections between the Party's leadership and its governance, the subject, object, nature, and content of the Party's leadership, as well as the behavioral boundaries, legal responsibilities, and regulatory paths of the Party's leadership, all constitute important parts of the theory of the Party's leadership, and this theory forms the cornerstone issue of the constitutional and rule of law theory of socialism with Chinese characteristics.

Secondly, Chinese rule of law discourse system must exhibit logical coherence, clear objectives, hierarchical clarity, scientific structure, and comprehensive content. It should closely revolve around the rule of law practice of socialism with Chinese characteristics, and focus on the Party's leadership, legislation, administration, judicature, law-abiding, and other rule of law operation links and specific social issues.

The Specific Connotations of "Building A Socialist Rule of Law System with Chinese Characteristics"

The socialist rule of law system with Chinese characteristics represents the legal manifestation of China's socialist system, with inherent consistency between the two. They are unified under the shared political framework and grand practice of "socialism with Chinese characteristics"(Wang, 2019, p. 6). This system serves as the normative expression of China's socialist institutional framework (Jiang, 2014). Thus, rule of law construction must solidify the rule of law system as its cornerstone.

Establishing a rule of law system constitutes the foundational project for modernizing state governance. General Secretary Xi Jinping emphasized at the Second Meeting of the Central Leading Group for Comprehensively Deepening Reforms the pivotal role of the rule of law in advancing the modernization of state governance systems and capacities, explicitly demanding that reforms be deepened along the track of the rule of law, which refers to the rule of law system itself (Li, 2014, p. 3). To comprehensively promote the rule of law means to take the rule of law as the basic way of governing the country and bringing national and social governance onto an institutionalized, standardized, and procedural track. In the governance of the country, the rule of law system is a crucial normative and institutional system (Jiang & Liu, 2019). The improvement and development of the system of socialism with Chinese characteristics must focus on the rule of law. The rule of law is the basic way for the modernization of national governance. The law-based governance system for socialism with Chinese characteristics is an important part of the system of socialism with Chinese characteristics, and the degree of its improvement determines the level of modernization of the national governance system and governance capacity. Meanwhile, the rule of law system is closely related to law-based governance by the Party. Law-based governance by the Party is the core and soul of the rule of law system (Li, 2014, p. 3). The rule of law is reflected in all aspects of the modernization of national governance, and building a socialist rule of law system with Chinese characteristics must be taken as an important lever for promoting the modernization of the national governance system and governance capacity. From a practical perspective, the "socialist rule of law system with Chinese characteristics" plays a pivotal role in deepening the comprehensive promotion of the rule of law. From a theoretical perspective, the concept and proposition of the "socialist rule of law system with Chinese characteristics" have a guiding significance for the innovation of the rule of law theory (Zhang, 2019, p. 10).

Since the 18th National Congress of the Communist Party of China, the rule of law system has become a core concept in the field of national governance. The 18th National Congress established the rule of law as the basic way of governing the country. The Fourth Plenary Session of the 18th Central Committee put forward the overall goal of comprehensively promoting the rule of law, which is to build a socialist rule of law system and a socialist rule of law country. General Secretary Xi Jinping profoundly expounded the scientific connotation of the socialist rule of law system, that is, "under the leadership of the Communist Party of China, adhering to the system of socialism with Chinese characteristics, implementing the theory of the rule of law for socialism with Chinese characteristics, forming a complete system of legal norms, an efficient system for the implementation of the rule of law, a rigorous system for the supervision of the rule of law, a strong system for the guarantee of the rule of law, and a sound system of intra-Party regulations" (*Decision of the Central Committee of the Communist Party of China on Several Major Issues Concerning Comprehensively Promoting the Rule of Law*, 2014, p. 4). The report of the 19th National Congress included the clarification of the overall goal of comprehensively promoting the rule of law into the "Eight Clarifications" of Xi Jinping Thought on Socialism with Chinese Characteristics for a New Era. The Decision of the Fourth Plenary Session of the 19th Central Committee took "adhering to and improving the socialist rule of law system with Chinese characteristics and enhancing the Party's ability to govern the country and exercise governance in accordance with the law" as an important task for the construction of democracy and the rule of law in the new era, reiterating the overall goal of comprehensively promoting the rule of law put forward by the Fourth Plenary Session of the 18th Central Committee.

The "rule of law system" is a legal concept with originality, timeliness, and representativeness, which General Secretary Xi Jinping has refined by pooling the wisdom of the entire Party. It is a core concept with rich and profound connotations, serving as the most representative and overarching one. It is also a major theoretical innovation in General Secretary Xi Jinping's new concepts, thoughts, and strategies for comprehensively promoting the rule of law (Zhang, 2019, p. 10). From the legal system to the rule of law system, there has been a fundamental transformation and improvement in the Chinese people's exploration and understanding of the governance path. The rule of law system is an organic unity of the "rule of law" in the value, factual, and formal aspects of the law. The socialist rule of law system is a systematic project in the true sense (Wei, 2013, p. 1). The process of building the socialist rule of law system with Chinese characteristics is a process of transformation and reform from the legal system to the rule of law system. It is an organic whole that is interconnected, mutually reinforcing, and inseparable, and represents a profound revolution in the rule of law. This revolution in the rule of law highlights the systematicness, integrity, and synergy of building the socialist rule of law system with Chinese characteristics (Jiang & Liu, 2019). Therefore, taking "building a socialist rule of law system with Chinese characteristics" as the cornerstone concept demonstrates the innovation and comprehensiveness of the socialist rule of law with Chinese characteristics.

"Building a socialist rule of law system with Chinese characteristics" has extremely clear implications. The socialist rule of law system with Chinese characteristics consists of five sub-systems: a complete system of legal norms, an efficient system for the implementation of the rule of law, a rigorous system for the supervision of the rule of law, a strong system for the guarantee of the rule of law, and a sound system of intra-Party regulations. Each sub-system is modified by an adjective: A "complete" system of legal norms means that the legal norm system should not only exist but also ensure "having laws to abide by" and "being well-founded in law". The legal norms should be interconnected and coordinated to achieve the unity of the legal system. An "efficient" system for the implementation of the rule of law means that the implementation of the rule of law must be "convenient and efficient" and ensure "strict compliance with the law". A "rigorous" system for the supervision of the rule of law means that supervision, as a means to control power, should "cover every aspect". A "sound" system of intra-Party regulations means that as an important part of the socialist rule of law system with Chinese characteristics, the system of intra-Party regulations is also constantly being improved to promote law-based governance of the country through governance of the Party in accordance with regulations. These five sub-systems form an integrated whole, jointly promoting the comprehensive advancement of the rule of law.

Establishing a Comprehensive Legal Norm System

In March 2011, the Standing Committee of the National People's Congress announced that the socialist legal system with Chinese characteristics had been established. Against the backdrop of an established legal system, it is still necessary to further improve the laws to make them more comprehensive. The Fourth Plenary Session of the 18th Central Committee of the Communist Party of China proposed to strengthen legislation in key areas. The 19th National Congress of the Communist Party of China pointed out that there had been a change in the principal contradiction in Chinese society. The people's demand for the law has shifted from "having laws to go by" to the pursuit of "good laws and good governance". With economic and social development, the people have higher requirements for democracy, the rule of law, fairness, justice, security, and the environment, and have new demands for the legal systems of the socialist market economy, intellectual property rights, data privacy, fiscal and tax, and finance. The laws in these areas must be further improved to better meet the people' aspiration for a better life. To this end, it is necessary to uphold the Party's leadership over legislation, promote democratic, scientific, and law-based legislation, give play to the leading role of the people's congresses in legislation, eliminate the legalization of departmental interests, and overcome local protectionism. It is also essential to improve the quality and efficiency of legislation.

Establishing an Efficient Rule of Law Implementation System

The rule of law implementation system refers to the institutional and regulatory system for law enforcement and legal application. The implementation of the rule of law requires strict law enforcement and fair justice that are impartial and unbiased to guide, regulate, and adjust people's behavior. The vitality of the law lies in its implementation, and the authority of the law also lies in its implementation. General Secretary Xi Jinping emphasized that "if laws are enacted but not implemented, left on the shelf, or implemented ineffectively as a mere formality, then no matter how many laws are formulated, it will be of no avail". Therefore, it is necessary to attach importance to the implementation of the rule of law to maintain and enhance its vitality. Requiring the rule of law implementation system to be "efficient" means that rule of law implementation should not only be effective but also efficient. To achieve this, it is necessary to improve China's administrative law-enforcement system and further promote the reform of the judicial system. It is essential to build a law-based government, promote law-based administration, and enforce laws in a strict, standardized, fair, and civilized manner. It is also necessary to deepen the reform of the judicial system, improve the operating mechanism of judicial power, reform the judicial management system, optimize the allocation of judicial functions and powers, improve the operating mechanism of judicial power, and build a fair, efficient, and authoritative judicial system.

Establishing a Rigorous Rule of Law Supervision System

Marxist jurisprudence has always adhered to the principle of power restriction, opposed all forms of corruption, exercised strict legal supervision over public power, and emphasized the control of power in accordance with the law (Li, 2015, p. 5). Regulating power in accordance with the law and strengthening the restriction and supervision of power operation are important aspects of comprehensively promoting the rule of law in China. The Communist Party of China has always regarded the restriction and supervision of power as a major issue in the construction of the Party and the country. At present, China has established a relatively rigorous supervision system consisting of intra-Party supervision, people's congress supervision, democratic supervision, administrative supervision, judicial supervision, audit supervision, social supervision, and public opinion supervision. However, with the advancement of Chinese rule of law modernization process, it is necessary to vigorously improve the supervision mechanism. Through institutionalized, standardized, and procedural mechanisms, enhance the intensity of supervision with the rigid constraints of the supervision system, form a synergy of supervision through the optimization and integration of the supervision system, improve the effectiveness of supervision through the coordination of the supervision system, and promote the establishment of a rigorous rule of law supervision system with more effective legal supervision.

Forming a Powerful Rule of Law Guarantee System

The rule of law guarantee system is a system composed of institutional norms including political guarantee, institutional guarantee, ideological guarantee, organizational guarantee, operational guarantee, talent guarantee, and cultural guarantee. A powerful legal guarantee system requires the formation of a guarantee element system that is structurally complete, mechanism-sound, resource-sufficient, and highly effective throughout the entire process of legislation, law enforcement, judicature, and law-abiding (Fu, 2015, p. 8). The leadership of the Party is a strong political guarantee for comprehensively promoting the rule of law in China. The socialist system with Chinese characteristics is a solid institutional guarantee for comprehensively promoting the rule of law. It is necessary to uphold the Party's leadership and continuously improve the socialist system with Chinese characteristics to provide political and institutional support for the rule of law system. Meanwhile, it is essential to further deepen the reform of the judicial system, promote the reform of the judicial management system below the provincial level, establish a judicial jurisdiction system that is appropriately separated from administrative divisions to ensure that judicial organs independently and impartially exercise judicial and procuratorial powers in accordance with the law. It is also necessary to expedite the establishment of a management system for judicial personnel that conforms to professional characteristics, scientifically and reasonably determine the quotas of judges and procurators, effectively provide financial and material guarantees, and build a high-quality rule of law workforce. A high-quality rule of law workforce is an organizational and talent guarantee for comprehensively promoting the rule of law, and the rule of law culture with Chinese characteristics is a rich cultural guarantee for comprehensively promoting the rule of law (Fu, 2015, p. 8). It is necessary to adhere to the cultivation of rule of law talents and the nurturing of rule of law culture. In the new era of socialism with Chinese characteristics, the people's aspiration for a better life must include the aspiration for fairness and justice (Zhuo, 2020). Ultimately, the rule of law guarantee system is to ensure social fairness and justice. Without fairness and justice, there will be no effective guarantee for the rule of law, and there will be no long-lasting peace and tranquility in society.

Forming a Comprehensive System of Intra-Party Regulations

Intra-Party regulations are not only important basis for governing the Party but also an important part of the socialist rule of law system with Chinese characteristics. To promote the rule of law in accordance with the law and manage the Party in accordance with regulations in a coordinated manner, it is necessary to continuously improve the system of intra-Party regulations while improving the national legal system, and achieve the connection and coordination between intra-Party regulations and national laws. "Intra-Party regulations are not only an important basis for governing the Party but also a powerful guarantee for building a socialist country under the rule of law" (*Decision of the Central Committee of the Communist Party of China on Several Major Issues Concerning Comprehensively Promoting the Rule of Law*, 2014). Therefore, incorporating the system of intra-Party regulations into the socialist rule of law system with Chinese characteristics is not only an important manifestation of the Chinese characteristics of the rule of law but also a major theoretical and practical breakthrough in comprehensively promoting the rule of law. (Xiao, 2016, p. 6) At present, the system of intra-Party regulations is still under construction. It is imperative to promote the rule of law in accordance with the law and manage the Party in accordance with regulations in a coordinated manner, and ensure the connection and coordination between intra-Party regulations and national laws. Requiring the system of intra-Party regulations to be "comprehensive" means that it must have some formal and substantial signs: It must cover all areas of Party building and Party work, meet the basic needs of governing the Party, with the formulation of basic and major intra-Party regulations completed, supporting intra-Party regulations being relatively complete, and the overall internal scientific and harmonious unity of the system of intra-Party regulations. Substantially, it should conform to China's basic national conditions and actual situations, and meet the actual needs of Party building and Party work (Yi, 2017, p. 7). It is essential to adhere to the organic unity of the rule of law and the management of the Party in accordance with regulations, and promote the comprehensive rule of law with a more comprehensive system of intra-Party regulations.

The rule of law system does not exist in isolation. The construction of the rule of law system cannot be discussed in isolation from other factors. Since the rule of law system is only a subsystem of the socialist system with Chinese characteristics, it can only function under the constraints of various social factors and must be coordinated with other institutional arrangements. The construction of the socialist rule of law system with Chinese characteristics must adhere to the Party's leadership. Strengthening and improving the Party's leadership over the construction of the rule of law system is the fundamental guarantee for the construction of the rule of law system.The construction of the rule of law system also involves the construction of many subsystems. The formation and improvement of the rule of law system must promote the various links of scientific legislation, strict law enforcement, fair judicature, and law-abiding by all citizens in a coordinated manner and do a good job in the internal coordination of the system. It is necessary to adhere to the combination of the rule of law and the rule of virtue, which means that in addition to the rule of law system, the role of the moral norm system also needs to be brought into play.

4.4 Conclusion

This chapter conducts an in-depth analysis of the basic composition of Chinese rule of law discourse system. In particular, through a detailed elaboration of the fundamental and cornerstone rule of law discourses, it reveals the internal logic and unique path of Chinese rule of law construction.

The fundamental rule of law discourse, with the core content of "the organic unity of the Party's leadership, the people being the masters of the country, and law-based governance", constitutes the theoretical basis of Chinese rule of law construction. This principle not only reflects the essential characteristics of the socialism rule of law with Chinese characteristics but also provides a solid theoretical foundation and practical guidance for Chinese rule of law construction.The Party's leadership is the most essential feature of the socialist rule of law with Chinese characteristics, ensuring the correct direction of rule of law construction. In China, the Party is the highest political leading force. The Party's leadership and the rule of law are not contradictory but complementary. The Party leads and promotes rule of law construction through governing the country in accordance with the constitution and laws, ensuring the authority and effectiveness of the rule of law. At the same time, the Party continuously promotes the organic unity of intra-Party governance by law and national governance by law through measures such as improving the institutional mechanism for formulating intra-Party regulations and enhancing the rule of law thinking and law-based governance capabilities of Party members and cadres. This leadership style not only reflects the Party's advanced nature and purity but also provides a strong political guarantee for Chinese rule of law construction. In practice, the Party's leadership runs through all links of legislation, law enforcement, judicial work, and law-abiding, ensuring the systematicness and coordination of rule of law construction. The people being the masters of the country is the essence and core of socialist democratic politics, emphasizing the people-centered nature of rule of law construction. In China, the people are not only participants in the rule of law but also beneficiaries of its achievements. Through the system of people's congresses, the fundamental political system, the people widely participate in the management of national and social affairs, realizing true democracy. This democracy is not merely formal but substantial. It enables the people to play a principal role in rule of law construction, ensuring the democracy and scientific nature of such construction. Law-based governance, as the basic strategy for the Party to lead the people in governing the country, is the only way to achieve modernization of national governance. It requires that all national work must be carried out in accordance with the law, and no organization or individual can enjoy privileges beyond the constitution. Law-based governance not only emphasizes the universal applicability of the law but also focuses on its fair implementation and effective supervision. By building a complete system of legal norms, an efficient system for law implementation, a strict system for law supervision, a strong system for law guarantee, and a sound system of intra-Party regulations, law-based governance provides a solid institutional foundation for the construction of the socialist rule of law with Chinese characteristics. Meanwhile, law-based governance continuously improves the level of the country's governance in accordance with the law by promoting the government's law-based administration and the fair judicial work of judicial organs. The cornerstone rule of law discourse, with the core content of "strengthening and improving the Party's leadership over law-based governance" and "building a socialist rule of law system with Chinese characteristics", provides a specific practical path and operational guidance for Chinese rule of law construction. "Strengthening and improving the Party's leadership over law-based governance" emphasizes the Party's central role in rule of law construction. It requires the Party not only to adhere to governing the country in accordance with the constitution and laws but also to continuously improve its ability and level of leading the rule of law. In practice, the Party integrates the spirit of the rule of law into all aspects of national governance by leading legislation, ensuring law enforcement, supporting judicial work, and taking the lead in abiding by the law. At the same time, the Party continuously promotes the organic unity of intra-Party governance by law and national governance by law through measures such as improving the institutional mechanism for formulating intra-Party regulations and enhancing the rule of law thinking and law-based governance capabilities of Party members and cadres, providing a strong political guarantee for Chinese rule of law construction. "Building a socialist rule of law system with Chinese characteristics" provides a specific path and goal for Chinese rule of law construction. It requires the construction of a complete system of legal norms, an efficient system for law implementation, a strict system for law supervision, a strong system for law guarantee, and a sound system of intra-Party regulations. These five sub-systems support and promote each other, jointly forming the complete framework of the socialist rule of law system with Chinese characteristics. In practice, China has improved the level of national governance in accordance with the law by continuously improving this system.

This chapter is not only a profound summary of Chinese rule of law practice experience but also a clear guide for future rule of law construction. In future rule of law construction, China will continue to adhere to the leading role of the fundamental rule of law discourse and continuously improve the supporting role of the cornerstone rule of law discourse, so as to promote the continuous improvement and development of the socialist rule of law system with Chinese characteristics and contribute more Chinese wisdom and Chinese solutions to global rule of law civilization.

References

Aristotle. (1983). *Politics* (W. S., Trans.). Commercial Press (pp. 167–168).

Central Literature Publishing House. (2015). *Xi Jinping: Selected quotations on comprehensively advancing the rule of law* (p. 34).

Central Literature Publishing House. (2016). *Selected important documents since the 18th national congress of the communist party of China (Volume II)* (pp. 12, 157–158).

Chen, Y., & Jiang, Q. (2015). An outline of the legal analysis of the leadership right of the Communist Party of China. *Legal System and Social Development*, 3.

Fu, Z. (2015). Forming a powerful legal protection system. *Qiushi*, 8.

Jiang, M. (2013). On the interrelationship between building a country ruled by law, a government ruled by law, and a society ruled by law. *Journal of LegalScience*, 6.

Jiang, B. (2014, November 1). How to build a socialist legal system with Chinese characteristics. *Guangming Daily*.
Jiang, T., & Liu, Y. (2019, March 21). New elements contained in China's "legal system". *Procuratorial Daily*.
Li, L. (2014). Building a legal system is a foundational project for promoting the modernization of national governance. *Modern Law Science*, 3.
Li, L. (2015). The theoretical foundation, guiding ideology, and basic composition of the socialist legal system with Chinese characteristics. *Chinese Journal of Law*, 5.
Liu, J. (2018). The vanity of discourse research and the reconstruction of discourse theory. *News Lovers*, 9.
Long, B. (2016). On the Party's leadership as the greatest advantage of the socialist system with Chinese characteristics. *Journal of Hunan University of Science and Technology (Social Science Edition)*, 5.
People's Publishing House. (2014). *Decision of the Central Committee of the Communist Party of China on several major issues concerning comprehensively promoting the rule of law* (p. 4).
Su, L. (1998). Modernization and the rule of law in China in the 20th century. *Chinese Journal of Law*, 1.
Tian, F. (2015). Party legalization in the process of building a country ruled by law. *Forum of Law*, 3.
Wang, T. (2015, March 15). Promoting the institutionalization and legalization of democracy: Learning from Comrade Xi Jinping's important speech at the celebration of the 60th anniversary of the founding of the National People's Congress. *People's Daily*.
Wang, J. (2017). The logical justification and practical orientation of the "Three Unifications" theory. *Law*, 5.
Wang, C. (2019). Taking on responsibilities in the practice of comprehensively advancing the rule of law and advancing along the path of socialist rule of law with Chinese characteristics. *Chinese Journal of Law*, 6.
Wei, Z. (2013). From the legal system to the legal system: On the basic construction of the socialist legal system with Chinese characteristics by the 18th National Congress of the Communist Party of China. *Journal of Beijing Administrative College*, 1.
Wei, S. (2019). The generation, evolution, and change of the conceptual system and social order. *Academics*, 5.
Xi, J. (2014). Conscientiously unifying our thoughts with the spirit of the Third Plenary Session of the 18th Central Committee of the Communist Party of China. *Qiushi*, 1.
Xi, J. (2017). *Securing a decisive victory in building a moderately prosperous society in all respects and striving for the great success of socialism with chinese characteristics for a new era: Report at the 19th national congress of the communist party of China* (pp. 20–23). People's Publishing House.
Xi, J. (2018, March 4). *Adhering to multi-party cooperation, developing socialist democratic politics, and uniting for the decisive victory in building a moderately prosperous society in all respects*. http://www.xinhuanet.com/polics/20181h/2018-03104/c_1122485786.htm
Xiao, J. (2016). On the basic composition of the intra-Party legal system. *Journal of the Central Party School of the Communist Party of China*, 6.
Yi, S. (2017). On the formation of a perfect intra-Party legal system. *Learning and Practice*, 7.
Zhang, W. (2016). Research on Xi Jinping's thought on the rule of law (Part II): The general theory of Xi Jinping's thought on the rule of law. *Legal System and Social Development*, 3.
Zhang, W. (2019). Promoting the construction of a law science system with Chinese characteristics at a new historical starting point. *Social Sciences in China*, 10.
Zhuo, Z. (2020, February 19). Adhering to and improving the socialist legal system with Chinese characteristics. *Study Times*.

Chapter 5
The Necessities, Practical Dilemmas and Mission of Innovation of Chinese Rule of Law Discourse

5.1 Introduction

In the context of today's globalization, the rule of law has become an important yardstick for measuring a country's governance level. As the world's largest developing country, Chinese rule of law construction not only concerns the stability and development of its domestic society but also showcases the country's soft power and image on the international stage. However, the international dissemination and influence of Chinese rule of law discourse have not yet matched its economic status and achievements in rule of law practice. Therefore, it is particularly urgent to promote the innovation of Chinese rule of law discourse and build a rule of law discourse system with Chinese characteristics. This chapter will delve into the strategic significance of innovating Chinese rule of law discourse and analyze the current practical dilemmas, aiming to provide ideas and directions for the construction and dissemination of Chinese rule of law discourse and help the socialist rule of law cause with Chinese characteristics shine on the international stage.

5.2 The Necessities

Scientifically and systematically constructing a rule of law discourse system with Chinese characteristics is a crucial step in promoting the modernization of the socialist rule of law with Chinese characteristics and accelerating the modernization of the country's governance capacity and governance system. It is also the only way to comprehensively implement the strategy of governing the country by law and realize the Chinese Dream of the great rejuvenation of the Chinese nation.

X. Dong, M. Zhang, *Chinese Rule of Law Discourse System*, Understanding China, https://doi.org/10.1007/978-981-95-6260-2_5

5.2.1 *Summarization of Rule of Law Experience and Acceleration of the Process of Rule of Law Modernization*

China's international rule of law discourse system, as a vivid carrier to showcase China's wisdom and experience in governance, needs to deeply explore the rich experience and glorious achievements accumulated in the development of the rule of law over more than 70 years since the founding of the People's Republic of China. Through careful refinement and summarization, creating a rule of law narrative that is both universal and rich in national characteristics can not only reflect on the process of rule of law construction during innovation but also significantly improve China's ability and level of rule of law modernization. At the same time, the maturity and improvement of the rule of law discourse are important indicators to measure the maturity of a country's rule of law construction. The construction of China's international rule of law discourse system helps us reach a rule of law consensus with the international community in a peaceful and co-building tone, ensuring the discourse power over the path of rule of law in international exchanges and cooperation and effectively safeguarding China's legal rights and rule of law dignity, thus creating a more favorable international atmosphere and environment for the process of rule of law modernization.

5.2.2 *Reconstructing Confidence in the Rule of Law Culture and Winning the Discourse Power in International Rule of Law Affairs*

China's international rule of law discourse is not only a symbolic marker of the rule of law ideology with Chinese characteristics but also a crucial force in reconstructing our confidence in the rule of law culture. During the construction process, it is necessary to be firmly rooted in China's national conditions, thoroughly explore and refine the wisdom and values of ancient Chinese rule of law culture. Meanwhile, the new situations and challenges in current domestic and international rule of law construction need to be closely integrated to create new expressions of the rule of law with Chinese characteristics that are both inclusive of international norms and deeply rooted in the local context. This process is not only an innovation of the rule of law with Chinese characteristics but also a transcendence of the simple application of Western rule of law discourses. Through this construction, China's international rule of law discourse can guide the review of the glorious journey of rule of law construction, address current challenges with rule of law wisdom, and facilitate looking forward to the future, thereby enhancing self-confidence and pride in rule of law construction. With an open, inclusive, confident, and composed attitude, the unique charm and value of China's socialist rule of law can be showcased to the world, and an independent and distinct rule of law image can be shaped. On this basis, China is more likely to win the discourse power on the international rule of law stage, gain fair and objective evaluations from the international community regarding Chinese rule of law development, and further promote the influence and status of Chinese rule of law cause on the international stage.

5.3 Practical Dilemmas

With the remarkable achievements continuously made in Chinese rule of law modernization, the rule of law discourse, as a manifestation of Chinese rule of law culture and ideology, urgently needs to adapt to the current situation and adopt systematic construction strategies. This is to firmly grasp the discourse power in international rule of law exchanges, touch the hearts of others with words and inspire them with actions, so as to establish an international rule of law status commensurate with China's comprehensive national strength and further promote the in-depth development of the modernization of socialist rule of law with Chinese characteristics. This urgent need poses new challenges and expectations for the construction of Chinese rule of law discourse system. Through in-depth research, the construction of Chinese rule of law discourse faces the following multiple dilemmas that need to be resolved urgently:

5.3.1 Difficulty in Reversing the Unfavorable Situation in the International Rule of Law Landscape

A country's rule of law discourse is closely linked to its legal system and rule of law practice, while a country's rule of law discourse power is closely related to its comprehensive national strength. However, China's current international rule of law discourse power and international influence do not match the achievements it has made in economic and rule of law construction. In international rule of law exchanges, China still faces the dilemma of "losing the voice". Since the 1990s, various theories about China have emerged one after another in the international community, including the "China threat theory" and the "China collapse theory", which deviate from the factual basis. The "dominance of Western discourse" in the international community poses challenges to the international dissemination of China's socialist rule of law discourse with Chinese characteristics.

5.3.2 Difficulty in Systematizing the Rule of Law Discourse

Despite the remarkable achievements in the rule of law construction over the more than 70 years since the founding of the People's Republic of China, in comparison with the long-standing rule of law history of Western countries, it is necessary to clearly recognize the objective facts that Chinese rule of law construction started late, has a shallow foundation, and faces arduous tasks. The rule of law practice is evolving at an astonishing pace. On one hand, there is a need to resolve the historical legacy issues, and on the other hand, emerging challenges have to be tackled. The core challenge in constructing the Chinese rule of law discourse system lies in how, based on national conditions, the rule of law discourse can be ensured to be updated in tandem with the rule of law practice. This entails continuously refining new topics in the rule of law discourse, highlighting Chinese characteristics, grasping the general laws of rule of law construction, keeping up with the times, seeking international recognition through commonalities, and promoting rule of law exchanges through unique features.

5.3.3 Difficulty in Innovating the Expression Forms of the Rule of Law Discourse

In the global rule of law discourse system, Western capitalist countries, especially the United States, occupy the high ground of the discourse power due to their profound rule of law heritage and economic strength. Western countries often view socialist rule of law countries, especially China, which adopt different development models, with suspicion, exclusion, and even hostility. As a result, China is frequently troubled by negative voices and reports in the international public opinion arena. Facing numerous challenges in the international rule of law community and the unequal discourse pattern, China urgently needs to construct a new form of international rule of law discourse that is both inclusive and able to carry forward the traditional values. It should use universal language expressions to meet the cognitive and emotional characteristics of diverse international audiences and break down ingrained prejudices. Meanwhile, it should use expressions with Chinese characteristics to build consensus domestically and showcase the profound wisdom of Chinese rule of law externally. This is not only an objective requirement for innovating the rule of law discourse but also a difficult problem that urgently needs to be solved.

5.3.4 Difficulty in Enhancing the Spreading Effectiveness of the Rule of Law Discourse

The formation of the international rule of law landscape characterized by "Western dominance and China's relative weakness" can be attributed to two main factors. On one hand, Chinese rule of law discourse system is still in the initial stage of construction. On the other hand, the international dissemination ability of Chinese rule of law discourse is insufficient, leading to a predicament where it is difficult to "reasonable arguments cannot be clearly articulated", "clearly articulated arguments fail to spread widely", and "widely spread arguments fail to resonate".

Specifically, firstly, there is insufficient emphasis on dissemination. Although China has repeatedly emphasized the importance of strengthening the dissemination of the Chinese rule of law discourse, overall, insufficient attention has been paid. The dissemination content lacks systematicness, and the means of expression lacks distinctiveness. Secondly, the dissemination approaches and means require innovation. Since Chinese rule of law discourse system is in its infancy, the dissemination is still mainly government-led, relying on limited channels such as mainstream media and academic dissemination in relevant fields. The private forces have not been effectively integrated, which greatly weakens the explanatory power, persuasiveness, and appeal of the rule of law discourse. Therefore, only through efficient dissemination can China's excellent rule of law culture give full play to its influence and enable China to effectively gain the rule of law discourse power.

5.4 The Missions

Since the 18th National Congress of the Communist Party of China, Chinese academia has paid increasing attention to the innovation of the rule of law discourse system with Chinese characteristics. The reason lies in that the scientific theory with Chinese characteristics, style, and features requires excellent discourse resources for inheritance. These excellent discourse resources carry the historical mission of spreading China's path, theory, system, and cultural confidence abroad. Therefore, scholars have gradually realized the important mission of innovating the rule of law discourse with Chinese characteristics. Specifically, it is manifested in the following aspects.

5.4.1 Writing the Chinese People's Own Legal Concept and Gaining the Right to Speak on the Rule of Law Internationally

Gustav Radbruch once said that each era must rewrite its jurisprudence. Therefore, contemporary China in the transitional period must also reshape its legal concept (Zheng, 2010, p. 128). A country's rule of law discourse is based on its legal system, and a country's right to speak on the rule of law is closely related to its comprehensive national strength. China's current international right to speak is not fully commensurate with its international economic status. Therefore, it is necessary to innovate the rule of law discourse system with Chinese characteristics, showcase and promote China's institutional advantages more on the international stage, and promote international recognition of China, especially the new achievements in the construction of the socialist rule of law with Chinese characteristics and the new development of the legal theory. This will enable China to firmly grasp the initiative in explaining and evaluating its own path of the rule of law.

5.4.2 Safeguarding the Security of the Socialist Rule of Law Ideology, Strengthening International Exchanges and Cooperation, and Enhancing China's International Soft Power

The concept of "soft power" was first put forward by Joseph Nye. He believed that "the United States has a large number of soft power resources and can effectively utilize them to achieve its expected goals." (Nye, 2013, p. 97) The Rule of Law discourse system carries a complete and rigorous ideological system that conforms to the interests of specific classes. "Especially when the right to speak is in the hands of specific groups, classes, countries, or even international groups, it may play an extremely important role in safeguarding their economic and political interests." (Luo, 2013, p. 5) In the era of globalization, the discourse pattern of "Western dominance and China's relative weakness" has not been fundamentally changed. Western countries are constantly exporting capitalist ideology, including capitalist rule of law thoughts and culture, in various ways. Therefore, it is necessary to safeguard the security of Chinese rule of law ideology. On the other hand, we cannot reject global rule of law dialogue and external rule of law exchanges and cooperation in the name of the locality of the socialist rule of law ideology. Some scholars have pointed out that "there are two discourse systems in China's internal and external publicity. At home, we talk about Marxism and socialism with Chinese characteristics, but abroad, we deliberately avoid Marxism and socialism and only talk about traditional Chinese culture and China's reform and opening-up." (Qin, 2012, p. 11) Therefore, currently, China needs to innovate the rule of law discourse system to condense rule of law thoughts, summarize rule of law experiences, and spread rule of law culture. It is vital to actively participate in the development of the world's rule of law civilization, keep "voicing" for development, broaden international exchange platforms, take advantage of favorable conditions such as international organizations, increase the "Chinese component" in the international rule of law right to speak, and enhance China's right to know, right to express, and right to participate in international affairs (Wang, 2015, p. 1).

5.4.3 Continuing to Promote the Sinicization of Marxism in an All-Round Way and Continuously Developing and Improving the Socialist Rule of Law with Chinese Characteristics

Innovating Chinese rule of law discourse system must adhere to inheritance and nationality, originality and contemporaneity, as well as systematicness and professionalism. At the same time, it must be guided by Marxism, which serves as the fundamental criterion distinguishing it from other rule of law discourse systems. In reality, some Chinese people uncritically accept Western rule of law discourses and theories in their entirety and even rely on Western ideas to bolster themselves. Therefore, how to safeguard Marxism and socialism with Chinese characteristics and rationally treat various social trends of thought has become an important part of safeguarding China's national security. Looking at the 70-year development process of New China, China has achieved a transformation from the revolutionary spirit of the rule of law to the currently advocated socialist concept of the rule of law (Yu, 2009, p. 5). When innovating Chinese rule of law discourse system, it is necessary to seek the "greatest common divisor" to build social consensus. However, this does not mean that we can abandon Marxism or forget the original aspiration and mission of the Communist Party of China, especially the most crucial historical mission of Marxism, such as realizing the free and all-round development of people and achieving common prosperity. These are the discourse resources that profoundly reflect the core value pursuit of socialism and must never be discarded.

5.5 Conclusion

In the era of globalization, the rule of law has become an important yardstick for measuring a country's governance effectiveness and international influence. As the world's second-largest economy and the largest developing country, Chinese rule of law construction not only concerns its domestic long-term stability but also shoulders the historical mission of conveying Chinese wisdom to the world and shaping the country's image. However, the international dissemination and influence of Chinese rule of law discourse still lag behind its economic status and achievements in rule of law practice. Therefore, constructing a rule of law discourse system with Chinese characteristics, style, and features has become an urgent need to enhance the country's soft power and participate in the reform of the global governance system. This chapter systematically analyzes the innovative paths of Chinese rule of law discourse in the new era from three dimensions: significance, practical dilemmas, and mission.

First, the innovation of rule of law discourse is a choice for promoting the modernization of national governance.

The construction of Chinese rule of law discourse system is a key driving force for promoting the modernization of the socialist rule of law with Chinese characteristics. On the one hand, by systematically sorting out the achievements and experiences of Chinese rule of law construction over the more than 70 years since the founding of the People's Republic of China, a rule of law narrative with both universality and national characteristics can be formed, contributing Chinese solutions to the global rule of law civilization. On the other hand, a mature rule of law discourse system is an important tool for winning the right to formulate international rules. Confronted with biases such as the "China threat theory" and the "China collapse theory" in the international community, China needs to participate in global rule of law dialogues in a peaceful and cooperative tone. By proactively setting topics and guiding the direction of discussions, China can gain the right to interpret and evaluate its rule of law path, creating a favorable international environment for the modernization of the rule of law.

Second, the Innovation of rule of law discourse faces multiple structural challenges. Currently, the construction of Chinese rule of law discourse system is still restricted by four major dilemmas: First, the situation of "Western dominance and China's relative weakness" in the international rule of law landscape has not been fundamentally reversed. Western countries, relying on their historical advantages and discourse dominance, have long dominated the formulation of international rule of law rules. China needs to break out of the "losing the voice" dilemma and strive for the right to formulate rules in emerging fields. Second, the content system of the rule of law discourse lacks systematicness. Since Chinese rule of law construction started relatively late, it is necessary to dynamically extract new topics while solving historical problems and addressing emerging challenges. Third, there is a lack of innovation in the form of discourse expression. Western countries spread the concept of the rule of law through soft channels such as film and television works and academic institutions, while China still mainly relies on government-led and academic dissemination. It is necessary to explore expressions that combine Chinese characteristics with international resonance. Fourth, the communication effectiveness needs to be improved urgently. At present, there is a dilemma of "reasonable arguments cannot be clearly articulated", "clearly articulated arguments fail to spread widely", and "widely spread arguments fail to resonate". It is necessary to integrate non-governmental forces and innovate communication means, such as using social media and international rule of law forums to enhance the penetration of the legal discourse.

Third, the innovation of rule of law discourse bears three historical missions. Looking to the future, Chinese rule of law discourse system needs to undertake three responsibilities: First, to compete for the international rule of law discourse power. By writing about the Chinese people's own rule of law concepts, China can break the Western dominance in the right to interpret the rule of law. Second, to safeguard ideological security and enhance soft power. In the context of globalization, it is necessary to avoid ignoring the actual situation of national development and blindly accepting the ideological system of Western capitalist rule of law in its entirety, as well as avoid the fragmentation of the rule of law discourse between domestic and international audiences. By innovating the rule of law discourse, China can build consensus both at home and abroad. For example, the rule of law cooperation under the Belt and Road Initiative can be transformed into a global public good. Third, to promote the Sinicization of Marxist legal theory. When absorbing the achievements of Western rule of law, China needs to adhere to the guiding position of Marxism and prevent falling into the misconception of "relying excessively on Western theories".

In conclusion, the innovation of the rule of law discourse in the new era is not only an inevitable choice for China to participate in global governance but also an important practice for promoting the mutual learning of rule of law civilizations. Only by using strategic determination to overcome practical dilemmas and cultural confidence to fulfill historical missions can China make its "Chinese voice" louder on the international rule of law stage and contribute rule of law wisdom to the construction of a community with a shared future for mankind.

References

Luo, H. (2013). Construction of the discourse system of the rule of law with Chinese characteristics. *Journal of the Party School of Tianjin Committee of the CPC*, 5.
Nye, J. 2013. *Soft power* (Ma, J., Trans.). CITIC Press (p. 97).
Qin, X. (2012). Ideas for constructing the academic discourse system with Chinese characteristics. *People's Tribune·Academic Frontiers*, 11.
Wang, J. (2015). Establishing the discourse power of the rule of law in China requires three-wheel drive. *People's Rule of Law*, 1.
Yu, Z. (2009). The evolution of the discourse of the rule of law in China since the founding of New China for 60 years. *Social Sciences in Xinjiang*, 5.
Zheng, Y. (2010). The essence of the practical legal concept: Starting from China in transition. *China Legal Science, 3*, 128.

Chapter 6
Basic Principles for the Innovation of Chinese Rule of Law Discourse

6.1 Introduction

A mature discourse system is often formed through long-term historical practice and development, and is closely related to the social system, historical traditions, and cultural heritage. Chinese rule of law discourse system has been formed and developed on the basis of the practice of socialism with Chinese characteristics. With the continuous deepening of reform and opening-up and the increasing expansion of international academic exchanges, Western rule of law theories and discourse systems have entered China through multiple channels, exerting a wide-ranging influence in the academic field. For a certain period, they became the theories and discourses that attracted considerable attention in the legal academia. In this process, Marxist legal theory, the rule of law theory of socialism with Chinese characteristics, and outstanding traditional Chinese legal thoughts have faced new challenges, and their influence has been somewhat undermined. The Western rule of law discourse system is underpinned by specific Western ideologies and values. Some of its viewpoints are presented in the form of the "theory of universal values", advocating concepts that seemingly transcend class and history. Influenced by this ideological trend, some domestic scholars have shown different cognitive biases. Some scholars overly revere Western rule of law theories and regard them as absolute standards. Others, in their research, neglect the uniqueness of the rule of law construction of socialism with Chinese characteristics and mechanically apply Western rule of law concepts and discourses to interpret China's development path and practical experiences, attempting to solve China's real-world problems and predict its future direction in this way. (Wang, 2013) Currently, in the international public opinion arena and academic discourse system, Western discourses still hold a relative dominant position, and this situation has not been fundamentally changed. China's legal academia must maintain a high level of theoretical confidence, enhance the awareness of academic innovation, and strengthen research on the innovation of

X. Dong, M. Zhang, *Chinese Rule of Law Discourse System*, Understanding China, https://doi.org/10.1007/978-981-95-6260-2_6

China's international rule of law discourse. It is necessary to use the discourse system with Chinese characteristics to interpret and summarize Chinese rule of law practices, experiences, theories, and paths. Therefore, this chapter explores the basic principles that must be followed in the innovation of Chinese rule of law discourse system towards the Belt and Road Initiative, aiming to lay a preliminary framework for the innovation of Chinese rule of law discourse system.

6.2 Principle of Being Rooted in Chinese Rule of Law Practice and Addressing China's Realistic Problems

The innovation of Chinese rule of law discourse system is neither a closed-concept deduction and logical demonstration, nor a form of "the doctrine of appropriation" from foreign models. Instead, it is an ideological expression activity closely related to the development of Chinese rule of law practice. The key lies in basing on Chinese rule of law practice, summarizing Chinese rule of law experience, and solving China's realistic problems. Without being rooted in Chinese rule of law practice, the innovation of the rule of law discourse system will be like a tree without roots and water without a source. The experience of rule of law development provides a solid foundation for the innovation of the rule of law discourse system, and the innovation of the rule of law discourse system, in turn, offers strong theoretical support for summarizing rule of law experience. It can be said that the purpose of innovating Chinese rule of law discourse system is to adhere to the Chinese path of rule of law, summarize Chinese rule of law experience, explain Chinese rule of law system, and improve Chinese rule of law theory. A series of key expressions of distinct Chinese rule of law discourses should be formed to enhance China's influence in international rule of law discourses and increase China's international rule of law discourse power. To achieve this goal, on the basis of accurately understanding the spirit of the central government, political discourses must be transformed into academic discourses, and the two should be organically combined rather than being separated or even opposed to each other.

On the one hand, confidence should be placed in Chinese rule of law practice. Although the rule of law of socialism with Chinese characteristics has experienced a tortuous process of selection, hesitation, growth, and development, overall, remarkable achievements have been made. The rule of law has become the basic way of governance in China. The socialist legal system with Chinese characteristics and the socialist rule of law system with Chinese characteristics have been formed and gradually improved. The combination of governing the country by law and governing the country by virtue, as well as the implementation of governing the country in accordance with the law and governing the country in accordance with the constitution, have provided rich real-world materials for the rule of law discourses of socialism with Chinese characteristics. Chinese rule of law practice also serves as a fertile ground and a rich mine for the innovation of China' s rule of law theory and is the source of innovation for China's international rule of law discourses. In fact, foreign insightful scholars are enthusiastic about researching it. Topics such as the "Chinese rule of law model", "Chinese rule of law practice and experience", and "China's international image in the rule of law" have gradually become hot topics in the foreign academic community. Regarding Chinese rule of law practice and experience, as well as the selection and inheritance of the Chinese rule of law path, the Chinese people are the most qualified and most likely to clarify these issues. Therefore, Chinese people should maintain the resolve, take on responsibilities, and achieve tangible results.

On the other hand, attention should be paid to China's real-world problems. Although remarkable achievements have been made in Chinese rule of law practice, it cannot be denied that there are still numerous problems. Legal theorists must uphold their sense of responsibility and mission, maintain a problem-awareness mindset, be adept at identifying problems, courageous in facing them head-on, and bold in solving them, rather than turning a blind eye to these issues. Since the development of China' s rule of law practice is an endless process, so is theoretical innovation. As old problems are resolved, new ones emerge. Humanity progresses precisely through the process of identifying and solving problems. Adopting a problem-oriented approach and focusing on the rule of law reality is the driving force behind the innovation of Chinese rule of law discourse system. Currently, the following issues need to be addressed: Firstly, how to accurately interpret the uniqueness of China's political system and political structure. The system of people's congresses, the system of multi-party cooperation and political consultation under the leadership of the Communist Party of China, the system of regional ethnic autonomy, and the system of community-level self-governance are not only different from those in Western countries but also significantly distinct from those in socialist countries such as the Soviet Union and Eastern European countries. China's socialist rule of law with Chinese characteristics must be in line with these political systems. These systems determine the characteristics that set China's socialist rule of law apart from that of other countries. China must accurately interpret these politically-characteristic systems using academic language. Secondly, how the rule of law can respond to the major themes of contemporary Chinese social development. Traditional rule of law theories and knowledge, based on their own systems and logical categorizations of disciplines or fields, have limited the theoretical perspective and the scope of knowledge. Therefore, an important direction for the innovation of China's socialist rule of law discourse system with Chinese characteristics is to use major issues in China's social development as a guide to form a new knowledge spectrum and solve a series of problems, such as the development and improvement of China's socialist democratic political system, the construction and improvement of China's socialist judicial system and judicial operation mechanism, and the strengthening and consolidation of community-level political power. Thirdly, how to achieve the simultaneous solution of diachronic problems in the construction of the rule of law (Gu, 2016). Different from Western countries with a long-standing rule of law tradition, Chinese rule of law construction started late, has the weak foundation, and faces heavy tasks. It has obvious super-stage characteristics, which have led to insufficient basic accumulations. For instance, the general legal belief among social members and their conscious attitude towards law-abiding, as well as the clear sense of rules in the whole society, are currently lacking in Chinese society. Therefore, recognizing the reality of insufficient basic accumulations in Chinese rule of law construction and meeting the requirements of the transcendent development of the rule of law are also the key points for the innovation of Chinese rule of law discourse system (Gu, 2012). Resolving the aforementioned issues requires not only maintaining confidence in the rule of law and adhering to a problem-oriented approach but also updating rule of law concepts. In conclusion, only by consistently maintaining a practical concern for Chinese issues can rule of law discourse possess enduring vitality.

6.3 Principle of Promoting the Essence of Chinese Culture and Absorbing Foreign Experiences in the Rule of Law

Undoubtedly, the innovation of Chinese rule of law discourse system requires full utilization of the excellent traditional Chinese cultural resources. Chinese rule of law discourse system should not only reflect the adherence to and development of the principles of scientific socialism but also inherit and promote the excellent genes of Chinese culture. When elaborating on the "Chinese characteristics", General Secretary Xi Jinping put forward the requirement of "four clarifications" in a systematic manner. That is, "It is necessary to clarify that due to different historical traditions, cultural heritages, and basic national conditions of each country and nation, their development paths must have their own characteristics; to clarify that Chinese culture has accumulated the deepest spiritual pursuits of the Chinese nation and is a rich nourishment for the Chinese nation's survival and growth; to clarify that the excellent traditional Chinese culture is the prominent strength of the Chinese nation and our deepest cultural soft power; to clarify that socialism with Chinese characteristics is rooted in the fertile soil of Chinese culture, reflects the will of the Chinese people, meets the requirements of China's and the era's development and progress, and has a profound historical origin and a broad realistic foundation" (Xi, 2013). This fundamentally determines the aspects from which we should strive to inherit and promote the essence of Chinese culture when constructing and innovating Chinese rule of law discourse system.

On the one hand, it is imperative to inherit the profound Chinese culture on the basis of grasping the advantages and characteristics of traditional Chinese academic language. As a symbol for expressing thoughts and values, language is relatively stable and has an unbreakable historical continuity. The traditional language that inherits the profound Chinese culture has unique advantages. Firstly, the unity of knowledge and action. Traditional Chinese language reflects the unity of theory and practice, as well as the unity of personality and scholarship. This unity determines that academic language has strong practicality and popularity. Even ordinary people without specialized education can master and use its core concepts. Secondly, it is vivid and intuitive. Most of China's traditional academic discourses are formed on the basis of personal life insights, different from the abstract and symbolized characteristics of Western academic language. This leads to a high degree of fit between traditional Chinese academic language and the real-life world. Thirdly, the meaning goes beyond words. Traditional Chinese academic discourses can well reflect the tension between the finiteness of language and the infiniteness of meaning, leaving infinite space for readers' life insights (Han, 2014).

On the other hand, it is necessary to adhere to the localization and sinicization of the context of rule of law discourse. The innovation of Chin's rule of law discourse needs to take contemporary Chinese society as the specific scenario, China's actual national conditions as the basic foothold, and the solution of practical problems in Chinese society as the goal. Even in the context of legal globalization, the construction of the rule of law must conform to China's long-term and overall interests and fit into China's existing institutional system, and cannot deviate from the dominant cultural values of Chinese society. China's contribution to the global legal civilization lies in the fact that China always adheres to a unique rule of law form rooted in traditional Chinese culture and provide inspiration and experience for other countries in the world with our own rule of law model.

The innovation of the rule of law discourse system of socialism with Chinese characteristics needs to be based on Chinese practice, grasp the essence of traditional Chinese culture, and at the same time, draw on and absorb all the achievements of global rule of law civilization. The innovation of the rule of law discourse system of socialism with Chinese characteristics should maintain a compatible discourse form. It is not only necessary to draw on the basic principles and general knowledge of the rule of law, but more importantly, to learn from the mature rule of law operation experiences of countries under the rule of law. However, when dealing with Western rule of law thoughts and resources, it is essential to maintain a clear sense of autonomy, use them prudently, and not be satisfied with or limited to certain existing conclusions. Vigilance should also be exercised against the political traps hidden behind the so-called "universality". The basic stance of Marxism should be adhered to, Western academic thoughts and views should be realistically dissected, the specific meanings of certain academic claims or rule of law views in specific situations should be examined, the true implications of concepts or propositions should be clarified, the attached social conditions should be identified, their connections with relevant ideological or theoretical systems should be analyzed, awareness of the "double standards" often used by Western countries should be raised, and the adaptability of these rule of law experiences and resources to China's other theories, practices, institutions, and cultures should be considered (Gu, 2012).

6.4 Principle of Improving the Scientific, Popular, and International Levels of the Rule of Law Discourse System

Currently, there are three forms of discourse in the field of the rule of law: overarching and guiding political discourse, esoteric academic discourse, and ambiguous yet popular and diverse common people's discourse. In terms of the discourse system, there is an urgent need to address two issues. Firstly, it is necessary to further resolve the issue of the broad masses of the people's recognition of the practice, path, and theory of the rule of law under socialism with Chinese characteristics. Secondly, it is required to solve the problem of how the Chinese model and form of the rule of law can be better understood by the international community to enhance China's influence in the international arena. Of course, to address these issues, it is essential to rely on facts, but at the same time, a fact-based discourse system is also needed. It can be said that the practice of the rule of law is the content and essence, while the rule of law discourse is the form and manifestation. Therefore, it is necessary to further improve the scientific, popular, and international levels of the rule of law discourse system.

For the scientific level of the rule of law discourse system, Chinese rule of law practice is a process of gradual development in twists and turns and keeps pace with the times. The scientific nature of the rule of law discourse system encompasses the scientific nature of both the form and content of the discourse, including the scientific nature of specific discourses and the scientific nature of the discourse structure. For example, in a series of discourses such as upholding the organic unity of Party leadership, people being the masters of the country, and governing the country according to law; adhering to the combination of governing the country according to law and governing the country with virtue; institutionalizing and legalizing democracy; promoting the integrated advancement of a law-based country, government, and society; governing in accordance with the law; constructing China's international rule of law system, and building a socialist rule of law country, the basic questions regarding the scientific nature of the rule of law discourse include which discourses constitute the fundamental and cornerstone discourses, which are the basic discourses, and whether they can form a logically rigorous and clearly-structured discourse system. The scientific nature of the rule of law discourse system will also promote the further development of the rule of law theory.

In terms of the popular level of the rule of law discourse system, this pertains to the foundation of the discourse system. As is well-known, the materials that constitute the contemporary Chinese rule of law discourse come from both the West and the practices of the Chinese people, which have been processed and transformed by legal practitioners, experts, and scholars. Therefore, the maturity of this discourse system largely depends on whether it can be accepted and trusted by the broad masses of the people, and further play a positive role in promoting social practice. So, how can the popularization of the Chinese rule of law discourse system be achieved? The following aspects can be considered: First, handle the relationship between written and oral discourses: Written discourses should maintain their unity, standardization, and solemnity. In real life, ordinary people are more likely to come into contact with, understand, and spread oral discourses. Therefore, to gain the understanding, recognition, and acceptance of the people, it is necessary to be good at transforming solemn, standardized, and unified written discourses into vivid and lively oral discourses. Second, handle the relationship between official and folk languages. Most official languages are derived from folk languages through processing, transformation, and adaptation. However, in real life, many people are reluctant to believe official discourses, and some even adopt a mocking and resistant attitude. Therefore, it is crucial to acknowledge this situation, analyze its causes, and take practical measures to bridge the gap between the two, enhancing their connection, communication, and integration. Third, handle the relationship between traditional and emerging languages. The discourse system is a natural evolutionary process, and even innovation is based on the original discourse system. However, due to the changes in the times and the emergence of new media such as the Internet, many new and fashionable languages have emerged. These emerging languages often intersect with oral languages and are widely loved by young people. Therefore, the emergence of emerging languages not only poses a challenge to traditional languages but also provides a good opportunity for their development. It is necessary to ensure the solemnity, standardization, and unity of the rule of law discourse system while actively learning emerging languages to promote the innovation and progress of the mainstream rule of law discourse (Li, 2012).

In terms of the internationalization of the rule of law discourse, it is necessary to carry out necessary formal packaging and transformation of Chinese rule of law discourse so that it can be understood by foreigners. By telling Chinese rule of law stories, introducing Chinese rule of law reality, explaining the origin and development of Chinese rule of law path, and presenting Chinese rule of law image, Chinese rule of law theory can be more widely disseminated in the world. To improve the internationalization level of the rule of law discourse, the following aspects need to be addressed. Firstly, it is essential to correctly understand and properly handle the relationship between the general and the particular, the universal and the specific. Interaction is based on commonalities. In international exchanges and external communication, it is necessary to identify certain commonalities as a basis. On the premise of these commonalities, the specific features of Chinese rule of law should be elaborated. Through communication, understanding can be deepened and consensus can be broadened. Secondly, in terms of communication methods, attention should be paid to studying the thinking patterns, hobbies and habits of foreigners. During the process of international communication, China should be good at telling stories, presenting facts and expounding principles, aiming for a natural and appropriate expression that unfolds smoothly. Regarding the issues they are concerned about, the basic stances and policies should remain firm, but the language used can be as gentle as possible. Thirdly, emphasis should be placed on enhancing the ability to exercise the right to speak. This mainly includes the following capabilities: the ability to set agendas, namely, establishing unique and advantageous topics originating from China, rather than merely responding passively to questions but proactively raising issues and setting agendas; the ability to frame narratives, which involves defining events, discerning responsibilities, making moral judgments, and proposing solutions; the ability to persuade through empathy, that is, placing oneself in others' shoes, changing perspectives, understanding both oneself and others, and fostering mutual understanding; and the ability to integrate communication, which not only includes the information gathering and dissemination capabilities across various media sectors such as news gathering, editing, and broadcasting within the news industry but also encompasses the integrated strength of other communication modes that coexist and complement news dissemination (Wu, 2014). What is national can become international, but it must be expressed in a language that people around the world can understand and easily comprehend in order to truly achieve the international dissemination of the rule of law discourse.

6.5 Conclusion

In the process of exploring the innovation of Chinese rule of law, it is not difficult to find that a mature discourse system plays a crucial and indispensable role in promoting rule of law practices, summarizing rule of law experiences, and expounding rule of law theories. Chinese rule of law discourse system has been formed over a long-term historical practice, based on China's unique social system, historical traditions, and cultural accumulations. Facing the complex situation of international public opinion and the dominant position of Western rule of law discourses, it is necessary to maintain a high level of theoretical awareness and confidence, and strengthen the innovative research on China' s external rule of law discourse.

During the innovation process, it is necessary to base on Chinese rule of law practices and address China's real-world problems. The innovation of the rule of law discourse system is not a closed exercise in conceptual deduction and logical demonstration, but an ideological expression activity closely related to the development of Chinese rule of law practices. Confidence in Chinese rule of law practice must be coupled with a concern for China's real-world problems. By summarizing rule of law experiences, responding to the themes of social development, and solving the diachronic problems in rule of law construction, a solid practical foundation can be provided for the innovation of the rule of law discourse system.

When constructing the rule of law discourse system, it is also crucial to uphold the essence of Chinese culture and absorb foreign rule of law experiences. Chinese culture embodies the deepest spiritual pursuits of the Chinese nation and serves as a rich source of nourishment for its continuous survival and development. In innovating the rule of law discourse system, it is necessary to inherit the profound Chinese culture and grasp the advantages and characteristics of traditional Chinese academic language. Meanwhile, an open attitude should be maintained to draw on and absorb all the achievements of the world's rule of law civilization. However, when drawing on Western rule of law thoughts and resources, it is crucial to maintain a clear sense of autonomy, exercise prudence in their application, and always remain grounded in China's realities and distinctive characteristics.

Finally, it is also of vital importance to improve the scientific, popular, and international levels of the rule of law discourse system. Scientificity requires that Chinese rule of law discourse system be logically rigorous and clearly structured; popularity means that Chinese rule of law discourse system should be acceptable and convincing to the general public; internationalization demands that Chinese rule of law discourse can be understood and recognized by the international community. By enhancing these three aspects, Chinese rule of law voice can be better spread, its rule of law image can be better presented, and its international rule of law discourse power can be strengthened.

In conclusion, the basic principles for the innovation of the rule of law under socialism with Chinese characteristics include basing on Chinese rule of law practices to address real-world problems, promoting the essence of Chinese culture and absorbing foreign rule of law experiences, and improving the scientific, popular, and international levels of the rule of law discourse system. These principles are interrelated and mutually reinforcing, jointly forming a framework for the innovation of Chinese rule of law discourse system. In future rule of law construction, these principles should continue to be adhered to in order to promote the continuous improvement and development of Chinese rule of law discourse system.

References

Gu, P. (2012). Construction of the contemporary Chinese discourse system of the rule of law. *Chinese Journal of Law*, 3.

Gu, P. (2016). Effectively handling the diachronic and synchronic contradictions in the development of the rule of law. *Judicature of China*, 2.

Han, X. (2014). Constructing an academic discourse system of philosophy and social sciences with Chinese characteristics. *Red Flag Manuscript*, 22.

Li, Z. (2012). Improving the scientific, popular and international levels of the Chinese discourse system. *People's Tribune*, 12.

Wang, W. (2013, December 20). Building a discourse system of philosophy and social sciences with Chinese characteristics. *China Social Sciences Today*.

Wu, X. (2014). The communication gap behind the struggle for discourse power. *International Communications*, 5.

Xi, J. (2013, August 21). Xi Jinping: Have the overall situation in mind, grasp the general trend and focus on major issues, and strive to do a better job in publicity and ideological work. *People's Daily*.

Chapter 7
Basic Paths for the Innovation of Chinese Rule of Law Discourse

7.1 Introduction

The construction of Chinese rule of law discourse system in the new era is a complex and systematic project with practicality, timeliness, and interactivity. In the multi-layered construction of the rule of law discourse system, it is imperative to firmly adhere to Xi Jinping Thought on the Rule of Law, remain unwavering in the path of rule of law with Chinese characteristics, tell the story of Chinese characteristics based on Chinese rule of law practices, seek common ground with an open mind, create expressions with historical wisdom, and make the voice of Chinese rule of law resonate with people through effective communication.

7.2 Clarifying the "Meta-theory"

Foucault profoundly revealed the assertion that "discourse is power" in *The Order of Discourse*, highlighting the core position of discourse in the power structure. In simple terms, discourse power refers to the ability to dominate international rule of law dialogue and communication by accurately elaborating, widely disseminating, and winning the general trust of the international community (Zhou et al., 2020, p. 338). For a long time, Western countries, relying on their strong comprehensive national strength and relatively well-developed discourse systems, have continuously promoted their rule of law concepts, theories, and cultures globally, especially to developing countries, gradually establishing a "Western-dominated discourse position" in the international community. Against this backdrop, the international community often tends to measure the rule of law development levels of other countries against the yardstick of Western rule of law discourse.

X. Dong, M. Zhang, *Chinese Rule of Law Discourse System*, Understanding China, https://doi.org/10.1007/978-981-95-6260-2_7

However, as the ancient Chinese saying goes, "Things are inherently different, which is the nature of things". Every country has its unique national conditions, historical, and cultural backgrounds. Based on its own national conditions and historical and cultural traditions, China has independently pioneered the path of socialist rule of law with Chinese characteristics. During the implementation of this innovative practice, it does not fully conform to the rule of law framework model dominated by the West. As a result, in international exchanges and dissemination, it has been subject to one-sided interpretations, unfounded accusations, and a certain degree of restrictions from some who uphold the Western-dominated rule of law discourse position. Meanwhile, since Chinese rule of law discourse system is still in the process of continuous improvement, its international communication ability and influence are still insufficient, leading to a certain degree of discourse deficiency in international rule of law dialogues. This deficiency not only affects the voice of Chinese rule of law on the international stage but also directly weakens China's discourse power and rule of law image in the international community.

To fundamentally reverse this unfavorable situation in rule of law discourse, it is essential to firmly establish confidence in the path, theory, system, and culture of socialist rule of law with Chinese characteristics. Clarifying the socialist rule of law theory with Chinese characteristics as the "meta-theory" for the construction of China' s rule of law discourse system is the key to strengthening rule of law confidence and maintaining strategic focus. This theory is the culmination of the long-term practical wisdom of Chinese rule of law construction. It originates from practice, guides practice, and is continuously enriched and developed in practice, featuring distinct Chinese characteristics and the spirit of the times.

In the process of constructing Chinese rule of law discourse system, this theory should serve as the cornerstone to ensure the scientific nature and comprehensiveness of the system. At the same time, attention should be paid to the innovation and transformation of discourse, converting the past slogan-style political language into rule of law language that combines universality and national characteristics, and conveying it to domestic and international audiences in a more vivid, specific, and accessible way. Through this approach, it can enhance the emotional, theoretical, and ideological identification of domestic and international audiences with the socialist rule of law with Chinese characteristics, thus breaking the international community's blind belief in Western rule of law theories and constructing a Chinese rule of law discourse system with strong persuasion, credibility, and appeal. Ultimately, China will convey the voice of its rule of law with greater confidence, gain discourse power in the international community regarding its rule of law, and make positive contributions to enhancing the country's rule of law image and international status.

7.3 Constructing Systematic Topics

The meticulous formulation of Chinese rule of law discourse is the key to constructing its rule of law discourse system. Law stands as the fruit of the wisdom born out of practice, and its vitality and credibility are deeply rooted in the fertile soil of rule of law practice. Only by closely following the development context of rule of law practice and continuously updating and enriching the topics of socialist rule of law with Chinese characteristics can China's international rule of law discourse maintain its vitality. If divorced from the solid foundation of Chinese rule of law practice, the innovation of China's international rule of law discourse system will become a tree without roots and water without a source, making it difficult to achieve sustainable and healthy development.

First, based on Chinese rule of law practice, clarify the characteristics of the national conditions. Currently, China is committed to promoting the modernization of the national governance system and governance capacity, actively exploring the path of modernizing the socialist rule of law with Chinese characteristics, and striving to build a law-based society, government, and country to achieve the Two Centenary Goals and the Chinese Dream of the great rejuvenation of the Chinese nation. Chinese rule of law discourse system should take this as the starting point and goal of discourse innovation, accurately explain to the international community the special national conditions and unique advantages of the socialist rule of law path with Chinese characteristics, and respect and understand the differences in the rule of law systems between China and other countries.

Second, take the "organic unity of upholding the Party's leadership, the people being the masters of the country, and governing the country according to law" as the fundamental discourse to elaborate on the uniqueness of China's political system and political construction. This concept clarifies the basic connotation of the political development path of socialism with Chinese characteristics and reflects the Chinese Communists' profound understanding of the laws of China's socialist political construction. Chinese rule of law discourse system should take this as the logical main line, set the discourse content reflecting important topics in Chinese rule of law practice, show the world the unique charm of China's political system and the remarkable achievements of its rule of law construction, and extract universally applicable principles from them to provide useful references for the rule of law construction of developing countries and contribute Chinese wisdom to the progress of human rule of law civilization.

Furthermore, accurately elaborate on the evaluation criteria for Chinese rule of law construction and gain the international discourse power in the rule of law. The international community often uses Western countries' rule of law theories as the standards to evaluate other countries' rule of law construction, which leads to misunderstandings and prejudices against the socialist rule of law path with Chinese characteristics. In the process of construction, Chinese rule of law discourse system should clearly expound the evaluation criteria for Chinese rule of law construction, emphasizing the status of the people as the main body in revolution, construction, and reform, as well as the principle that the people share the fruits of revolution, construction, and reform. By highlighting that improving people's well-being is the criterion for judging the success of rule of law construction, China can break the evaluation system dominated by Western countries, strengthen the essential features of China's democratic politics, and promote the international community to make a fair evaluation of the socialist rule of law with Chinese characteristics.

Finally, pay attention to China's real-world problems and set up issues for the synchronic solution of diachronic problems. Chinese rule of law construction started late, has a weak foundation, and faces heavy tasks. It needs to address the diachronic and synchronic contradictions brought about by rapid development. For example, there are contradictions between advanced legal systems and relatively backward rule of law culture construction, challenges in coordinating the relationship between democracy and the rule of law, and issues such as international dissemination of China's national rule of law discourse and enhancement of the legal team's professionalism. The innovation of China's international rule of law discourse system should adhere to a problem-oriented approach, set up topics around these real-world problems, and continuously accumulate, summarize, and refine China's experience and practices. By demonstrating the process and achievements of Chinese rule of law construction, China can dispel the "China threat theory" and the resistance from other countries that may arise in rule of law exchanges, and at the same time provide Chinese experience and wisdom for global rule of law governance and the maintenance of the rule of law order.

7.4 Standardizing the Translation

Constructing the Chinese rule of law discourse system is a systematic project. If the discourse system is compared to an ideological edifice, the bricks and stones that make up this building are concepts and categories. A discourse system is not simply a random collection of words but an organic combination of concepts or categories supported by theories and with specific connotations. Concepts and categories play a fundamental role in the construction of a discourse system. Terminology serves as the linguistic markers of concepts and categories. Generally speaking, when people acquire new knowledge and ideas, they tend to rely on their existing experiences to understand unknown issues. For instance, when we study foreign theories and ideas, we interpret them according to the Chinese understanding structure and way of thinking, and digest and transform foreign ideological theories based on our own cultural traditions and understanding structures. The same principle applies when foreign and Western audiences try to understand China.

Chinese rule of law terminology refers to the concepts and core cultural terms, in the form of words or phrases, that are created or constructed by the Chinese nation, condensing Chinese legal philosophical thoughts, humanistic spirit, ways of thinking, and values. These terms frequently appear in our legal practice and serve as the foundation and means of expressing the ideas of China's modernized rule of law.

The numerous and diverse legal terms with Chinese characteristics are of fundamental significance for understanding contemporary Chinese legal thoughts, legal culture, values, knowledge systems, and the legal reality in China. The essence of the thoughts contained in these terms is the result of the Chinese nation's exploration and rational thinking about law and society over thousands of years, embodying the Chinese nation's legal wisdom, reflecting the nation's deepest spiritual pursuits, as well as the depth and breadth of its rational thinking. The humanistic ideas, ways of thinking, and values they contain have become a kind of "life gene" deeply embedded in the blood of the Chinese people, internalized into the common character and beliefs of the Chinese nation, and have thus supported the Chinese nation's legal civilization for thousands of years. At the same time, they are also the practical expressions of the new path of Chinese-style modernization in the rule of law, and the key for other countries and ethnic groups in the world to understand the contemporary Chinese path of the rule of law. Only by accurately understanding the subtle connotations of these terms can one truly understand the long-standing Chinese legal civilization and the new path of Chinese-style modernization in the rule of law at a profound level.

In international communication practices, Chinese-characteristic terms often fail to retain their original connotations and extensions during cross-cultural translation, frequently resulting in the loss of some meanings or the addition of new ones. For instance, the term "科学" (kēxué) frequently appears in China's political discourse, with its English equivalent being "science". However, when we refer to the "Scientific Outlook on Development", inquire whether "decisions are scientific", or assess whether "practices are scientific", the term "科学" transcends its literal translation as "science" or "scientific", becoming virtually synonymous with correctness, precision, rationality, systematicity, and reasonableness. In contrast, English-speaking audiences typically interpret the term within its original semantic scope, often associating it solely with the natural sciences upon hearing "science".

Similarly, the "one-China principle" has been mistranslated by some foreign media outlets as the "one-China policy". The term "原则" (yuánzé, principle) denotes the rules or standards that underpin speech or conduct, representing rationalized phenomena derived from long-term empirical summaries. In contrast, "政策" (zhèngcè, policy) refers to the action guidelines formulated by a state or political party to achieve specific historical objectives, carrying a greater degree of uncertainty. More critically, the "one-China principle" emerged from the Chinese people's righteous struggle to safeguard national sovereignty and territorial integrity, resting on an unshakable factual and legal foundation. It constitutes the basis and prerequisite for achieving peaceful reunification and must not be conflated with the so-called "one-China policy", which avoids making an explicit statement. Therefore, the precise translation of rule of law terminology holds paramount importance for the construction of China's international rule of law discourse system.

In practice, on the one hand, it is essential to take the initiative and have Chinese experts proficient in foreign languages serve as the main translators. Only in this way can the connotations and denotations of the terms be accurately translated. On the other hand, it is equally important to leverage international expertise by inviting foreign scholars to meticulously review, revise, and polish the translations. Only in this way can the translations be truly understood by foreign audiences in cross-cultural communication. After the foreign experts have made their revisions, the main translators should deliberate repeatedly to ensure that the revised terms are consistent with the original meanings. When necessary, they should have in-depth discussions with the foreign experts to find the most exquisite and vivid translations.

In summary, the work of sorting out, translating, and spreading rule of law terminology is a fundamental project for the international spreading of Chinese legal culture. In the new era, to strengthen the capacity for international communication, comprehensively enhance the effectiveness of international communication, and establish international rule of law discourse power commensurate with China's comprehensive national strength and international status, it is necessary to develop a standardized version of the translation of Chinese legal terminology. This will reveal the true essence of Chinese culture to the world, deepen exchanges and mutual learning between different civilizations, and promote the better spreading of Chinese legal culture globally.

7.5 Shaping New Expressions

In the global rule of law discourse system, Western capitalist countries, by virtue of their profound rule of law heritage and economic strength, have occupied the high-ground of discourse power. Towards countries with different development models, especially socialist rule of law countries like China, the West often holds a certain degree of suspicion and exclusion, which has led China to be frequently troubled by negative voices and reports in the international public opinion arena. Facing numerous challenges in the international rule of law community and the disadvantaged position in the discourse landscape, China urgently needs to construct a new form of rule of law discourse that is both inclusive and able to inherit and carry forward the traditional values.

On the one hand, China should actively absorb new rule of law concepts and knowledge from Western countries, aiming to have a comprehensive understanding, and closely integrate them with China's national conditions to clearly elaborate China's positions and propositions. The rule of law theory originated in the West and is the crystallization of its long-term governance experience, with Western liberal rule of law as a representative. Liberal rule of law closely links the rule of law with freedom, which has promoted the stability of the capitalist economy and social order. With the advancement of globalization, the rule of law has become a consensus in human society. Marx and others, while criticizing the capitalist rule of law, also affirmed its achievements, believing that liberal rule of law is a significant progress in human civilization. General Secretary Xi Jinping pointed out that "the rule of law is one of the important achievements of human civilization. The essence and gist of the rule of law have universal significance for national governance and social governance in all countries. We should learn from and draw on the excellent achievements of the rule of law civilization in the world". (Zhang, 2023) The biggest difference between the socialist rule of law theory with Chinese characteristics and the Western capitalist rule of law theory lies in the basic national conditions. The socialist public ownership system and the dominant position of the people require the socialist rule of law with Chinese characteristics to safeguard the freedom of the vast majority of people. When learning from the Western liberal legal theory, it is crucial to closely combine national conditions and the actual needs of rule of law development, dialectically analyze the contradictions in the capitalist rule of law system, and construct rule of law concepts with Chinese characteristics with an innovative thinking that transcends the limitations of liberal rule of law. This does not mean a complete negation of Western rule of law, but rather exploring a rule of law path suitable for China's national conditions through exchanges. The socialist rule of law theory with Chinese characteristics adheres to the organic unity of the people being the masters of the country and governing the country according to law, resolving the potential conflicts between the rule of law and democracy. At the same time, through the combination of governing the country according to law and governing the country according to virtue, and the unity of formal rule of law and substantive rule of law, it promotes the mutual complementarity between law and morality. These core concepts should become the central content of China's international legal discourse system construction, demonstrating Chinese rule of law position of "integrating Chinese and Western rule of law thoughts" and providing inspiration and reference for the international community in rule of law development.

On the other hand, China needs to deeply explore and integrate traditional and modern rule of law resources, trace the evolution of Chinese rule of law concepts, and highlight the unique wisdom and charm of Chinese rule of law. In the process of integrating the essence of traditional culture, reflecting the general laws of the development of human rule of law civilization, and the practice of the socialist rule of law with Chinese characteristics, Chinese rule of law discourse system will be able to create new expressions and concepts that are both "integrating Chinese and Western rule of law thoughts" and "rooted in the local context", and tell influential Chinese rule of law stories with persuasive Chinese voices. The Chinese nation has a long history and a profound cultural heritage. Traditional Chinese culture contains rich rule of law wisdom and resources, among which the people-centered ideology, the ideology of benevolent governance, and the ideology of rule by virtue are particularly prominent. The people-centered ideology emphasizes putting the people at the center and is the core of ancient Chinese political thought. The political concept of the Chinese people being the masters of the country and the people-centered principle is an inheritance and development of the people-centered ideology. The ideology of benevolent governance was initiated by Confucius and further developed by Mencius. It requires rulers to implement benevolent governance extensively, reduce corvée, lower taxes, and carry out moral education. The pursuit of good laws and good governance in the construction of the socialist rule of law with Chinese characteristics is an embodiment and sublimation of the ideology of benevolent governance. The ideology of rule by virtue, as another essence of traditional

Chinese political culture, emphasizes that rulers should set an example, pay attention to self-cultivation and diligence in government, attach importance to moral education of the people, implement "governing the country by virtue", and stress the priority of virtue over punishment. The path of the socialist rule of law with Chinese characteristics adheres to the combination of governing the country according to law and governing the country according to virtue, which is an inheritance and sublimation of the traditional ideology of rule by virtue. In the process of constructing Chinese rule of law discourse system, traditional discourses in traditional culture that transcend time and space, have universal values and cultural significance should be deeply explored and combined with the socialist rule of law theory with Chinese characteristics to integrate traditional cultural and modern rule of law discourse resources. By telling the story of the inheritance and innovation of Chinese rule of law concepts in practice, a "locally-rooted" Chinese discourse system can be precisely forged, enabling the world to understand China's wisdom and achievements in the process of rule of law development.

7.6 Conclusion

The construction of Chinese rule of law discourse system is a complex and systematic project that combines practicality, timeliness, and interactivity. Its core objective is to convey China's unique rule of law concepts and practical experiences to the world in a scientific, systematic, and innovative way, thereby enhancing China's voice and influence in the international rule of law arena. In this process, it is necessary to be guided by Xi Jinping Thought on the Rule of Law, firmly adhere to the path of socialist rule of law with Chinese characteristics, base on Chinese rule of law practices, seek international consensus with an open-minded and inclusive attitude, innovate the means of expression by drawing on historical wisdom, and make the voice of Chinese rule of law resonate with people through effective communication strategies.

Clarifying the "meta-theory" of Chinese rule of law discourse is the foundation for constructing the discourse system. For a long time, Western countries, by virtue of their strong comprehensive national strength and relatively well-developed discourse systems, have established the so-called "Western discourse dominance" in the international community. As a result, the international community often uses Western rule of law discourses as a yardstick to measure the rule of law development levels of other countries. However, each country has its own unique national conditions, historical, and cultural backgrounds. Based on its own national conditions and historical and cultural traditions, China has independently pioneered the path of socialist rule of law with Chinese characteristics. Nevertheless, this innovative practice has been deliberately distorted, smeared, and suppressed by some countries. Meanwhile, Chinese rule of law discourse system remains imperfect, with insufficient international communication capabilities and influence, leading to a lack of voice in international legal dialogues. To reverse this situation, it is imperative to strengthen self-confidence in the path, theory, system, and culture of socialist rule of law with Chinese characteristics. The theory of socialist rule of law with Chinese characteristics should be regarded as the "meta-theory" for the construction of the rule of law discourse system. This theory is rooted in China's long-term rule of law construction practices, featuring distinct Chinese characteristics and contemporary features. Constructing the discourse system on this foundation, with an emphasis on discourse innovation and transformation, can enhance the recognition of socialist rule of law with Chinese characteristics among both domestic and international audiences, break the blind faith in Western rule of law theories, and construct a Chinese rule of law discourse system with strong persuasion, credibility, and appeal.

Carefully formulating systematic topics for Chinese rule of law discourse is the key to constructing the discourse system. Law is the crystallization of practical wisdom, and the topics of Chinese rule of law discourse should closely follow the development context of rule of law practice. Based on Chinese rule of law practice, it is necessary to clarify the characteristics of the national conditions. With the goals of promoting the modernization of the national governance system and governance capacity, and building a law-based society, government, and country, it is imperative to accurately elaborate on the special national conditions and unique advantages of the path of socialist rule of law with Chinese characteristics. Taking the "organic unity of the leadership of the Communist Party of China, the people being the masters of the country, and law-based governance" as the fundamental discourse, it is necessary to expound on the uniqueness of China's political system and political structure, demonstrate the charm of China's political system and the achievements of rule of law construction, and extract universally applicable principles to provide references for the rule of law construction of developing countries. Accurate elaboration should be provided on the evaluation criteria for Chinese rule of law construction, with emphasis placed on the status and role of the people. It is essential to break free from the evaluation system dominated by Western countries and encourage the international community to make a fair assessment of the socialist rule of law with Chinese characteristics. Attention should be directed towards China's real-world problems, with the establishment of topics aimed at the simultaneous resolution of diachronic issues. Topics should be formulated around the contradictions and challenges encountered in Chinese rule of law construction. By summarizing China's experiences and practices, valuable Chinese wisdom and insights can be offered for global rule of law governance and the maintenance of the rule of law order.

Standardizing the translation of Chinese rule of law terminology is an important part of constructing the discourse system. A discourse system is composed of an organic combination of concepts and categories, and terms are the linguistic markers of concepts and categories. Chinese rule of law terms condense Chinese rule of law philosophical thoughts, humanistic spirits, ways of thinking, and values, which are of great significance for understanding contemporary Chinese rule of law. In international communication practice, there are often deviations in the connotation and denotation of Chinese-characteristic terms during cross-cultural translation. Therefore, accurate translation of rule of law terms is crucial. In practice, on the one hand, Chinese experts proficient in foreign languages should be the main translators to accurately translate the connotation and denotation of terms. On the other hand, foreign experts should be engaged to review, revise, and polish the translations to ensure that the translations can be truly understood by foreign audiences in cross-cultural communication. The main translators should also deliberate repeatedly and fully discuss with foreign experts to find the most exquisite translations. Constructing a standard version for the translation of Chinese legal terms is a basic project for deepening exchanges and mutual learning among different civilizations and promoting the spread of Chinese rule of law culture to the world.

Shaping new expressions for Chinese rule of law discourse is an inevitable requirement for constructing the discourse system. In the global rule of law discourse system, Western capitalist countries hold a dominant position in terms of discourse power and take a skeptical and exclusive attitude towards socialist rule of law countries like China. Facing these challenges and the unequal discourse pattern, China needs to construct new forms of rule of law discourse that is inclusive and carries forward the traditional heritage. On the one hand, China should actively absorb new Western rule of law concepts and knowledge, closely integrate them with China's national conditions, and clearly expound its positions and propositions. When drawing on Western liberal rule of law theories, a dialectical analysis of the contradictions in the capitalist rule of law system should be conducted. An innovative mindset should be adopted to construct rule of law concepts with Chinese characteristics, demonstrating Chinese rule of law stance of "integrating both Chinese and Western concepts of rule of law". On the other hand, China should deeply explore and integrate traditional and modern rule of law resources and trace the evolution process of Chinese rule of law concepts. The people-centered thought, benevolent governance thought, and rule by virtue thought in traditional Chinese culture have provided rich wisdom and resources for the construction of the socialist rule of law with Chinese characteristics. By combining the timeless and universally valuable discourses in traditional culture with the socialist rule of law theory with Chinese characteristics, new expressions and concepts that "integrate Chinese and Western elements" and are "rooted in the local context" can be created, enabling China to tell influential stories about its rule of law with a persuasive voice.

In conclusion, the basic path for innovating Chinese rule of law discourse requires the coordinated promotion of multiple aspects, such as clarifying the "meta-theory", setting up systematic topics, standardizing the translation of rule of law terms, and shaping new expressions. Through these efforts, China can enhance the international dissemination capacity of its rule of law discourse, strengthen its discourse power and influence in the international rule of law arena, and make positive contributions to advancing the development of global rule of law civilization.

References

Zhang, W. (2023, December 15). Profoundly grasp the essence of confidence in the rule of law. *Guangming Daily*, 11.

Zhou, Y., Lin, J., Zhang, Q., et al. (2020). *Research on the innovation of the discourse system of the rule of law with Chinese characteristics*. People's Publishing House.

Chapter 8
The Global Propositions of Chinese Rule of Law Discourse in the New Era

8.1 Introduction

Rule of law discourse is a linguistic symbol system created through the application of rule of law thinking, with the fundamental functions of manifesting the spirit of the rule of law and promoting its ideals. Generally speaking, as a symbolic representation of ideology, rule of law discourse not only functions as an internal symbolic language but also serves to express ideological concepts and facilitate cultural education (Zhou et al., 2020: 1). The socialist rule of law discourse with Chinese characteristics represents an aggregate of ideas, theories, cultures, and languages that integrate the fundamental principles of Marxism with the specific realities of China's new path towards modernization of the rule of law, as well as with the excellent traditional Chinese legal culture. It is a concentrated exposition of the rule of law thinking and spirit inherent in the path of socialist rule of law with Chinese characteristics.

President Xi Jinping has stated, "The path of socialist rule of law with Chinese characteristics embodies the achievements and experiences of socialist rule of law construction and represents the sole correct path towards building a socialist country governed by law". Rooted in the excellent traditional Chinese legal culture and aligned with China's actual conditions and national circumstances, this path is the result of the unremitting exploration and struggle of the Chinese people since modern times. It encompasses profound historical logic and embodies profound historical wisdom, making a unique contribution to the progress of human rule of law civilization and representing a new form of human rule of law civilization.

The global propositions of the socialist rule of law discourse with Chinese characteristics serve as a practical response to the epochal question of "What is happening in the world, and how should we respond?" It serves as a comprehensive and effective remedy for addressing global challenges and advancing the transformation of the global governance system, forming an integral part of Xi Jinping Thought on

X. Dong, M. Zhang, *Chinese Rule of Law Discourse System*, Understanding China, https://doi.org/10.1007/978-981-95-6260-2_8

Socialism with Chinese Characteristics for a New Era. Therefore, a profound understanding, translation, and dissemination of the connotations and practical significance of these global propositions are of immense worldwide importance. They enable us to accurately grasp the internal logic of Xi Jinping Thought on Socialism with Chinese Characteristics for a New Era, elucidate the value orientation of China' new path towards modernization of the rule of law to the world, contribute Chinese wisdom to the progress and development of human rule of law civilization, and provide China's solutions to drive the reform of the global governance system.

This chapter explores the following key issues related to the global propositions of the socialist rule of law discourse with Chinese characteristics: First, the historical context: The world is undergoing profound changes unseen in a century, and there is a growing call within the international community for reform of the global governance system. Second, the core essence: Advocating for the diversity and interactivity of human rule of law civilizations. Third, the primary objectives: Promoting the democratization, legalization, and rationalization of international relations. Fourth, the methods of struggle: Coordinating the advancement of domestic rule of law and international rule of law, employing legal means in international struggles, and resolutely safeguarding national sovereignty, security, and development interests. Fifth, the action agenda: Practicing true multilateralism, maintaining world peace, promoting common development, and advancing the building of a community with a shared future for mankind.

8.2 Context of the Era

The contemporary world is undergoing profound changes unseen in a century. The deepening trends of multipolarity, economic globalization, social informatization, and cultural diversification have increasingly intertwined and interdependent relations among nations. The rapid rise of emerging markets and developing countries has contributed to a more balanced distribution of international power, with peace and development emerging as the themes of our time. However, the world also faces a multitude of global challenges: regional hotspots and conflicts persist, and non-traditional security threats such as terrorism, cybersecurity, major infectious diseases, and climate change continue to spread, making the challenges humanity faces increasingly complex and variable. Yet, the existing global governance system is becoming increasingly ill-suited to the evolving landscape and trends of international society, leading to a growing chorus of calls for its reform.

Looking at the world today, instability and uncertainty remain prominent issues. In the realm of international politics, a multipolar trend is evident. Since the beginning of the new century, the collective rise of a large number of emerging market and developing countries has significantly altered the balance of international power, triggering structural changes in the international political and economic landscapes. This has led to a collective panic, he rise of hegemonism and power politics, and the frequent creation of conflicts and confrontations by unilateralist nations. These actions interfere in the internal affairs of other countries, undermining their legitimate rights and interests, and exacerbating North-South tensions. In global governance, this is particularly evident in the competition for voice and discourse. Moreover, international and regional security situations are becoming increasingly complex, with geopolitical conflicts arising continuously and terrorist threats persisting. Behind the turmoil and conflicts in the Middle East, the Syrian war, and the Russia-Ukraine conflict, among others, lies the the geopolitical strategies of major powers, which is the fundamental catalyst for these upheavals. The resulting surge in populism and refugee issues has plunged human security and development into a new round of crises. All these factors contribute to the formidable challenges in global governance.

In the field of international economy, development remains the main theme in the international economic arena, and economic globalization continues to be the overarching trend. However, since the global financial crisis in 2008, the world economy has been severely hit, with global economic growth slowing down and the wealth gap between the North and the South widening. The ongoing spread of the COVID-19 pandemic across the globe has further pushed the world economy into recession. On the other hand, the collective rise of emerging markets and developing countries such as China, India, Brazil, Russia, and South Africa has become an irreversible trend of the times, becoming the driving force for world economic development. Nevertheless, the growth of emerging market forces has also led to continuous global trade frictions. In addition to the changes in the international economic power balance, economic sanctions have intensified in recent years. This is incompatible with the trend of economic globalization, disrupting the normal development of the world economic order and creating an unfair situation for other markets and currencies. Moreover, the increasing risks and uncertainties of the world economic downturn have also brought many hidden dangers to world economic development.

In the field of environmental and security, problems in the field of environmental security are emerging one after another, and the security situation is becoming increasingly complex. Terrorism is on the rise within the territories of European and American countries, posing continuous threats. Africa and the Middle East have become high-incidence areas for terrorist activities. With the advancement of technology, terrorism has become increasingly networked, internationalized, and even globalized. The problem of world poverty remains prominent, with a huge wealth gap between the North and the South. This has led many countries and regions to fall into turmoil or face terrorist threats. Frequent "black swan events" in the Internet field have made cybersecurity an increasingly serious global issue that threatens the information security of countries and their people. The environment and resources also face numerous challenges. Issues such as global warming, air pollution, marine pollution, energy crises, and water shortages are becoming increasingly severe, demanding joint efforts and coordinated governance from all countries. The interweaving of such traditional and non-traditional security issues has made the challenges in global governance even more daunting.

In the face of the current paralysis and ineffectiveness of the global governance mechanism, the CPC Central Committee with Comrade Xi Jinping at its core, based on respecting objective laws and grasping the development trend, shoulders the responsibility of a major country with a development concept that embraces a shared future. While creating a new path for the modernization of the rule of law with Chinese characteristics, it has also put forward a series of global propositions and practical measures to promote the reform of the global governance system. Firstly, respect the diversity of world cultures, abandon ideological biases, achieve peaceful coexistence on the basis of mutual respect and seeking common ground while reserving differences, and promote the development of human rule of law civilization through exchanges and mutual learning. Secondly, adhere to the concept of global governance featuring extensive consultation, joint contribution and shared benefits, abandon the outdated concepts of the Cold-War mentality and zero-sum game, uphold mutual respect and understanding, enhance mutual learning and trust, resolve differences through negotiation and dialogue, jointly address global challenges, and jointly build a better future for mankind, so that people of all countries can enjoy development opportunities and achievements. Thirdly, practice true multilateralism, adhere to the core values and basic principles of multilateralism, safeguard the international system with the United Nations at its core and the international order based on international law, promote the democratization, legalization and rationalization of international relations, respect the equal sovereignty of all countries, be rule-based, fairness-oriented and win-win-targeted, and promote the building of a community with a shared future for mankind. At the practical level, China actively promotes the building of a new type of international relations centered on cooperation and win-win results, and strives to build a peaceful and stable international development environment with an open and inclusive attitude; adheres to the opening-up strategy of "mutual benefit and win-win results", endeavors to create new platforms for opening-up, creates a new pattern of all-round and diversified opening-up, and actively builds an open world economy. To promote the building of a community with a shared future for mankind, President Xi Jinping has announced a number of practical cooperation measures on a series of major international occasions, actively developed global partnerships, expanded the convergence of interests with other countries, and promoted cooperation. In addition, adhering to the principle of extensive consultation, joint contribution and shared benefits, he has called on all people of insight to jointly build the Belt and Road Initiative, and promoted the establishment of a new cooperation platform featuring policy connectivity, facilities connectivity, unimpeded trade, financial integration and people-to-people and cultural exchanges. This not only provides continuous impetus for economic growth in countries along the Belt and Road, but also contributes "Chinese wisdom" and "Chinese solutions" to promoting the reform of the global governance system and addressing common challenges for the future of mankind.

As an increasing number of developing countries gain influence and voice within the global governance system, a growing array of Chinese initiatives are ascending to the level of international consensus. Concurrently, numerous Chinese propositions are coalescing into collective international action, and an abundance of

Chinese solutions are inspiring the direction of human progress. Consequently, the global governance system is progressively moving towards a more equitable and rational direction (Wang, 2019).

8.3 Advocating for the Diversity and Interactivity of Human Rule of Law Civilization

The diversity of human civilization is a fundamental characteristic of the world and a source of human progress. Rule of law civilization is an integral part of human civilization, the core content of human political civilization, and an important indicator of the progress of human civilization. It plays a role in safeguarding and promoting the entire social civilization of humanity, including both material and spiritual civilization.

The profound significance of Xi Jinping Thought on the Rule of Law lies in the fact that, based on upholding Marxist historical materialism, it grasps the distinct historical characteristics exhibited by the development process of global rule of law civilizations across different ethnic groups, nations, and regions, and expounds in depth the principle of diversity in the development of global rule of law civilizations.

8.3.1 The Diversity of Rule of Law Civilization as an Inherent Attribute of Human Civilization

Throughout the long course of historical development, while each nation and country has been creating its own civilization, differences in geography, climate, social systems, economic development levels, historical cultures, etc., have led to variations in the development levels, methods, and paths of civilizations across countries. This natural disparity has not only made human civilization as a whole present a flourishing diversity of human civilization but also manifested varying degrees of uniqueness. This is a natural law and an objective outcome of the development of human civilization. Rule of law civilization has been nurtured in the soil of this diverse human civilization, thus taking on a rich and colorful array of forms.

The diversity of human civilization determines the diversity of the connotations of human rule of law civilization. Since ancient times, China has developed the Chinese legal system, which stands out uniquely in the history of world legal systems and has accumulated profound legal cultures. Different from the Continental legal system, the Anglo-American legal system, the Islamic legal system, etc., the Chinese legal system was formed under specific historical conditions in China, demonstrating the great creativity of the Chinese nation and the profound heritage of Chinese legal civilization. Meanwhile, the Chinese legal system embodies the spirit and wisdom of the Chinese nation, and there are many excellent ideas and concepts worthy of our inheritance. Strategies such as the governance strategy of transitioning from ritual to law and emphasizing both ritual and law, the people-centered concept that “the people are the foundation of the state, and when the foundation is stable, the state is secure”, the value pursuit of “a society without lawsuits and harmony as the most precious”, the cautious penal ideology of prioritizing morality over punishment and practicing prudent punishment with moral guidance, the equal concept of “judging cases based on laws and punishing in proportion to the crime”, and the principle of lenient punishment aimed at protecting the vulnerable such as widows, orphans, the elderly, children, and women, all highlight the wisdom of excellent traditional Chinese rule of law culture (Xi, 2021a). The rule of law civilization in Western society originated from the political and legal practices of the ancient Greek city-states of Athens. It was not until the 17th and 18th centuries during the founding process of capitalist society that the legal world view centered around the “rule of law” began to prevail. The emergence of ideas such as the “rule of law”, “equality before the law”, “judicial independence”, “liberty and equality”, and “natural rights” greatly enriched Western rule of law thinking. Rule of law civilization has achieved modernization through such a process of collision and integration between the East and the West.

The diverse cradles of human civilization and unique historical trajectories have led to different paths and approaches in the pursuit of the rule of law civilization, thus giving rise to various rule of law models. As Xi Jinping emphasized in 2019, “There is no identical political system in the world, nor is there a political system model applicable to all countries”. In modern times, the rule of law in the UK gradually took shape during the long-standing struggle to limit royal power. Through judicial practices that safeguard human rights, the UK Constitution was gradually formed, presenting a model of rule of law development centered around the judiciary. France’s rule of law model was profoundly influenced by the late eighteenth century French Revolution and the ideas of Rousseau, manifesting as a model centered around legislation. It emphasizes that the parliament, representing the sovereignty of the people, should enact laws to safeguard human rights and freedoms. The rule of law model in the United States inherits the historical traditions of the common law system and is also deeply influenced by the modern European Enlightenment ideas. On the one hand, the United States takes the Constitution as the foundation of the nation, highlighting the use of a written constitution to safeguard citizens’ liberties and rights (Chen, 2019). On the other hand, through the constitutional review system, the United States has established a rule of law model centered around the judiciary. Chinese rule of law model has been developed on the basis of absorbing the achievements of the existing rule of law civilization of the Chinese legal system. It is a socialist rule of law path with Chinese characteristics that suits China’s national conditions, which has been developed through the continuous theoretical exploration and practical innovation of the Communist Party of China. That is, it adheres to the leadership of an advanced political party, upholds the principal position of the people, combines the rule of law with the rule of virtue, and proceeds from China’s actual situation. It is precisely because of the different civilizational institutions and national conditions around the world that different paths of rule of law development have emerged, further leading to the formation of various distinctive political systems and rule of law frameworks. As a result, human civilization shines with diversity and splendor.

8.3.2 *The Interactivity of the Rule of Law Civilization: An Important Source for Promoting the Development of Human Civilization*

The diverse development of human civilizations has converged into the historical torrent of human civilization. The progress of human civilization draws continuous and powerful impetus from the diverse development of various national civilizations through their rise and fall, as well as exchanges and interactions. Therefore, Xi Jinping strongly advocates promoting exchanges and mutual learning among civilizations, stating that "Civilizations become colorful through exchanges, draw on each other's strengths through exchanges, and develop through mutual learning (Xi, 2020a: 468)." Moreover, "The rule of law is one of the important achievements of human civilization. The essence and gist of the rule of law have universal significance for national governance and social governance in all countries. We should learn from and draw on the excellent achievements of the rule of law civilization around the world (Xi, 2015a)."

First of all, human civilizations are not isolated from each other. The diversity of human civilizations determines the inherent necessity of exchanges and mutual learning among civilizations (Xi, 2021a: 65). Since their inception, various human civilizations have carried out different forms of interaction and exchange in different social interactions and economic activities. With the rapid development of science and technology, the significant improvement of communication methods, and the increasing advancement of economic globalization, exchanges among human civilizations have gradually broken through the boundaries of time and space, as well as the spiritual and cultural barriers. The level, depth, and breadth of these exchanges have all been greatly enhanced. The exchanges and mutual learning of the rule of law civilization have also injected vitality into the development process of human rule of law civilization. The Chinese civilization has formed an open-ended system in the process of continuous collision and interaction with other civilizations, absorbing fresh energy and nutrients directly or indirectly. "From the eastward spread of Buddhism and the integration of Islam and Confucianism in history, to the introduction of Western learning, the New Culture Movement, and the spread of Marxism and socialist ideas into China in modern times, and then to the all-round opening-up since the reform and opening-up, the Chinese civilization has always been rejuvenated through inclusive learning (Xi, 2020a: 471)."

Secondly, diverse human civilizations are equal, and exchanges and mutual learning must be carried out on the basis of the principle of equality. Xi Jinping (ibid.: 468–469) once mentioned in a speech: "Each civilization is deeply rooted in its own living soil, embodying the extraordinary wisdom and spiritual pursuits of a country and a nation, and all have their own values. Humans only differ in skin color and language, and civilizations only differ in their rich variety, but there is absolutely no distinction of high or low, superiority or inferiority… We should uphold equality and respect, discard arrogance and prejudice, deepen our understanding of the differences between our own civilization and other civilizations, and promote exchanges, dialogues, and harmonious coexistence among different civilizations." The history of human civilization also tells us that although various civilizations differ in their historical lengths, there is no distinction of high or low, superiority or inferiority. All civilizations should be equal and deserve equal respect. For the continuous development of the rule of law civilization, it is necessary to view all human civilizations equally, recognize the reality of the long-term coexistence of different social systems and different rule of law cultures, adhere to the concept of diversified development, seek common ground while reserving differences, integrate with each other in the process of collision, learn from each other's strengths and make up for each other's weaknesses. This not only conforms to the objective reality of the diversity of human civilizations but also represents the internal law of the continuous development of human rule of law civilization and is the inevitable path to promote the continuous improvement of human civilization. Practice has proven that the rule of law civilization of socialism with Chinese characteristics has unique advantages and strong vitality. To build a socialist country under the rule of law, it is necessary to unswervingly follow the path of socialist rule of law with Chinese characteristics.

Lastly, human civilization is inclusive. An attitude of inclusiveness and integration should be advocated, where people seek common ground while reserving differences and uphold the principle of harmony without uniformity. "As there are more than 200 countries and regions, over 2500 ethnic groups, and more than 7 billion people on this planet, it is impossible to have uniformity. Such differences should not become obstacles to communication, let alone reasons for confrontation. The diversity of different civilizations, systems, and paths, along with exchanges and mutual learning, can provide strong impetus for the progress of human society. We should be less arrogant and prejudiced and more respectful and inclusive, embrace the rich diversity of the world, strive to seek common ground while putting aside differences, learn from each other's strengths, and pursue harmonious coexistence and win-win cooperation (Xi, 2020a: 458)." Xi Jinping's thought on the diversity of world civilizations, on the one hand, affirms the diversity, differences, contradictions, and conflicts of human civilizations. On the other hand, it reiterates the respect for the autonomy of each nation in choosing its own development path and model. It opposes the hegemonic ideology of "self-centeredness" in the process of the development, construction, and innovation of civilizations. It respects the independence and diversity of various rule of law civilizations of humanity, overcomes prejudice and misunderstanding with an all-embracing and inclusive attitude, resists various forms of extremism and nationalism, and promotes global cooperation. Only when all civilizations in the world are inclusive and seek common ground while reserving differences can human civilization achieve development in peace and harmony. As President Xi Jinping (2020b) emphasized, "We should foster a sense of community with a shared future where everyone has a stake in each other, breaking free from the mindset of small-circle thinking and zero-sum games, and embrace the concept of a global family and win-win cooperation. We should abandon ideological disputes, avoid the trap of civilizational conflicts, respect the development paths and models independently chosen by each country, and let the diversity of the world become an inexhaustible driving force for the progress of human society and the natural state of the colorful human civilization."

Xi Jinping Thought on the Rule of Law, building upon and developing Marxist legal thought, proposes the concept of diversity in human legal civilizations based on a scientific understanding of the objective laws governing the development of human civilization and a profound grasp of the essential characteristics and operational patterns of conflicts among civilizations. This concept has become an integral part of Xi Jinping Thought on Socialism with Chinese Characteristics for a New Era. Xi Jinping emphasized, "There is no one-size-fits-all specific development model or an unchanging path to development in the world. The diversity of historical conditions determines the diversity of development paths chosen by different countries (Gong, 2021)." In leading the Chinese people on the path to realizing the Chinese Dream of national rejuvenation, the Communist Party of China has, based on the internal logic of Chinese civilization, rooted itself in China's cultural soil, adhered to the objective laws of modern civilization's development, respected and embraced the diversity of world civilizations, and upheld exchanges and mutual learning among human civilizations. By seeking consensus through exchanges and achieving development through mutual learning, China has creatively blazed a new trail of Chinese-style modernization of the rule of law. While exploring its own path to the rule of law, China has also provided a platform for exchanges and mutual learning among different legal civilizations. For instance, the Belt and Road Initiative proposed by President Xi Jinping in 2013 has offered an international cooperation platform for promoting mutual benefit and win-win outcomes among countries, attracting participation from numerous nations. Spanning across Asian, European, and African countries, the Belt and Road traverses diverse cultural landscapes, including Confucian, Christian, and Islamic cultures, and connects different legal systems such as the Continental Law System, the Common Law System, and the Islamic Law System. In advancing the Belt and Road strategy, China has actively promoted exchanges and mutual learning among different rule of law civilizations, addressing the challenge of "clash of civilizations" and fostering mutual complementarity and common development among diverse civilizations.

8.4 Promoting Democracy, the Rule of Law, and Rationality in International Relations

In today's world, the international landscape is evolving at an accelerated pace. With the rise of the comprehensive strength of emerging market economies and developing countries, the global governance system inherited from the end of World War II is becoming increasingly incompatible with the profound changes in international power dynamics. Meanwhile, new global governance issues are constantly emerging. Human society is facing numerous challenges such as climate change, the prevention and control of major infectious diseases, international governance of cyberspace, and the refugee crisis. The current global governance system is functioning inadequately, and its flaws are becoming increasingly apparent. Therefore, the reform of the global governance system has become an irresistible trend. Since the 18th National Congress of the Communist Party of China, based on a profound understanding of the global trends of the times and the development trends of human civilization, the CPC Central Committee with Comrade Xi Jinping at its core has creatively put forward the concept of global governance featuring extensive consultation, joint contribution, and shared benefits. This concept provides a "good prescription" and contributes Chinese wisdom to the reform of the global governance system and the solution of global governance problems.

8.4.1 Adhering to the Concept of Global Governance Featuring Extensive Consultation, Joint Contribution, and Shared Benefits

The concept of global governance featuring extensive consultation, joint contribution, and shared benefits is the basic concept and proposition for China's active participation in the reform and construction of the global governance system. It is an important part of Xi Jinping Thought on Diplomacy, following the independent diplomatic stance of previous generations of Chinese Communists, inheriting and developing China's peaceful foreign policy, and adhering to the diplomatic concept of friendly consultation and seeking common ground while reserving differences. It is a governance concept that stands at a historical height, grasps the global trend, and is based on the interests of the people, with rich and unique connotations.

(1) **The connotations of the concept of global governance featuring extensive consultation, joint contribution, and shared benefits**

The concept of global governance featuring "extensive consultation, joint contribution, and shared benefits" elaborates on the new type of international relations, state-to-state relations, and interest relations in the new era characterized by mutual interdependence in the new era. It also elaborates on the new connotations of a peaceful world in the new era. It integrates the concepts of equality of sovereignty, equality of rights, equality of opportunities, and equality of rules into the reform process of the global governance system, and provides a "Chinese prescription" for comprehensively eliminating the four deficits, narrowing the development gap, improving global governance, and solving global governance problems.

(I) Extensive consultation refers to the democratization of global governance.

In the report to the 19th National Congress of the Communist Party of China, Xi Jinping (2017: 66) pointed out that "China pursues a vision of global governance featuring extensive consultation, joint contribution, and shared benefits. It advocates greater democracy in international relations and stands for equality among all countries, big or small, strong or weak, rich or poor." This means that in global governance, all countries, regardless of their size or strength, enjoy equality of opportunity, equality of rights, and equality of rules. On the basis of equality, countries communicate and understand each other. Promoting consensus through extensive consultation is the foundation for achieving global governance. Equality of opportunity means that in all fields of global governance, when facing common problems and challenges of humanity, every sovereign state, as an equal member of the international community, has an equal opportunity to participate in decision-making, express its demands and positions, and enjoy the outcomes of governance. Equality of rights means that every sovereign state in the international community enjoys the rights conferred by international law and undertakes the obligations assigned to sovereign states by the international community. Equality of rules means opposing hegemonism, nationalism, and pragmatism, as well as "double standards" in the face of international rules. All sovereign states should be required to abide by international rules without discrimination. As President Xi Jinping (2021: 72) emphasized, "In the international community, law should be the common yardstick. There is no law that applies only to others but not to oneself, nor is there any law that applies only to oneself but not to others. There should be no double standards in the application of law."

Extensive consultation acknowledges differences and seeks consensus. There are more than 200 countries and regions in the world, which differ to varying degrees in terms of historical background, economic development level, legal system, religious belief, cultural traditions, etc. These differences inevitably lead to conflicts of civilizations and divergences of interests. However, global challenges and governance problems are of a global nature, as they are not only the dilemmas faced by a single country or a region but also go beyond the governance scope and capacity of a single sovereign state. Therefore, they require the joint efforts and common governance of all countries. Xi Jinping has also emphasized on many occasions that "the future of the world should be jointly decided by all countries, international rules should be jointly written by all countries, global affairs should be jointly managed by all countries, and development outcomes should be jointly shared by all countries". Therefore, only through common consultation on the basis of respecting differences and seeking common ground while reserving differences can we expand the space for cooperation, reach political, economic, and social development consensuses on global governance, and ultimately achieve the goal of win-win cooperation in terms of interests.

(II) Joint contribution is the path to global governance.

Joint contribution is the fundamental path for countries to achieve global governance on the basis of extensive consultation and consensus. The core of joint contribution lies in the word "joint", which means that all countries should jointly participate in global construction, jointly promote cooperation, jointly assume obligations in the process of global governance, jointly address global governance challenges, achieve common development, and share common outcomes. One aspect of joint contribution is to jointly address global challenges. In the era of globalization, the world has become an organically-connected whole, forming a development community where countries are intertwined. Countries are interdependent, mutually restricting and influencing each other. Facing global governance challenges and dilemmas, no country can stay immune. Many challenges are difficult to be tackled independently. This requires countries to adhere to the concept of joint contribution, cooperate whole-heartedly, give full play to their respective strengths, and achieve win-win results through mutual complementarity. However, it should also be noted that there are still differences in capabilities and development levels between developing countries and developed countries. Under the same goal, they should assume common but differentiated responsibilities.

The other aspect of joint contribution is to bring about changes in the global governance system. The world is undergoing profound changes unseen in a century. The international landscape is evolving rapidly. The trends of multi-polarization and economic globalization are deepening. The balance of international power is becoming more equitable. The global governance system and multilateral cooperation mechanisms are being challenged by protectionism and unilateralism. To promote the building of an international community featuring peace, development, cooperation, and win-win results, the global governance mechanism urgently needs reform. The concept of joint contribution put forward by Xi Jinping advocates that all countries jointly establish an international system with the United Nations at its core and an international order based on international law. Xi Jinping (2017) pointed out that "The United Nations is the most universal, representative and authoritative inter-governmental international organization and should play a central role in global governance. Under the current circumstances, the role of the United Nations needs to be strengthened rather than weakened." Therefore, jointly building a new international order with the United Nations at its core means promoting the innovation and improvement of the global governance system on the basis of safeguarding the international status of the United Nations, promoting equality of rights, rules and opportunities, enhancing the representation and voice of emerging market economies and developing countries, ensuring the equal right of all countries to participate in rule-making, and striving for more equal and fair development opportunities (Xi, 2015b).

(III) Sharing is the goal of global governance

Joint contribution serves as the foundation for sharing, and the ultimate aim of joint contribution is sharing. The primary connotation of sharing is that all sovereign states jointly share the development achievements in global governance across economic, cultural, ecological, and other domains through collaborative governance.

Xi Jinping (2015b) emphasized that "All countries should be participants, contributors, and beneficiaries of global development. It is unacceptable that only one or some countries develop while others do not." In other words, the outcomes of global governance should be fairly and justly shared among the participants in extensive consultation and joint contribution, achieving win-win cooperation and common development. This is the core of Xi Jinping's concept of extensive consultation, joint contribution, and shared benefits. Xi Jinping's sharing concept not only serves as the driving force for countries to actively participate in extensive consultation and joint contribution but also acts as an important guarantee for promoting the governance concept of extensive consultation and joint contribution. Only by fully ensuring that all countries enjoy equal rights, equal opportunities, and equal rules in sharing the construction achievements of global governance can the foundation of trust among countries be further consolidated, the team for joint contribution be strengthened, the trend of globalization be more stable, global development be more balanced, and the construction achievements be more equitably distributed to the people of all countries, thus enabling the prosperity of human development.

Xi Jinping's concept of extensive consultation, joint contribution, and shared benefits is a development concept put forward in response to the new domestic and international situations in the new era and a governance concept adapted to the reform of the global governance mechanism. The sharing concept reflects the urgent aspirations and development needs of emerging market economies and developing countries to break the monopoly of Western countries in global governance and actively participate in the global governance process. It is an effective means to balance the competition for voice between developing and developed countries and a prescription for promoting the world towards fairness and justice. As the largest developing country, China actively promotes the reform of the global governance system while advancing national governance and self-construction. China always adheres to the global governance concept of extensive consultation, joint contribution, and shared benefits, pursues an open strategy of mutual benefit and win-win results, strives to create a friendly and stable international environment, actively builds global partnerships, and fosters consensus. Through the Belt and Road Initiative, China realizes policy coordination, infrastructure connectivity, unimpeded trade, financial integration, and people-to-people bonds among countries, creates new platforms for international cooperation, promotes world economic development with new ideas, deepens regional cooperation, builds a community of shared interests and a community with a shared future for mankind, and achieves win-win cooperation and common development.

(2) **The value of the global governance concept of extensive consultation, joint contribution, and shared benefits**

The global governance concept of extensive consultation, joint contribution, and shared benefits represents China's wisdom contributed to actively participating in the reform and construction of the global governance system, providing a Chinese solution to addressing governance challenges faced by the world. It is also an integral part of Xi Jinping Thought on Socialism with Chinese Characteristics for a New Era, possessing profound theoretical and practical value.

(I) The global values of extensive consultation, joint contribution, and shared benefits have profound theoretical value

Firstly, the global values of extensive consultation, joint contribution, and shared benefits inherit and develop the diplomatic theory of socialism with Chinese characteristics. At the dawn of New China's founding, the CPC leadership, represented by Mao Zedong and Deng Xiaoping, proposed adhering to an independent and peaceful foreign policy after a profound examination of domestic and international situations. This policy ensured that China would handle domestic and foreign affairs independently, without interference or coercion from imperialism, regardless of the complexity and difficulty of the external environment. Building on this diplomatic philosophy, Premier Zhou Enlai creatively proposed the Five Principles of Peaceful Coexistence at the Bandung Conference, which gained widespread recognition and became one of the essential principles for international interactions. After the reform and opening-up, facing a complex international landscape, Deng Xiaoping further advanced the development concept of "seeking common ground while reserving differences" and proposed "set aside disputes and conduct joint development" based on the peaceful foreign policy. In today's turbulent world, Xi Jinping, while inheriting China's peaceful foreign policy, consistently upholds the diversity of world civilizations, respects global diversity, and adheres to the development concept of seeking common ground while reserving differences. With a great spirit of inclusivity, he further proposed the global governance concept of "extensive consultation, joint contribution, and shared benefits", promoting consensus and bridging differences through friendly consultations. Based on mutual respect, equality, and mutual benefit, China seeks development and achieves win-win outcomes with countries worldwide. The global governance concept of extensive consultation, joint contribution, and shared benefits not only inherits and develops the wise diplomatic philosophies of successive generations of Chinese Communists but also enriches the theory of major-country diplomacy with Chinese characteristics. Moreover, it aligns with the trends of the times and the theme of development, bringing momentum and opportunities for reforming the world governance system.

Secondly, the global values of extensive consultation, joint contribution, and shared benefits have enriched Xi Jinping Thought on Socialism with Chinese Characteristics for a New Era. In today's world, challenges persist, and humanity finds itself in an era of escalating risks. The global economy is sluggish, the shadow of financial crises lingers, the development gap continues to widen, armed conflicts occasionally erupt, and non-traditional security issues such as climate change, cybersecurity, and refugee crises are spreading continuously. Moreover, anti-globalization trends such as unilateralism, protectionism, and hegemony are on the rise, undermining the international order and impacting the global governance system and multilateral mechanisms. The CPC Central Committee, with Xi Jinping at its core, has responded to these trends and grasped the pulse of the times by proposing the global governance concept of extensive consultation, joint contribution, and shared benefits to address global governance challenges. This concept advocates for equal consultation and concerted cooperation among nations, injecting vitality and dynamism into the promotion of democratization, rule of law, and rationalization in global governance, as well as the advancement of world peace and development. This represents China's approach to global governance, embodying Chinese vision, characteristics, and style. It signifies an innovation and development within Xi Jinping Thought on Socialism with Chinese Characteristics for a New Era, offering insightful reflections and unique perspectives on major issues concerning human development. Furthermore, it expands the pathways for developing countries to achieve modernization, providing choices and opportunities for nations and peoples seeking development while maintaining their independence.

(II) The global governance concept of extensive consultation, joint contribution and shared benefits boasts rich practical value

Firstly, the global values of extensive consultation, joint contribution and shared benefits promote the transformation of the global governance system. As emerging market countries rise rapidly and the comprehensive strength of developing countries increases, the power balance in international relations has changed. The existing global governance system dominated by developed countries can no longer cope with the new changes in the world order. The ideologies of hegemonism and unilateralism have seriously hindered the progress and development of the world. Therefore, the global governance system, governance mechanisms and the structure of discourse power urgently need to be updated and improved. The proposal of the global governance concept of extensive consultation, joint contribution and shared benefits is a comprehensive prescription for the ills of world governance, addressing both the symptoms and root causes. It supplements and improves the existing world governance pattern and global governance theories, and points out the development direction and provides institutional guarantees for the reform of the global governance system. In today's world, countries are closely interconnected, and every nation is a participant, contributor and beneficiary in world governance. Each country should adhere to the concept of win-win cooperation, uphold equality in rights, opportunities and rules in international cooperation and international affairs, break through the monopoly barriers in world governance, enhance the international status and discourse power of emerging markets and developing countries, and guide the global governance system towards greater fairness and rationality. Thus, it can achieve greater synergy in development and shared benefits for all.

Secondly, the global values of extensive consultation, joint contribution and shared benefits promote China's Belt and Road Initiative. To deepen reform and build a new pattern of win-win opening-up, Xi Jinping put forward the Belt and Road Initiative in 2013, which has built a new platform for international cooperation on connectivity and added new impetus for common development.

Xi Jinping (2020a: 486) pointed out that "Jointly building the Belt and Road meets the internal requirements of the reform of the global governance system, demonstrates the awareness of a community with a shared future featuring mutual assistance and shared responsibilities, and provides new ideas and solutions for improving the reform of the global governance system." "The purpose of the Belt and Road Initiative is to focus on connectivity, deepen practical cooperation, jointly address various risks and challenges faced by humanity, and achieve mutual benefit, win-win results and common development" (ibid: 490). The proposal of the global governance concept of extensive consultation, joint contribution and shared benefits provides fundamental guidelines and important policy guarantees for the implementation of the Belt and Road Initiative. To promote the Belt and Road Initiative, it is necessary to adhere to dialogue and consultation to resolve differences and plan for overall development. By adhering to the principle of extensive consultation, joint contribution and shared benefits, through various forms of cooperation such as bilateral, trilateral and multilateral cooperation, the Belt and Road should be built into the broadest international cooperation platform that conforms to the trend of economic globalization. More countries should be encouraged to participate, leveraging the advantages of synergy, promoting the integration of the world economy, achieving common development for all mankind and realizing the great vision of a community with a shared future for mankind.

8.4.2 Upholding Fairness and Justice and Promoting Democratization, the Rule of Law and Rationalization in International Relations

Fairness and justice serve as the value yardstick for the development and progress of human civilization, the value criterion for shaping a more just and reasonable international order, and the value guidance for the in-depth advancement of the reform and construction of the global governance system. Xi Jinping (2018d: 389) pointed out that "Global governance featuring fairness and justice is a prerequisite for the common development of all countries." In today's world, issues such as unbalanced development, governance dilemmas, the digital divide, and the deficit in fairness are becoming increasingly prominent. These problems clearly indicate that addressing issues of fairness and justice and promoting global governance based on fairness and justice are not only the inevitable requirements for establishing a more just and reasonable international order but also an important and unavoidable issue for all countries. In the process of promoting the reform of the global governance system, only by upholding fairness and promoting justice can we build a beautiful world of fairness and justice and amplify the positive energy in international relations. "Fairness and justice are the lofty goals pursued by people around the world in the field of international relations. In today's international relations, fairness and justice have far from been achieved" (Xi, 2018d: 133). Therefore, in promoting the reform of the global governance system, it is necessary to safeguard international fairness and justice, reform institutional arrangements in the global governance system that run counter to fairness and justice, create an international environment of fairness and justice, and jointly strive to build a global governance system that is fair and just.

(1) **Jointly promoting the democratization of international relations**

The fundamental spirit of the democratization of international relations is to oppose power politics and unilateralism. It advocates that all countries in the world jointly address international issues and govern international affairs through equal consultations. In international affairs, the Five Principles of Peaceful Coexistence must be adhered to, and the law of the jungle where the strong prey on the weak should be discarded. Regardless of size, wealth, or strength, all countries are equal members of the international community. They are not only equal in terms of rights and interests but also equal in international rules, and all enjoy the equal right to participate in regional and international affairs. The democratization of international relations is the call of the times and the key and prerequisite for building a harmonious world, promoting lasting world peace, common development, and the progress of civilization. Without the democratization of international relations, multi-polarization and globalization will go astray, a just and reasonable new international order cannot be established, and the lofty goals of world peace and development will be difficult to achieve. Xi Jinping (ibid.) pointed out that "The destiny of the world must be jointly determined by the peoples of all countries, and international affairs should be jointly discussed and handled by the governments and peoples of all countries. The idea of monopolizing international affairs is outdated, and any attempt to do so is bound to fail." After experiencing the baptism of the pandemic, people around the world have a clearer understanding that the Cold-War mentality and zero-sum games should be abandoned, and any form of "new Cold War" and ideological confrontation should be opposed. Countries should treat each other equally and respect one another. Matters within a country's sovereignty should be managed only by its government and people, and global affairs should be jointly discussed and addressed by the governments and peoples of all countries.

Sovereignty is the fundamental symbol of a country's independence and the fundamental manifestation and reliable guarantee of national interests. Sovereign equality is the most important norm regulating relations between countries over the past few centuries and the primary principle followed by the United Nations and all its agencies and organizations. Upholding fairness and justice in international relations and global governance requires first and foremost safeguarding the principle of sovereign equality of countries. This is the most important norm in international relations and the primary principle that global governance must follow. President Xi (2018b: 273) pointed out that "We should uphold the principle that all countries, big or small, strong or weak, rich or poor, are equal. We should respect the right of peoples of all countries to independently choose their own development paths, oppose interference in other countries' internal affairs, and safeguard international fairness and justice." While seeking its own development, each country should actively promote the common development of other countries. The long-term development of the world cannot be based on the situation where some countries become increasingly wealthy while others remain poor and backward for a long time. "The practice of shifting crises onto neighbors, benefiting oneself at the expense of others is both immoral and unsustainable (ibid.)." Promoting the reform of the global governance system is a common task for the international community, and the principle of extensive consultation, joint contribution, and shared benefits should be adhered to. All countries should work together to properly address various issues and challenges. "We should firmly support relevant countries in steadily advancing major domestic political agendas in accordance with the law, firmly support all countries in safeguarding political security and social stability, and resolutely oppose external forces from interfering in the internal affairs of member states under any pretext (Xi, 2020c)." China firmly safeguards its own sovereignty, security, and development interests and also supports other countries, especially developing countries, in safeguarding their sovereignty, security, and development interests. China adheres to the principle of non-interference in other countries' internal affairs and will not impose its will on others. No matter how strong it becomes, China will never seek hegemony.

To achieve fairness and justice in the international community, Xi Jinping (2018c: 444; 2018b: 303) has particularly emphasized the need to uphold the correct view of justice and interests. He has repeatedly stressed that "when developing relations with developing countries and neighboring countries, we should establish a correct view of justice and interests. Politically, we should adhere to justice, uphold fairness, and prioritize morality. Economically, we should pursue mutual benefit, win-win results, and common development." "Upholding the correct view of justice and interests, we should always be reliable friends and sincere partners of developing countries." We should combine justice with interests, with justice taking precedence. "Only by taking both justice and interests into account can we achieve both; only by balancing justice and interests can we achieve a win-win situation."

The establishment of a new international political and economic order is an important institutional guarantee for promoting the democratization of international relations. The process of realizing the democratization of international relations is the process of breaking the unequal old international order and establishing a just and reasonable new international order. The establishment of a new international order is the goal of the democratization of international relations, and the establishment of the new international order itself is a manifestation of the democratization of international relations. The current old international order is highly unreasonable. In essence, it serves to maintain the international exploitation of monopoly capital and the hegemonic status of Western powers. It is the hegemonism and power politics that seriously hinder world peace and development. The establishment of a new international order will enable all countries in the world to participate in the process of economic globalization on an equal footing, fundamentally change the unequal status of developing countries in the international community, ensure that all countries share the "dividends" of globalization, and ultimately achieve harmonious coexistence and common development among all countries in the world.

(2) **Jointly promoting the rule of law in international relations**

The establishment of a just and reasonable international order is an aspiration and ideal that humanity has long pursued. Xi Jinping (2018a: 291) emphasized that "we should create a future that upholds the rule of law, fairness, and justice. We need to enhance the status and role of international law in global governance, ensure the effective observance and implementation of international rules, adhere to democracy, equality, and justice, and build an international rule of law system." The Central Leadership Collective with Xi Jinping at its core coordinates both the domestic and international situations, comprehensively considers the two major tasks of national governance and international governance, and actively promotes the positive interaction between domestic rule of law and international rule of law. In the era of globalization, the boundaries between the domestic and international spheres are becoming increasingly blurred, with enhanced interpenetration and interaction, and accelerated mutual influence and transformation. The value orientation and political wisdom in domestic and international governance are highly unified. In essence, the two types of rules, domestic and international, with law as the main content, are also interrelated.

As an external manifestation and logical extension of the concept and basic strategy of comprehensively governing the country according to law, Xi Jinping advocates upholding the rule of law and safeguarding international fairness and justice in global governance, which also conforms to the growing trend of the rule of law in international relations. "The establishment of international mechanisms, the observance of international rules, and the pursuit of international justice have become the consensus of most countries." Regarding China's relationship with the world, China positions itself as a builder of world peace, a contributor to global development, and a defender of the international order. "The rule of law is an important achievement of human political civilization" (Xi, 2018a: 486). Upholding the spirit of the rule of law and promoting the rule of law in international relations are inherent requirements for the transformation of the global governance system. The international order is a set of norms and behavioral rules, and international law is its most typical carrier. As an important means to maintain the international order, countries are increasingly using institutional rules to coordinate their relations and resolve interest conflicts. "We should encourage all parties to abide by international law and generally recognized basic principles of international relations in international relations, and use uniformly applied rules to distinguish right from wrong, promote peace, and pursue development" (Ibid: 134).

Therefore, it is necessary to enhance the status and role of international law in global governance and ensure the effective observance and implementation of international rules. All countries have the responsibility to safeguard the authority of international rule of law, balance rights and obligations, exercise rights in accordance with the law, and fulfill obligations in good faith. In response to the "double—standard" approach of some Western countries towards international rule of law, where they always claim to be the "spokespersons" of international law and the "world judges", using international law when it suits them and discarding it when it doesn't, Xi Jinping (2018c: 540) clearly pointed out that "the vitality of law also lies in fairness and justice. Countries and international judicial institutions should ensure the equal and unified application of international law, avoid double-standards, and not 'selectively apply' it. It is imperative to truly achieve 'impartiality and integrity, the path of righteous governance'." Advancing the reform of the global governance system necessitates ensuring the equal and unified application of international law, opposing the distortion of international law, and opposing acts of infringing on the legitimate rights and interests of other countries and undermining international peace and stability in the name of "rule of law". The rule of law is governance by rules. With the in-depth advancement of global governance reform, it is imperative to continuously improve the international rule system to ensure the fairness and reasonableness of the international order and the fairness and justice of human society. Therefore, it is essential to adhere to the rule-based approach and improve global governance. As Xi Jinping (2020a: 459) emphasized, "Strengthening global governance based on rules is a necessary prerequisite for achieving stable development. Rules should be jointly formulated by the international community, not determined by who is stronger or more powerful. We should not practice pragmatism or double-standards, using rules when they suit us and discarding them when they don't." In the international community, law should be the common yardstick. There is no law that only applies to others but not to oneself, nor is there a law that only applies to oneself but not to others. International law not only confers rights on countries but also imposes obligations on them. A country enjoys the rights and interests conferred by an international treaty by concluding it and must also assume corresponding international obligations. The relations and interests among countries can only be coordinated through institutions and rules, not by the power of the strong. The vitality of law lies in its implementation. All countries have the responsibility to safeguard the authority of international rule of law, exercise rights in accordance with the law, and fulfill obligations in good faith. Countries should fulfill their international law obligations in good faith. All valid treaties are binding on the parties and must be fulfilled by them in good faith. A party to a treaty cannot invoke its domestic law as a reason for non-performance of the treaty. When there is a conflict between the obligations of a United Nations Member State under the Charter and its obligations under any other international agreement, the obligations under the Charter shall prevail. China is an advocate and defender of international rule of law. It honors its commitments, does not practice exceptionalism, opposes the distortion of international law, and opposes acts of infringing on the legitimate rights and interests of other countries and undermining peace and stability in the name of "rule of law".

(3) **Jointly promoting the rationalization of international relations**

Countries are closely interconnected, and humanity shares a common future. Xi Jinping (2019: 169) pointed out that "we should promote the development of a new type of international relations featuring mutual respect, fairness, justice, and win-win cooperation." Only through win-win cooperation can countries accomplish significant, beneficial, and sustainable undertakings. If some countries become increasingly wealthy while others grow increasingly impoverished, long-lasting peace and prosperity in the world will be unattainable. The rapid development of a large number of developing countries has become an irresistible historical trend in the current world process. The Western-dominated situation in the global governance structure and system can no longer be sustained, and the competition for the dominance of global governance and international rule-making is extremely fierce. This will surely have a profound impact on the reform process of the global governance system. Xi Jinping (2018a: 384) noted that "the global governance structure is determined by the international power balance, and the reform of the global governance system stems from the changes in the international power balance." Therefore, to promote the reform of the global governance system, it is necessary to reflect the profound changes in the international structure, firmly safeguard the common interests of developing countries, adhere to the principle of extensive consultation, joint contribution, and shared benefits, actively promote the innovation of global governance rules, and strive to enhance the status and role of developing countries in the global governance system. Efforts should be made to vigorously promote the reform of the unjust and unreasonable arrangements in the global governance system, reform the governance structures of international economic and financial institutions such as the International Monetary Fund and the World Bank, and increase the representation and voice of developing countries. The Doha Round negotiations should be further promoted to safeguard the legitimate rights and interests of the vast number of developing countries and ensure equal opportunities, rules, and rights for all countries in international economic and trade activities and international economic cooperation.

Xi Jinping (2018a: 260) emphasized that China is a responsible major country. "We should proceed from China's national conditions, maintain our positioning as a developing country, and combine safeguarding China's interests with safeguarding the common interests of developing countries." The purpose of the reform of the global governance system is to make global governance develop in a direction that more balancedly reflects the will and interests of most countries, especially emerging market countries and developing countries, so as to better reflect the changes in the international structure, meet the practical needs of addressing global challenges, and conform to the historical trend of peace, development, cooperation, and win-win results. It is normal for countries to have differences, which should be properly resolved through dialogue and consultation. There can be competition among countries, but it must be positive and benign, and moral and international norms should be adhered to. Major countries should act in a befitting manner, provide more global public goods, assume major-country responsibilities, and demonstrate major-country leadership. China actively participates in the reform and construction of the global governance system, promotes the reform of the unjust and unreasonable arrangements in the global governance system, and endeavors to make the global governance system more balanced in reflecting the will and interests of most countries. As a participant, promoter, and leader in the reform process of the global governance system, China plays a constructive role. It actively participates in and strives to lead international rule-making, promotes the formation of a fair, reasonable, and transparent international rule system, firmly safeguards the common interests of developing countries, enhances the status and role of developing countries in the global governance system, boosts China's voice and influence in the reform of the global governance system, and makes every effort to contribute Chinese wisdom and Chinese solutions to the improvement of the global governance system.

8.5 Utilizing the Rule of Law as a Means in International Struggles

Since the 18th National Congress of the Communist Party of China, the Central Committee with Comrade Xi Jinping as the core has coordinated the overall strategy for the great rejuvenation of the Chinese nation and the profound changes unseen in the world in a century. From the strategic height of the long-term stability of the Party and the country, it has systematically planned and, with the construction of the socialist rule of law system with Chinese characteristics as the starting point, comprehensively promoted the rule of law, coordinated the advancement of domestic and international rule of law, so as to better use domestic and international rules to safeguard national sovereignty, security, and development interests. Xi Jinping (2022) pointed out that "the world has entered a period of turbulence and transformation, and international competition is increasingly manifested as a struggle over systems, rules, and laws. We must strengthen the construction of the foreign-related legal system, improve the efficiency of foreign-related law enforcement and judicial work, and resolutely safeguard national sovereignty, security, and development interests."

8.5.1 Accelerating the Formation of a Sound Foreign-Related Rule of Law System

The foreign-related rule of law system is a foreign-related governance system formed by the principles, rules, and institutions formulated by a country to regulate foreign-related legal relations, and it is an important part of a country's rule of law system. The *Decision of the Central Committee of the Communist Party of China on Several Major Issues Concerning Comprehensively Advancing the Rule of Law* adopted at the Fourth Plenary Session of the 18th Central Committee clearly put forward for the first time in a Party document that "we should strengthen foreign-related legal work. In line with the continuous deepening of opening-up, we should improve the foreign-related legal system and promote the construction of a new open economy system." The Fourth, Fifth, and Sixth Plenary Sessions of the 19th Central Committee also put forward a series of new measures for strengthening foreign-related rule of law work and made important strategic arrangements for strengthening the construction of the foreign-related rule of law system.

(1) **Strengthening legislation in foreign-related fields**

As an important source of the foreign-related legal system and a crucial link in the rule of law system, the perfection degree of legislation in foreign-related fields directly affects the effective implementation of foreign-related rule of law work. Since the Third Plenary Session of the 11th Central Committee of the Communist Party of China, China's foreign-related rule of law work has made remarkable progress. A number of important foreign-related laws and regulations have been successively formulated, such as the *Law on Sino-foreign Equity Joint Ventures*, the *Law on Foreign-funded Enterprises*, the *Law on Sino-foreign Cooperative Joint Ventures*, the *Customs Law*, the *Foreign Trade Law*, and the *Law on the Application of Laws in Foreign-related Civil Relations,* providing legal basis and rule of law guarantee for the in-depth advancement of reform and opening-up. With the deepening of China's opening-up, the fierce competition brought about by the scientific and technological revolution and industrial technological transformation, and the new challenges posed by global issues such as economic crises, environmental threats, and cyber security to global governance work, new requirements have been put forward for China's foreign-related rule of law construction work. Therefore, the *Plan for the Construction of the Rule of Law in China (2020–2025)* issued by the Central Committee of the Communist Party of China (2021b) clearly proposed that "we should strengthen legislation in key fields, emerging fields, and foreign-related fields." At present, China's legislation work in foreign-related fields should focus on improving China's foreign investment law, establishing and improving a unified management system for foreign investment access and a supervision system for post-entry operations, perfecting systems such as the national security review of foreign investment, anti-monopoly review, the national technology security list management, and the unreliable entity list, and enhancing the ability to prevent and respond to overseas security risks; improving the foreign-related economic and trade legal system, perfecting the legal systems in aspects such as market access and supervision, property rights protection, and the credit system, and creating a market-oriented, law-based, and internationalized business environment; improving the overseas investment management system, establishing and improving an overseas investment consulting service and risk early-warning mechanism, and constructing a legal service system for foreign aid to provide rule of law guarantee for Chinese citizens and enterprises to "go global".

(2) **Accelerating the construction of the legal system for the extraterritorial application of Chinese laws**

The extraterritorial application of domestic laws actually represents the extraterritorial extension and expansion of a country's sovereign power, thereby endowing domestic laws with extraterritorial validity. Xi Jinping (2020d: 257) has repeatedly emphasized that "we should accelerate the construction of the legal system for the extraterritorial application of Chinese laws to provide a legal basis for China's foreign-related law-enforcement and judicial activities." Currently, economic globalization is encountering headwinds, and there is a rising trend of protectionism, unilateralism, and hegemonism, seriously undermining international rule of law and disrupting the world order. Therefore, accelerating the construction of the legal system for the extraterritorial application of Chinese laws is not only an inevitable requirement for blocking and countering the improper extraterritorial application of foreign laws but also an inevitable choice for safeguarding China's sovereignty, security, and development interests. At present, although China has promulgated laws and departmental regulations for blocking and countermeasures, such as the *Anti-Foreign Sanctions Law*, the *Measures for Blocking the Improper Extraterritorial Application of Foreign Laws and Measures*, and the *Regulations on Entity Lists*, the legal system for the extraterritorial application of Chinese laws is still incomplete. It is necessary to further strengthen research on countermeasure theories and practices, and promptly establish laws for the extraterritorial application of domestic laws and their supporting mechanisms. It is necessary to clarify the standards, conditions, and procedures for the extraterritorial application of China's existing laws, strengthen foreign-related law-enforcement and judicial work, refine the details, discretion standards, and operating procedures of foreign-related administrative law-enforcement, improve the foreign-related judicial mechanism, enhance the transparency and credibility of judicial work, and strengthen the accuracy and authority of the extraterritorial application of Chinese laws, so as to make it a legal weapon for effectively safeguarding China's national security and interests and powerfully countering foreign unilateral sanctions and "long-arm jurisdiction."

(3) **Improving the foreign-related legal service system**

A sound and comprehensive foreign-related legal service system serves as a crucial legal safeguard for Chinese citizens and enterprises venturing abroad and engaging in foreign relations. It is also an indispensable part of China's foreign-related rule of law system. The Fourth Plenary Session of the 18th Central Committee of the Communist Party of China clearly stated that it is necessary to "strengthen foreign-related legal services, safeguard the legitimate rights and interests of Chinese citizens and legal persons overseas as well as those of foreign citizens and legal persons in China, and protect the rights and interests of overseas Chinese in accordance with the law". In 2016, the Ministry of Justice, the Ministry of Foreign Affairs and other departments jointly issued the *Opinions on Developing Foreign-related Legal Services*, proposing specific measures for the development of foreign-related legal services in multiple fields, including serving major national development strategies, diplomatic work, and combating transnational crimes. The Fourth Plenary Session of the 19th Central Committee of the Communist Party of China further proposed to "establish a legal affairs system for foreign-related work, strengthen the research and application of international law, and improve the rule of law level of foreign-related work", putting forward new requirements for foreign-related rule of law work under the new situation.

In 2019, the General Office of the CPC Central Committee and the General Office of the State Council issued the *Opinions on Accelerating the Construction of the Public Legal Service System*, clearly stating the need to establish and improve a legal verification mechanism. Through the establishment of a unified database of Chinese laws and regulations, a database of national legal information, and an expert database, it provides legal verification services and consultation on foreign laws for Chinese citizens and enterprises, helping them understand relevant foreign legal systems, and guiding enterprises and citizens to consciously abide by local laws and regulations and use legal means to safeguard their legitimate rights and interests when going global. By improving the construction of foreign-related legal service institutions, promoting the establishment of international commercial mediation organizations, and creating internationally renowned arbitration institutions, it actively provides legal services for major national economic and trade activities and all-round opening up.

8.5.2 Enhancing the Capacity to Engage in International Struggles through Rule of Law Mechanisms

The rule of law is an important part of a country's core competitiveness and a significant symbol of shaping the image of a global power. Meanwhile, the rule of law has increasingly become an important means in international struggles and great-power games. Xi Jinping (2019, 2020d: 256–257) has also emphasized on multiple occasions: "As China moves towards the world and participates in international affairs as a responsible major country, it must be adept at using the rule of law. In external struggles, we should take up legal weapons, occupy the high-ground of the rule of law, and have the courage to say no to those who undermine and disrupt the order." "We should place greater emphasis on rule of law responses, speak and act in accordance with rules to safeguard China's political and economic security, as well as the legitimate rights and interests of Chinese enterprises and citizens."

(1) **Actively participating in the formulation of international rules**

Xi Jinping (2018a: 259) pointed out: "Over the past few hundred years, the way for great powers to compete for interests and hegemony through war, colonization, and the division of spheres of influence has gradually evolved into a way for countries to coordinate relations and interests through institutional rules." Against the backdrop of significant changes in current international rules, China's active participation in the formulation of international rules is not only about providing public goods for global governance and contributing Chinese wisdom and Chinese value as solutions but also an important path to compete for international discourse power and rule-making power and safeguard China's national sovereignty, security, and development interests. Currently, there is a serious imbalance between China's discourse power in international rule-making and its national strength. Therefore, China should be guided by Xi Jinping's thought on foreign-related rule of law, uphold the value concept of national-interest orientation, and actively strive for international rule-making power to promote the improvement of the international rule system and international rule of law. First, it is essential to strengthen the research and application of international law. Only by deepening the research on international law can China more flexibly apply international law, promote theoretical innovation and development of international law, and enhance the ability to participate in international dialogues and resolve international affairs with international rule of law thinking, international legal principles, and rules. Second, China should actively participate in international affairs and provide Chinese wisdom for global public issues of common concern to all countries, such as environmental pollution, resource and energy security, cybersecurity, and the prevention of major infectious diseases, and become an active participant and promoter in global governance. Third, China should actively engage in international talks and activities of international organizations, strive to put forward fair and reasonable Chinese solutions, and voice China's opinions in the formulation and reform of international rules. Fourth, China should widely absorb like-minded international partners to jointly establish new type international organizations, lead the formulation of international rules, and serve as an important supplement to the existing international governance system to address the failure of the global governance system.

(2) **Strengthening the cultivation of foreign-related rule of law talents**

Xi Jinping (2015b) emphasized that "we should strengthen capacity building and strategic investment, enhance theoretical research on global governance, and attach great importance to the cultivation of talents in the field of global governance." On one hand, foreign-related rule of law talents serve as the talent guarantee for China to thoroughly promote opening-up and implement national strategic plans such as the Belt and Road Initiative. On the other hand, participating in global governance also requires a large number of foreign-related rule of law talents who are familiar with the guidelines and policies of the Party and the state, understand China's national conditions, can proficiently use foreign languages, are well-versed in international rules, and are proficient in international negotiations. The cultivation of foreign-related rule of law talents is a systematic project that involves multiple disciplinary systems such as law, politics, economics, and foreign languages, and it requires a talent cultivation mechanism with perfect institutions and a sound system.

Currently, there is a relative shortage of foreign-related rule of law talents in China who are good at handling foreign-related legal affairs and participating in resolving international legal disputes. The scale and quality of the existing foreign-related legal talents are also difficult to meet the historical process of China moving closer to the center of the world stage. The cultivation mechanism for rule of law talents is not yet perfect, and there is an obvious shortage of international law talents in important international positions. Therefore, it is necessary to further strengthen the cultivation of foreign-related rule of law talents, innovate the cultivation mechanism for foreign-related rule of law talents, and establish a normalized and standardized cultivation system for foreign-related rule of law talents. In April 2022, the Ministry of Justice, in conjunction with other departments such as the Ministry of Education, issued the *Notice on Implementing the Foreign-Related Arbitration*

Talent Cultivation Project. This not only makes specific arrangements for innovating the cultivation mechanism for foreign-related arbitration talents and optimizing the cultivation path for foreign-related arbitration talents but also represents a highly beneficial attempt to build a team of high-quality and professional foreign-related arbitration talents.

(3) **Strengthening international cooperation in law enforcement and justice**

Currently, the rule of law has become an important means of national governance and global governance. As the global crime situation becomes more complex, there is an urgent need for countries to strengthen international collaboration to address global challenges. Therefore, international rule of law cooperation has also become an important means for countries to handle international affairs. The Fourth Plenary Session of the 18th Central Committee of the Communist Party of China put forward three types of international rule of law cooperation:

Firstly, actively carry out international law enforcement and security cooperation and continuously improve the legal foundation for security cooperation. It is necessary to abide by the laws of one's own country and ensure the equal and unified application of international law without double-standards. Information sharing and joint actions should be strengthened to jointly combat terrorist forces, ethnic separatist forces, religious extremist forces, and various forms of organized transnational crimes such as drug trafficking and smuggling, human trafficking, and cybercrimes. Secondly, deepen international cooperation in the judicial field. On the basis of respecting national sovereignty and abiding by international law, countries should promote international judicial cooperation in areas such as extradition, repatriation of criminal suspects, collection and transfer of evidence, and transfer of sentenced persons within the framework of friendly and mutually-beneficial cooperation. Thirdly, strengthen international anti-corruption cooperation and increase efforts in recovering stolen assets and fugitives overseas, as well as extradition and repatriation. At present, China has signed more than 140 judicial assistance agreements with over 70 countries, which has effectively improved the efficiency of case handling.

8.6 Practicing True Multilateralism

Multilateralism is an effective path to safeguard peace and promote development. Its essence lies in jointly discussing international affairs and jointly shaping the future and destiny of the world by all countries. For a long time, China has held high the banner of multilateralism, actively participated in multilateral activities centered around the United Nations, and extensively joined multilateral treaties and international conventions, making significant contributions to maintaining world peace and promoting common development.

The world today is undergoing profound changes unseen in a century. Although peace and development remain the themes of the era, the world still faces numerous problems and challenges. Unilateralism and protectionism still prevail in some countries, constantly affecting the stability and development of the international community. The world economy is experiencing the most severe recession since World War II. Cultural soft-power elements such as ideology, values, and moral principles have increasingly become the main battlefield for competition among countries. Global issues such as climate change, environmental pollution, and major infectious diseases continue to threaten the survival of all mankind. These problems are intertwined and mutually exacerbated, posing common difficulties and challenges on the path of human progress. At the same time, the trend of world multipolarization remains unchanged, and economic globalization has shown new resilience. The call for maintaining multilateralism and strengthening communication and cooperation has become even stronger. Since the 18th National Congress of the Communist Party of China, General Secretary Xi Jinping has put forward the major initiatives of building a community with a shared future for mankind and building a new type of international relations, taking into account the direction of world development and the future and destiny of humanity. These initiatives have expanded and deepened the concept and practice of multilateralism in the new era, winning high praise and wide support from the international community.

8.6.1 Practicing True Multilateralism Requires Upholding the Concept of a Community with a Shared Future for Mankind and Adhering to the Common Values of all Mankind, Including Development, Equity, Justice, Democracy, and Freedom

A world of peaceful development should accommodate different forms of civilizations and must be inclusive of diverse paths to modernization. After the baptism of the pandemic, people around the world have become more clearly aware that the Cold-War mentality and zero-sum game must be abandoned, and any form of "new Cold War" and ideological confrontation must be opposed. It is imperative to vigorously promote the common values of all mankind, compete on the basis of fairness and justice, build an open-world economy, firmly safeguard the multilateral trading system, refrain from setting up discriminatory and exclusive standards, rules, and systems, and avoid building high walls that cut off trade, investment, and technology. We should engage in a track-and-field race where everyone strives to catch up and improve together, rather than a gladiatorial fight of mutual attacks and survival of the fittest. Some developed countries often show self-serving tendencies in the construction and operation of relevant multilateral mechanisms. This "selective multilateralism" follows the logic of prioritizing national interests, which is inconsistent with the realization of the common interests of humanity and hinders the deepening of multilateral cooperation and the unity of the international community. China advocates upholding the concept of a community with a shared future for mankind and taking the promotion of common development among countries and the solution of the problem of unbalanced global development as an important agenda for international multilateral cooperation. In the established multilateral systems, all countries should act in accordance with the corresponding rules and procedures, safeguard the authority and effectiveness of multilateral systems, and should not pick and choose according to their own will when fulfilling obligations and abiding by rules. International rules should be jointly observed by all countries, and there should be no exceptions. Furthermore, multilateral systems should undergo continuous innovation and improvement in practice to better coordinate national actions and address challenges, rather than being treated as tools to be utilized or discarded at will.

8.6.2 *Practicing True Multilateralism Requires Adhering to International Law as the Foundation and Earnestly Upholding a System, Order, and Rules that Ensure Fairness and Justice*

As an ancient Chinese saying goes, "Law is the starting point of governance." The international community should be governed in accordance with the rules and consensus reached by all countries, rather than being dictated by one or a few countries. There is only one international system in the world, which is centered around the United Nations. There is only one international order, which is based on international law. And there is only one set of rules, which are the basic norms of international relations based on the purposes and principles of the Charter of the United Nations. The United Nations has evolved into the most universal, representative, and authoritative international organization in the world today. It is a symbol of multilateralism and the core of multilateral mechanisms. The Charter of the United Nations is widely recognized as the fundamental norm governing relations between countries. Without these international norms jointly formulated and universally recognized by the international community, the world would eventually descend into the law of the jungle, bringing catastrophic consequences to humanity. When addressing international issues, one should not act from the so-called "position of strength" to pursue hegemony, power politics, and bullying. "Bullying the weak" is not multilateralism. China firmly adheres to the rule of law in international relations and unswervingly safeguards the international system centered around the United Nations, the international order based on international law, and the basic norms of international relations based on the purposes and principles of the Charter of the United Nations. Multilateral institutions are platforms for practicing multilateralism and the basic framework for safeguarding it. Their authority and effectiveness should be maintained. It is essential to coordinate and regulate the relations between countries through institutions and rules and oppose the practice of the strong bullying the weak. The multilateral mechanism centered around the United Nations not only represents the progress of the international community but also marks a new era, where the principle of "all countries, big or small, are equal" is no longer an empty slogan. If one's mindset remains stuck in the old era and always tries to oppress other countries by relying on strength, it will only lead to counterproductive results and arouse public outrage.

8.6.3 *Practicing True Multilateralism Requires Firmly Opposing "Pseudo-Multilateralism"*

"Pseudo-multilateralism" ostensibly claims to uphold multilateralism, but in essence, it aims to form "exclusive cliques" and engage in bloc politics. It even attempts to divide the world by forcing countries to take sides based on ideology, thereby undermining the international order and creating confrontation and division. Some Western countries regard multilateral institutions as tools for individual or a small number of countries to consolidate or expand their dominance in the world. They often draw lines based on ideology, excluding the majority of countries. Through multilateral institutions, they impose their values, norms, and rules on other countries, seriously undermining the sovereign equality of other countries and their right to have a say in world affairs. Multilateralism should not be closed and exclusive. The so-called multilateralism within small cliques deviates from the original intention and essence of multilateralism. It is a form of "pseudo-multilateralism" that uses the name of multilateralism to pursue unilateralism. It is necessary to adhere to the principles of openness and inclusiveness and avoid creating closed and exclusive groups. As Xi Jinping (2021b) pointed out, "The essence of multilateralism is that international affairs should be handled through joint consultation, and the future and destiny of the world should be jointly determined by all countries". Creating "exclusive cliques" and instigating a "new Cold War" in the international arena, excluding, threatening, and intimidating others, and frequently resorting to decoupling, supply disruptions, and sanctions, artificially isolating or even severing connections, will only push the world towards division and confrontation. A divided world is unable to address the common challenges faced by humanity, and confrontation will lead humanity into a dead-end. China firmly opposes the acts of the strong bullying the weak, shifting blame, distorting facts, and using the name of multilateralism to pursue unilateralism. China also firmly opposes using international rules as tools to maintain one's own hegemony, selectively applying rules according to one's own interests, and practicing "selective multilateralism". The world needs justice, not hegemony. Currently, the once-in-a-century changes in the world and the COVID-19 pandemic are intertwined. The international landscape is evolving at an accelerated pace, and the period of instability and adjustment continues. Against the complex international backdrop, multilateralism faces numerous challenges. True multilateralism is in line with the trends of democratization and the rule of law in international relations. It advocates equality among countries, big or small, and promotes the handling of inter-state relations through cooperation, negotiation, and consultation rather than through power politics, force, or coercion. "Pseudo-multilateralism" such as bloc politics and exclusive cliques runs counter to true multilateralism and goes against the trend of the times and the expectations of the people.

8.6.4 Practicing True Multilateralism Requires the Joint Support and Maintenance of all Members of the International Community, and in Particular, the Contributions and Examples of Major Powers

Multilateralism in modern international relations originated from humanity's efforts to address common issues. In a world where countries are increasingly interconnected, no country, regardless of how powerful it is, can remain immune from global challenges or single-handedly solve the problems facing the world. Instead, countries need to attach strategic and principled importance to multilateral cooperation and multilateral institutions. Multilateralism is not a groundless concept but a product that meets the requirements of the era of economic globalization and world multi-polarization. To revitalize multilateralism, major world powers should serve as exemplary adherents of the purposes and principles of the UN Charter, leaders in abiding by international rules, and pioneers in providing necessary international public goods for global well-being. In particular, major world powers should lead the international community to firmly establish the concept of a community with a shared future for mankind, hold high the banner of openness, inclusiveness, cooperation, and win-win results, and uphold the common values of all humanity, including peace, development, fairness, justice, democracy, and freedom. They should further deepen and expand the connotation and extension of multilateralism. As Xi Jinping (2021b) pointed out, "Multilateralism in the 21st century should uphold its core values and basic principles while also innovating and looking towards the future. It is necessary to reform and improve the global governance system on the basis of extensive consultations and consensus-building, taking into account the changes in the world pattern and the need to address global challenges." Safeguarding and practicing true multilateralism is an inevitable choice for humanity to address global challenges and solve global problems, and it is of great significance for human peace and development. China is firmly committed to the core values and basic principles of multilateralism. Based on the changes in the world pattern and with a view to addressing global challenges, China continuously enriches the practice of multilateralism in the new situation. Standing on the right side of history and on the side of human progress, China is constantly writing new chapters in safeguarding and practicing multilateralism.

8.7 Promoting the Building of a Community with a Shared Future for Mankind

The Earth is the only home for humanity to survive on. Cherishing and protecting it is the only option for mankind. There is only one Earth, and all countries share one world. In March 2013, during a speech at the Moscow State Institute of International Relations in Russia, Xi Jinping (2018a: 5) first clearly put forward the concept of building a community with a shared future for mankind. He pointed out that "in this world, countries are more interconnected and interdependent than ever before. Humanity lives in the same global village, in the same time space where history and reality converge. We are increasingly becoming a community with a shared future where everyone's interests are intertwined". In a series of subsequent speeches, Xi Jinping (ibid: 29) further emphasized that "common development is an important foundation for sustainable development and is in the long-term and fundamental interests of the people of all countries. Since we live in the same global village, we should firmly establish the awareness of a community with a shared future". He also proposed to "build a new type of international relations featuring win-win cooperation and forge a community with a shared future for mankind" (Xi, 2021b). Moreover, he put forward the ideas of building a "China-ASEAN community with a shared future", "firmly establishing the awareness of an "Asia-Pacific community with a shared future", "building a community with a shared future between China and Latin America", "forging a community with a shared future in the neighborhood", "moving towards an Asian community with a shared future", "forging a community of shared interests among the BRICS countries", "moving towards a China-Africa community with a shared future", "jointly building a community with a shared future in the cyberspace", "jointly building a community with a shared future for universal security", "working together to build a Shanghai Cooperation Organization community with a shared future", "jointly building a community with a shared future between man and nature", and "jointly building a global community of health for all" (Xi, 2018a: 29), etc.

On October 18, 2017, in the report to the 19th National Congress of the Communist Party of China, Xi Jinping clearly stated that "We call on the people of all countries to work together to build a community with a shared future for mankind and create an open, inclusive, clean, and beautiful world that enjoys lasting peace, universal security, and common prosperity". On December 1, 2017, in the keynote speech at the High-level Dialogue between the Communist Party of China and World Political Parties, Xi Jinping (2018a: 510) clearly explained the basic meaning of the community with a shared future for mankind: "As the name suggests, a community with a shared future for mankind means that the future and destiny of every nation and every country are closely linked. We should stand together through thick and thin, share weal and woe, and strive to turn the planet where we were born and grew up into a harmonious big family, and turn the aspirations of people around the world for a better life into reality". Therefore, to understand the general trend of world development, keep up with the trend of the times, promote the international order and the international system to develop in a more just and reasonable direction, and promote the building of a community with a shared future for mankind so that the torch of peace can be passed down from generation to generation, the driving force for development can be continuous, and the light of civilization can shine brightly, which are the ardent expectations of the people of all countries in the world.

8.7.1 Promoting the Building of a Community with a Shared Future for Mankind Reflects the Objective Laws of Human Social Development

In the long history of human social development, the contradictory movement between productive forces and forms of social interaction has formed an organically linked sequence. The process of the transformation of history into world history, which began in the early modern era, is rooted in the historical progress of social productive forces and the resulting changes in the mode of production. Since the advent of the modern world, the scope of activities through which different ethnic groups influence one another has been expanding day by day. The previous isolated and self-contained states of ethnic existence have gradually been broken, and all ethnic groups have been incorporated into an integrated and interconnected development network. As a result, isolated or fragmented history has begun to transform into an integrated or unified one, which has given rise to the emergence of modern international law and the establishment and development of the international system. Xi Jinping adheres to the application of the basic principles of Marxist historical materialism and the theory of world history, conducts in-depth investigations into the evolution of human social political civilization and international order since the modern era, and analyzes the course of changes in international relations from the *Peace of Westphalia* more than 360 years ago to the *Geneva Conventions* more than 150 years ago, from the *Charter of the United Nations* more than 70 years ago to the Bandung Conference more than 60 years ago. By summarizing the history of human society in the past more than 100 years, he has reached an important conclusion: Peace and development are the common aspirations of all mankind, and the establishment of a just and reasonable international order is the goal that humanity has been constantly striving for. However, this task remains unaccomplished to this day (Xi, 2018a: 415). Therefore, it is imperative to follow the historical trend and the will of the people, promote the building of a community with a shared future for mankind, and make unremitting efforts to achieve the lofty goals of world peace and development and to establish a more just and reasonable international order and global governance system.

8.7.2 The Major Strategic Thought of Promoting the Building of a Community with a Shared Future for Mankind Embodies the Common Values of all Mankind

Civilization is the soul of a country and a nation. The civilization of each country and nation is deeply rooted in the profound social soil of its own country and nation, embodying the concepts, spirits, and wisdom of that country and nation. However, there are undoubtedly certain common value factors among different civilizational systems in different temporal and spatial contexts. As human social interactions increase and expand, the common value factors hidden behind different civilizational systems are bound to manifest themselves in various ways and through various channels. These common value factors undoubtedly reflect the universal rational requirements of human social interaction practices.

Standing at a new historical starting point of promoting the building of a community with a shared future for mankind, Xi Jinping (2018a: 253; 2021c) refines and summarizes the common value norms of human society accumulated in the process of human civilization development, and incisively elaborates on the common value benchmarks of human society. He profoundly points out that "peace, development, fairness, justice, democracy, and freedom are the common values of all mankind". "We should carry forward the common values of all mankind, namely, peace, development, fairness, justice, democracy, and freedom, advocate exchanges and mutual learning among different civilizations, and promote the development of human civilization". This important thought reflects the unremitting pursuit of the progress of human civilization, embodies the common value concerns of all mankind, and highlights the lofty humanistic spirit of "When the Great Way prevails, a just society is shared by all". Thus, it establishes the common human values that the building of a community with a shared future for mankind should follow. The proposal of the common values of all mankind, including peace, development, fairness, justice, democracy, and freedom, clearly expresses Xi Jinping's political value norms for building a new type of international relations featuring win-win cooperation. It promotes and expands the positive energy in international relations, effectively leads the construction of a fair and just beautiful world, greatly enhances the appeal of international morality, and fully demonstrates China's wisdom in responding to "the questions of the world".

8.7.3 The Major Strategic Thought of Promoting the Building of a Community with a Shared Future for Mankind Embodies the Precious Treasures of Human Political Civilization and International Relations Norms

Xi Jinping (2018a: 417) pointed out that "Looking back at the history since modern times, the establishment of a fair and reasonable international order has been the goal that mankind has been tirelessly pursuing". In the process of the transformation from history to world history since modern times, the pattern of international relations has undergone profound changes, and the international system has changed several times. Historically, basic norms of international relations such as sovereign equality, reconciliation and consultation, rule of law justice, openness and inclusiveness, and humanitarianism have emerged, which have profoundly changed the basic appearance of international social life.

Xi Jinping has a profound insight into the historical trajectory of changes in the international order system and carefully grasps the basic value orientations of international conventions and international legal documents with landmark significance in the more than 300-year process since modern times. He emphasizes that a series of recognized principles accumulated in the evolution of international relations, such as the principle of equality and sovereignty established by the *Treaty of Westphalia* and the Five Principles of Peaceful Coexistence advocated by the Bandung Conference, "should serve as the basic guidelines for building a community with a shared future for mankind" (Xi, 2018c: 539). Xi Jinping further points out that sovereign equality is the most important norm for countries to regulate their relations with each other over the past few hundred years, and it is also the primary principle followed by the United Nations and all its agencies and organizations; communication and consultation are effective strategies for resolving differences, and political negotiation is the fundamental way to resolve conflicts; international conventions and international legal instruments should be effectively implemented, and all countries have the responsibility to safeguard the authority of international rule of law. Therefore, Xi Jinping (ibid.) emphasizes that "the destiny of the world should be jointly decided by all countries, international rules should be jointly written by all countries, global affairs should be jointly governed by all countries, and the fruits of development should be jointly shared by all countries". Thus, China's proposal for building a community with a shared future for mankind inherently inherits, promotes, and develops the outstanding achievements of human political civilization and the basic norms of international justice since modern times.

8.7.4 Promoting the Building of a Community with a Shared Future for Mankind Necessitates Firmly Upholding and Practicing True Multilateralism

Generally speaking, multilateralism refers to an institutionalized form of coordinating relations among three or more countries in the field of international relations. In contrast, unilateralism mainly refers to the bullying behavior of a particular major power in a dominant position in the international system, which acts willfully, pursues self-interests, and treats other countries rudely in international affairs. Upholding multilateralism and opposing unilateralism is a historical product of promoting the democratization of international relations and forming a more just and reasonable international order after World War II. In today's volatile era, global common challenges emerge in an endless stream, and the interconnections, cooperation, and interdependence among countries are becoming increasingly closer. Upholding and practicing multilateralism is an inherent requirement for countries to jointly address global challenges and promote the reform of the global governance system under the historical conditions of profound changes in the world pattern.

Since the 18th National Congress of the Communist Party of China, Xi Jinping has profoundly expounded on the great significance of upholding multilateralism on many important occasions and put forward a series of major political propositions for upholding and developing multilateralism, which have played an important role in promoting global governance and maintaining international order. Facing the complex situation of the accelerated evolution of the international pattern and the interweaving of the pandemic and the once-in-a-century changes, with a broad global vision and a firm sense of responsibility as a major power, Xi Jinping has reaffirmed China's firm commitment to multilateralism and clearly advocated multilateralism, pointing out the way forward for the world at a crossroads in history. Xi Jinping (2018c: 539, 547; 2021b) pointed out that "Multilateralism is an effective path to safeguard peace and promote development"; "The essence of multilateralism is that international issues should be discussed and resolved jointly by all, and the future and destiny of the world should be jointly determined by all countries". Multilateralism in the twenty-first century should uphold the right principles and make innovations, and look forward to the future. It is necessary to adhere to the core values and basic principles of multilateralism, and also base on the changes in the world pattern and focus on the needs of addressing global challenges. The global governance system should be reformed and improved on the basis of extensive consultation and consensus-building. This concise yet profound statement reveals the essence of multilateralism and its requirements of the times. In today's world, unilateralism is strongly resisted by the international community, and upholding and practicing multilateralism is receiving more and more support. In this situation, some countries are starting to use multilateralism as a guise to form "small cliques" and provoke a "new Cold War" in the international arena, engage in ideological confrontation, and often impose sanctions or threaten with sanctions and decoupling. Their aim is to pursue unilateralism in the name of multilateralism and create a world of division and confrontation. In response, Xi Jinping (2021c) has specifically emphasized that "We must uphold true multilateralism and promote the development of the global governance system in a more just and reasonable direction". "The world needs true multilateralism. All countries should act in accordance with the purposes and principles of the UN Charter. They should not practice unilateralism or hegemonism, and should not form small cliques or engage in ideological confrontation in the name of multilateralism". It is crucial to "uphold true multilateralism". Therefore, to uphold and practice true multilateralism, it is essential to adhere to the concept of a community with a shared future for mankind, abide by the common values of all humanity, including peace, development, fairness, justice, democracy, and freedom. It is necessary to uphold openness and inclusiveness instead of closure and exclusivity, get rid of ideological prejudices, and resolutely oppose hegemonism and bullying acts. It is imperative to be based on international laws and rules instead of self-centeredness, firmly safeguard the international system with the United Nations at its core, firmly safeguard the international order based on international law, firmly safeguard the basic norms of international relations with the purposes and principles of the UN Charter as the cornerstone, firmly safeguard the authority of the United Nations and its core role in international affairs, and firmly safeguard the multilateral trading system with the World Trade Organization at its core. Every nation should resolutely oppose the jungle law of the strong preying on the weak pursued by some countries, advocate consultation and cooperation instead of conflict and confrontation, pursue a win-win, multi-win, and mutually beneficial cooperation concept, reject the narrow-minded policies of self-interest, and discard the old concepts of the Cold-War mentality and zero-sum game. In this way, we can turn our global village into a big stage for common development rather than an arena for mutual wrestling (Xi, 2018b: 276), and promote the formation and development of a more just and reasonable international order.

The innovative concept of promoting the building of a community with a shared future for mankind embodies the outstanding achievements of Chinese civilization and the common values of all humanity. It reflects the historical changes in the relationship between China and the world in the new era. Once put forward, it has resonated strongly on a global scale, been incorporated into numerous UN agreements and the declarations and outcome documents of international multilateral mechanisms, and triggered positive responses at the national level, in regional contexts, and in major global fields. It has received increasingly extensive recognition and support from the international community, demonstrating strong international influence. It is evolving from an idea into action and constantly moving towards the goal of building a community with a shared future for mankind. As Xi Jinping pointed out (2020d: 276), "Since the 18th National Congress of the Communist Party of China, we have put forward the concept of promoting the building of a community with a shared future for mankind, which has been widely welcomed and highly appraised by all parties and incorporated into a series of UN resolutions. We should build on the momentum and act in accordance with the trend, firmly safeguard the international order and international system centered around the purposes and principles of the UN Charter, and contribute Chinese wisdom and Chinese solutions to the reform and development of the global governance system".

8.8 Conclusion

Rule of law discourse is a product of the development of the rule of law to a certain stage. In a sense, rule of law discourse is a rational expression. The emergence of rule of law discourse is a manifestation of the progress of human civilization, and the dissemination of rule of law discourse is conducive to the advancement of the civilization of the rule of law. Only in a society where the rule of law is realized can there be a systematic and complete expression of rule of law discourse.

In today's world, the strategic overall situation of the great rejuvenation of the Chinese nation and the profound changes unseen in a century interact organically and influence each other, profoundly affecting the process of the transformation of the global governance system. The peaceful rise of contemporary China has not only historically changed the relationship between China and the world but also significantly altered the development pattern and trend of the current world.

The birth of the socialist rule of law civilization with Chinese characteristics is a profound revolution in the process of human rule of law civilization. It inherits the outstanding achievements of human rule of law civilization, creates a brand-new rule of law civilization system different from the previous ones, represents a fundamental change in human social rule of law civilization, and is a historical transcendence of Western capitalist rule of law civilization.

Firstly, the socialist rule of law civilization with Chinese characteristics is a Chinese form of rule of law civilization created based on China's national conditions and its own historical development.

Comrade Deng Xiaoping pointed out that "we should integrate the universal truth of Marxism with China's specific reality, blaze our own trail, and build socialism with Chinese characteristics. This is the basic conclusion we have drawn from our review of our long-term historical experience". Given the different national conditions of each country, the paths to the modernization of the rule of law also vary. China is the world's largest developing country, and the development of the modernization of the rule of law in the Chinese style is precisely based on this basic national condition. Building a socialist country under the rule of law in a large eastern country like China, which is vast in territory, large in population, and complex in national conditions, is by no means an easy task. It is imperative to adhere to proceeding from reality, highlighting Chinese characteristics, and reflecting the characteristics of the times. The path of socialist rule of law with Chinese characteristics is a path that suits China's national conditions, conforms to the laws of the rule of law, and has Chinese characteristics, which has been explored under the leadership of the Communist Party of China. This path adheres to the leadership of the Communist Party of China and the socialist system with Chinese characteristics. The leadership of the Party is the soul of the socialist rule of law with Chinese characteristics and the greatest difference between our rule of law and that of Western capitalist countries. At the same time, this path of the rule of law adheres to the principal position of the people, promotes the coordinated advancement of law-based governance of the country, law-based exercise of state power, and law-based government administration, and promotes the integrated development of a country, government, and society under the rule of law, continuously driving China's socialist rule of law construction to achieve historical achievements and undergo historical changes.

Since the reform and opening-up, through continuous efforts, China has achieved a historical transformation from a highly centralized planned economy to a dynamic socialist market economy and from a closed or semi-closed state to all-round opening up. It has created two remarkable miracles that have amazed the world: rapid economic development and long-term social stability. The Chinese nation has witnessed a great leap from standing up, getting rich to becoming strong, expanding the path for developing countries to achieve modernization and providing a brand-new option for countries and nations that aspire to both rapid development and the preservation of their own independence. One of the crucial reasons why contemporary China has been able to create these two miracles is that it adheres to and expands the new path of the modernization of the rule of law in China, strengthens the construction of the state system and legal system of socialism with Chinese characteristics, and develops the socialist rule of law civilization with Chinese characteristics. This demonstrates the significant superiority and strong vitality of the new form of human rule of law civilization. As General Secretary Xi Jinping emphasized, China's practice has shown the world a truth: "There is not just one path of the Western institutional model for governing a country and promoting its modernization. Countries can definitely blaze their own trails".

Secondly, the socialist rule of law civilization with Chinese characteristics is the contemporary form of Chinese rule of law civilization with rich historical and cultural resources.

The path of socialist rule of law with Chinese characteristics has a profound historical and cultural tradition. In the historical process of realizing the great rejuvenation of the Chinese nation, the Chinese nation is bound to explore a new form of civilized development. Over more than 5000 years of civilized development, the Chinese nation has given rise to a time-honored legal culture, formed a unique legal spirit, established a rule of law civilization system that reflects the legal wisdom and rational spirit of the Chinese nation, founded the unique Chinese legal system in the world's legal history, and accumulated profound national legal culture. In the excellent traditional Chinese legal civilization system, there are many outstanding ideological concepts, institutional arrangements, and national governance experiences of the Chinese nation for maintaining national stability and prosperity. They are of great value for promoting the modernization of the rule of law in the Chinese style and building the socialist rule of law civilization with Chinese characteristics, and serve as a profound historical foundation for creating a new form of human rule of law civilization. For example, Chinese rule of law civilization is rich in the ideology of governing the country with both virtue and law. General Secretary Xi Jinping pointed out that "a distinct feature of the path of socialist rule of law with Chinese characteristics is the combination of governance according to law and governance according to virtue, emphasizing that both the rule of law and rule of virtue should be promoted simultaneously and with equal emphasis". Under the leadership of the Communist Party of China, the Chinese people have created the socialist rule of law civilization with Chinese characteristics, which is the inheritance and revival of the Chinese legal system in the contemporary era and the reshaping of the contemporary Chinese legal system. It marks the creative transformation and innovative development of the tradition of Chinese rule of law civilization.

Thirdly, the socialist rule of law civilization with Chinese characteristics is a brand-new form of world rule of law civilization that surpasses the West and looks towards the future.

The Communist Party of China has united and led the Chinese people in a century-long struggle. Especially over the past four decades since the reform and opening-up, it has blazed and developed the path of socialism with Chinese characteristics, enabling Chinese civilization to achieve a new stage of development like a phoenix rising from the ashes. Since modern times, when the Western intellectual circle discusses the forms and evolution of human civilization, there has been a prevalent trend of thought called the "Theory of Western-centered Civilization". This trend of thought holds that the evolution of human civilization is a historical process from simplicity to complexity and from a lower level to a higher level. Western civilization represents and dominates the main trend of human civilization's evolution, and non-Western civilizations will inevitably follow a development path roughly similar to that of Western civilization. According to this idea, China's reform would inevitably lead to the adoption of Western governance models, but it is now obvious that this is an illusion. The socialist rule of law civilization with Chinese characteristics is a new model, and its achievements reflect the brand-new characteristics of human rule of law civilization. It is a brand-new form different from the Western "liberal rule of law civilization".

Facing the "question of the world" in the context of the once-in-a-century changes in the world, "What has happened to the world and what should we do?", Chinese Communists represented by Xi Jinping, with the great theoretical courage of Marxism, based on China's practice of rule of law construction and carrying forward the excellent traditional Chinese legal culture, have clearly put forward the global proposition of the rule of law discourse of socialism with Chinese characteristics:

The diversity of civilizations determines the inherent necessity of exchanges and mutual learning among civilizations. The development of human rule of law civilization does not have only one model, and different rule of law civilizations are all the crystallization of human governance wisdom. China advocates a concept of civilization featuring equality, mutual learning, dialogue, and inclusiveness, and holds that different rule of law civilizations can engage in mutual exchanges and learning. While exploring its own rule of law path, China also provides a platform for exchanges and mutual learning among different rule of law civilizations.

Adhere to the global governance concept of extensive consultation, joint contribution and shared benefits, and promote the democratization, legalization and rationalization of international relations; practice true multilateralism; carry forward the common values of all mankind, including peace, development, fairness, justice, democracy and freedom, and promote the building of a community with a shared future for mankind. General Secretary Xi Jinping profoundly pointed out that "as the name suggests, a community with a shared future for mankind means that the future and destiny of every nation and every country are closely linked. We should stand together through thick and thin and share weal and woe. We should strive to build the planet where we were born and raised into a harmonious big family and turn the aspirations of people around the world for a better life into reality". It can be seen that the concept of building a community with a shared future for mankind does not aim to suppress or eliminate the "others". Instead, it hopes to achieve common development with the "others", respect the well-being of all mankind and promote the progress of human civilization. Therefore, the global proposition of the socialist rule of law discourse with Chinese characteristics clearly conveys to the world China's proposition on the direction of world development and the future and destiny of mankind, and has become an ideological banner leading the progress of human civilization.

References

Chen, H. (2019). Exploration and contributions of the Chinese path to the rule of law civilization. *Southeast Academic Research, 6*, 20–28.

Gong, P. (2021). The internal logic of the new path of Chinese-style modernization of the rule of law. *Law Science, 10*, 3–4, 14.

Wang, L. (2019, September 2). Socialism with Chinese characteristics can stand firm and go far. *Guangming Daily*.

Xi, J. (2015a). Accelerating the construction of a socialist country under the rule of law. *Qiushi*, 1.

Xi, J. (2015b). Working for common and sustainable development and being partners for win-win cooperation: Speech at the UN Sustainable Development Summit. *People's Daily*.

Xi, J. (2017). *Securing a decisive victory in building a moderately prosperous Society in all respect and striving for the great success of socialism with Chinese characteristics for a new era*. People's Publishing House.

Xi, J. (2018a, June 11). Carry forward the "Shanghai Spirit" and build a community with a shared future. *People's Daily*, 003.

Xi, J. (2018b). *Carry forward the global governance concept of extensive consultation, joint contribution and shared benefits. In On adhering to promoting the building of a community with a shared future for mankind*. Central Party Literature Press.

Xi, J. (2018c). *Carry forward the five principles of peaceful coexistence and build a beautiful world of win-win cooperation*. In *On adhering to promoting the building of a community with a shared future for mankind*. Central Party Literature Press.

Xi, J. (2018d). *Jointly build a community with a shared future for mankind. In On adhering to promoting the building of a community with a shared future for mankind* (p. 415). Central Party Literature Press.

Xi, J. (2019). Firmly uphold cultural confidence and build a strong socialist culture country. *Qiushi*, 12.

Xi, J. (2020a). *Xi Jinping: The governance of China (Volume III)*. Foreign Languages Press.

Xi, J. (2020b, November 11). Carrying forward the "Shanghai Spirit", deepening solidarity and cooperation, and building an even closer community with a shared future. *People's Daily*.

Xi, J. (2020c). *On upholding and promoting comprehensive law-based governance*. Central Party Literature Press.

Xi, J. (2020d, September 23). It is essential to foster an awareness of a community with a shared future and a win-win concept of cooperation: Xi Jinping delivers an important speech at the General Debate of the 75th Session of the United Nations General Assembly. *Beijing Youth Daily*.

Xi, J. (2021a, June 2). Strengthening and improving international communication to present a true, multi-dimensional, and comprehensive image of China. *People's Daily*.

Xi, J. (2021b). Unswervingly follow the path of socialist rule of law with Chinese characteristics to provide strong legal guarantees for comprehensively building a modern socialist country. *Qiushi*, 5.

Xi, J. (2021c). Let the torch of multilateralism illuminate humanity's path forward: Special address at the "Davos Agenda" Dialogue of the World Economic Forum. *Contemporary Party Members*, 3.

Xi, J. (2022). Adhering to the path of socialist rule of law with Chinese characteristics and better promoting the construction of the socialist rule of law system with Chinese characteristics. *Qiushi*, 4.

Zhou, Y., Lin, J., Zhang, Q., et al. (2020). *Research on the innovation of the discourse system of socialist rule of law with Chinese characteristics*. People's Publishing House.

Chapter 9
Planning of Chinese Rule of Law Discourse in the New Era

9.1 Introduction

Since the Belt and Road Initiative was put forward in 2013, it has gradually become an important global platform for promoting the community with a shared future for mankind, achieving a significant transformation from a Chinese initiative to an international consensus and from theory to practice. In the process of Belt and Road construction, the rule of law is indispensable. How to build a Chinese rule of law discourse system that not only conforms to the development trend of global economic governance but also meets the characteristics of the Belt and Road Initiative is a major issue currently faced by China.

National language capacity refers to the language proficiency a country needs to handle various domestic and international affairs. It is an integral part of a nation's core competitiveness and plays a crucial role in national construction, development, and security. In the current context of deep-rooted globalization and with China and its citizens increasingly involved in international political, economic, and cultural affairs, enhancing national language capacity not only helps boost the country's "soft power" but also contributes to strengthening its "hard power". It safeguards the legitimate rights and interests of the nation and its citizens, enabling them to have a voice on the international stage. Among national language capacity, the ability of international rule of law discourse is an extremely important component. Strengthening the construction of a country's the capacity of international rule of law discourse will contribute to the establishment of a professional and service-oriented team of international rule of law discourse. This, in turn, can safeguard national security, protect citizens' rights; participate in rule-making, and promote opening-up; develop legal services, and conduct legal exchanges. Therefore, it is self-evident that leveraging the Belt and Road Initiative, a global platform for cooperation and exchange, to strengthen the construction of a country's international

X. Dong, M. Zhang, *Chinese Rule of Law Discourse System*, Understanding China, https://doi.org/10.1007/978-981-95-6260-2_9

communication capacity and international discourse system, and to enhance the country's ability of international rule of law discourse is of great significance.

Therefore, this chapter first elaborates on the new tasks and missions of Chinese rule of law discourse planning in the new era. It specifically introduces relevant issues such as the disciplinary origin of language planning in the field of Chinese law, the dilemmas and goals of Chinese rule of law discourse planning in the new era. Then, taking the Belt and Road Initiative as a global platform for cooperation and exchange, based on the construction of China's ability of international rule of law discourse, it systematically explores Chinese rule of law discourse planning for the Belt and Road. This mainly includes the connotation of Chinese rule of law discourse under the Belt and Road Initiative, the difficulties and challenges it faces, and the research framework and content of Chinese rule of law discourse planning for the Belt and Road. Thirdly, it discusses the translation policy for the Belt and Road. Currently, as China moves closer to the center of the world stage, China's translation cause has reached a new starting point. It is facing unprecedented development opportunities and also shoulders greater responsibilities and missions. For this reason, this chapter mainly sorts out the definition and research status of China's domestic translation policies, and conducts forward-looking thinking on the research content of China's Belt and Road translation policies. Finally, it implements the translation policy in translation planning. Combining the characteristics of the Belt and Road construction, with the goal of meeting the needs of "people-to-people connectivity" and spreading Chinese rule of law discourse, it systematically constructs China's translation planning research suitable for the Belt and Road. Based on four dimensions of discourse planning, status planning, education planning, and communication planning, it determines the main levels and specific language problem areas of the Belt and Road translation planning research from three levels: macro, meso, and micro, in order to enhance China's ability of rule of law discourse.

9.2 New Tasks and Missions

The Fourth Plenary Session of the 19th Central Committee of the Communist Party of China summarized the historical experiences in the formation, development, and improvement of the socialist system with Chinese characteristics and the national governance system over the 70-year history since the founding of the People's Republic of China and more than 40 years of reform and opening-up, especially since the 18th National Congress of the CPC. It clearly pointed out that "building a socialist rule of law system with Chinese characteristics and a socialist country under the rule of law is an inherent requirement for upholding and developing socialism with Chinese characteristics" (Feng, 2019). The rule of law discourse system with Chinese characteristics is an ideological and value-belief system composed of theories and beliefs reflecting China's practice and experience of rule of law. It centrally expresses the Chinese nation's self-understanding of the rule of law in building socialism with Chinese characteristics. It shoulders the mission of exploring the truth and legitimacy of the rule of law and strives to have a voice in the international legal field and establish a significant rule of law discourse power (Zhu, 2017, p. 27). The discipline of language planning has a history of more than 60 years. The entire significance of this discipline lies in solving and coordinating the problems of language communication and interaction in human society (Shen, 2019, p. 36). Language planning is one of the necessary ways to achieve "language interoperability", protect and promote language and cultural diversity, and drive the innovative development of global governance concepts, thus continuously contributing Chinese wisdom and strength to the improvement of global governance. Mr. Li (2018) advocates that as the scope and depth of global governance increase, Chinese linguistics should continuously broaden its horizons and shift from ontological research to discourse research. The rule of law discourse planning with Chinese characteristics is an important symbol of the modernization of the national governance system and governance capacity, and it contributes valuable Chinese wisdom to the improvement of global governance and the construction of a community with a shared future for mankind.

9.2.1 Disciplinary Origins of Language Planning in the Legal Field in China

Language planning in the legal field is a real-world, problem-oriented issue that involves multiple disciplines (at least including linguistics, law, literature, communication studies, education, and sociology, etc.). It is also one of the new areas for language competition and the dissemination of cultural soft power (Dong, 2015). Language has always held an important position in the legal field. In the West, there is a saying, "The law is simply a matter of linguistics."

In the initial stage of the discipline, language corpus planning was the main task of language planning. Corpus planning refers to the transformation of the language itself, aiming to promote the continuous standardization and improvement of legal language so that it can effectively perform the language functions assigned by status planning. This includes dictionary compilation, grammar explanation, term revision, and the improvement and standardization of the writing system. As Professor Liao (2008), a legal linguist, said, "Legal language civilization is an extremely important and indispensable part of the rule of law civilization The law must first standardize language before it can effectively regulate human behavior. The era of the rule of law construction calls for research on legal language standardization…".

After the late 1970s, with the in-depth development of the immigration wave and the civil rights movement, people paid more and more attention to ethnic relations and ethnic issues related to language. Using language legislation or formulating language policies to solve language problems had become an important decision for multi-ethnic countries around the world at that time. Language legislative reform and language policy research became new hotspots in sociolinguistic research. For example, in 1969, the Canadian Parliament passed *The Official Languages Act*, declaring that English and French have equal status and effect. In 1987, the Australian Federal Department of Education promulgated *The National Policy on Languages*, designating English as the national and official language of Australia while emphasizing the protection and research of indigenous languages (Dong, 2015). *The Law of the People's Republic of China on the Standard Spoken and Written Chinese Language* is China's first specialized law on language and writing. The law stipulates that all current languages and writing systems in China have equal status, and Mandarin Chinese and standard Chinese characters are the national common language and writing. In ethnic autonomous areas and areas where ethnic minorities live in compact communities, the national common language and writing can be used simultaneously with the local common ethnic minority languages and writing.

In terms of language education planning (acquisition planning), Dong (2015) believes that the research on language acquisition planning in the legal field does not refer to the study of the national or official language established by law, but to the study of legal language itself. As a language for specific purposes, legal language is different from ordinary language and has its own characteristics. The language acquisition planning in the legal field aims to serve specific professional work with language (English). Therefore, the curriculum is set up to meet the specific needs of learners, and the focus of learning lies in the language (grammar, vocabulary, register), discourse, and genre appropriate to this profession.

In the late 1970s and early 1980s, some Chinese universities offered courses in legal English. Professor Zhang's research (2019) shows that the discipline of legal English in China has gone through three development stages: the initial and formative stage, the exploratory and diversified development stage, and the stage of rapid development and the formation of an independent disciplinary status. After nearly 40 years of development, the disciplinary system of legal English has become increasingly mature and gradually shows the nature of an independent discipline. The prominent sign is the increasingly complete talent-cultivation system. Now, a complete legal English talent-cultivation system from undergraduate bachelor's degrees, master's degrees to doctoral degrees has been formed.

Since the mid-to-late 1980s, language planning has undergone a post-structuralist transformation. Ruiz (1984) formally proposed the concept of language as a resource. Under the influence of this concept, Chinese language planning has gradually shifted from focusing on language structure and status to planning activities at the level of language use and application, both in theory and practice. The concept of language function planning has gradually taken shape (Li & Wang, 2019). For example, in terms of translation planning: Du, Zhang, and Yuan (2004), Dong (2021), Qu (2012), etc. have all pointed out the importance of research on the standardization of legal translation dissemination. Dong (2018) further pointed out that "Legal translation contributes Chinese wisdom to global governance. The dissemination planning of translation includes not only the dissemination subject (the selection of foreign translators and cooperation with foreign publishing institutions), but also the dissemination purpose, content, media, ideas, target audience, structure, channels, recipients, effects, and environment. The dissemination planning of translation needs comprehensive and overall consideration, thus having comprehensive and overall characteristics."

9.2.2 Special Areas of Legal Discourse Planning

The analysis of legal discourse can be traced back to the study of rhetoric in ancient Greece. In the 1970s, forensic linguistics was formally and widely recognized as an independent discipline. The comprehensive development of linguistics and law has provided nourishment for the full-fledged development of forensic linguistics, and the research results of legal discourse have gradually been applied in legal practice (Zhang & Zhang 2019). After the 1970s abroad, there has been an emphasis on the dynamic study of legal language as a process, that is, the analysis of the pragmatic and discursive aspects of legal discourse. For example, the analysis of legal language as a tool, and the research on the relationship between legal discourse and power from the perspective of sociolinguistics, etc. In China, the study of the legal discourse system began in the 1980s. Among them, legal translation and court interpretation activities have been the top priorities in the development of legal discourse research in recent years. Many monographs have been published in this field, such as *Case Studies and Comments on English-Chinese Legal Translation* (Li, 2011), *Legal Text Translation* (Dong, 2021), *Court Interpretation* (Dong, 2021), *Case-based Coursebook on Legal English Translation* (Dong, 2015), and *Research on Legal Translation* (Qu, 2018). Although discourse research has always been an important area in applied linguistics, it did not attract the attention of language planning research for a long time. In the past decade or so, discourse research has gradually become an important method in language planning and language policy research, playing a crucial role in innovating the research methods of language planning (Shen, 2019).

Generally speaking, a country's legal discourse refers to the legal language behavior and expression carried out by individuals or collectives, either from the private or official sectors, through top-down or bottom-up approaches, with the fundamental purpose of safeguarding the country's legal rights and interests, promoting the legal spirit, and spreading the legal culture. According to the nature of the discourse subject, legal discourse can be divided into official state legal discourse and civil legal discourse. Their common goal is to enhance the international rule of law discourse power of the sovereign state. Rule of law discourse power has two meanings: Firstly, it is the right of rule of law discourse. That is, the discourse subject should have the right and qualification to express their opinions and participate in the handling of legal affairs in the legal field. Secondly, it is the rule of law discourse power, which means that the discourse subject has the dominance and influence over the discourse in a certain legal field or scope. With the collapse of the Western colonial system, as "late-developing countries" in the legal field, nation-states gradually realized in the process of imitating and learning from the legal concepts and rule of laws of the Western world that legal discourse planning and legal discourse power have increasingly become important tools to counter Western powers and gain the initiative in discourse.

9.2.3 *Dilemmas in the Planning of Chinese Rule of Law Discourse*

Over the 40 years of reform and opening-up, China has become the world's second-largest economy after the United States. However, the improvement of comprehensive national strength has not enabled China to gain a corresponding discourse status globally. It is necessary to clearly recognize that the international rule of law discourse power is based on the mature internal attributes and intangible external influence of a country's rule of law discourse system. China's planning and construction of the rule of law discourse still face both "domestic troubles and external threats".

From an external perspective, on the one hand, influenced by political factors, the game of international rule of law discourse power is, to a large extent, a game of political discourse power. The unbalanced situation of international rule of law discourse power will continue to exist for a long time. On the other hand, due to differences in historical traditions, religions, ethnic groups, politics, and economies, there are multiple conflicts among the rule of law traditions and legal cultures of different countries. It is necessary to overcome the barriers in political systems, civilizations, and cultures, and the effective achievement of interest relations also requires setting reasonable rules according to the actual situation. The strong Western rule of law discourse power comes with its developed economic strength and complete rule of law. In contrast, China is in an "awkward situation" of inherent deficiency in discourse ability.

From an internal perspective, the planning of the rule of law discourse with Chinese characteristics (the construction of the discourse system) is still in its initial stage, and the overall domestic rule of law environment is not mature enough, which is manifested in many aspects:

Firstly. the domestic legal theory circle and legal practice circle still find it difficult to break free from the shackles of Western rule of law ideology. Introducing and absorbing Western liberal rule of law theories played a positive role in promoting Chinese rule of law construction for a certain period. However, any rule of law theory must be integrated into specific national conditions and cultures. Blindly copying Western theories cannot lead to the path of planning the rule of law discourse with Chinese characteristics, nor can it help solve the actual problems faced by Chinese rule of law, let alone form its own disciplinary system, academic system, and discourse system.

Secondly, the socialist rule of law in general can basically meet the needs of China's current economic and social development. However, when it comes to competing for international rule of law discourse power, there is still a wide gap between the construction of Chinese rule of law and that of developed countries. Meanwhile, the level of law-based administration of governments at all levels in China does not meet the requirements of implementing the rule of law in the new era.

Thirdly, the legal education model in China is rigid, and the innovation ability of legal talents is insufficient. Currently, legal education in China is challenged by both the government and the market and has many problems. For example, there is a contradiction between the expansion of the scale of legal education and the guarantee of its quality. The disciplinary system of law lacks focus and characteristics. The knowledge structure of legal teaching staff is single, emphasizing theory over practice. The legal curriculum system focuses on examinations, and the cultivation of legal talents is divorced from legal professions. There is a shortage of high-end and foreign-related legal talents, with limited international exchanges and international perspectives, and they lack the practical ability to handle international legal affairs and international competitiveness.

Fourthly, China has not yet established a platform for international communication and promotion of its rule of law discourse. A platform is the carrier and channel for expressing discourse and an important aspect of building international rule of law discourse power. There are various types of platforms. For example, establishing international organizations and setting international agendas are basic platforms for discourse competition, while platforms represented by think-tanks, media, legal journals, and legal associations are important supplementary forces and play a significant role.

9.2.4 Goals of the Planning for Chinese Rule of Law Discourse

The planning for Chinese rule of law discourse with Chinese characteristics in the new era should include the following three tasks: First, continuously promote the innovation of the rule of law theory, constantly construct, enrich and improve the basic content of the rule of law discourse system with Chinese characteristics, and enhance the confidence in the rule of law culture. Second, participate in global governance and contribute Chinese rule of law wisdom to the construction of a community with a shared future for mankind. Third, implement the "strategy of promoting the rule of law globally" to improve the internationalization level of Chinese rule of law discourse and convey China's right to speak in the field of the rule of law to the world (Zhu, 2017, p. 27).

Innovating the Rule of Law Theory and Enhancing the Confidence in the Rule of Law Culture

Cultural confidence is a more fundamental, profound and lasting strength in the development of a country and a nation. "Discourse is a constituent element of society and culture. Every use of language will affect the changes and re-creation of society and culture, including power relations (Liu & Cui, 2010, p. 501)."

The construction of Chinese rule of law discourse with Chinese characteristics for the Belt and Road Initiative is rooted in the profound atmosphere of traditional Chinese culture. With the modernity, openness and inclusiveness of its legal thoughts and concepts, it absorbs the essence of traditional Chinese legal thoughts and the civilization of modern Western rule of law construction. After a complex process of inheritance, transplantation, exchange, conflict and integration, it has formed the socialist rule of law concept, rule of law system, rule of law culture, legal education and research with Chinese characteristics. It has achieved independent innovation and creation with Chinese subjectivity and localization, and has become a typical example for the rule of law construction or transformation of third-world countries. China has become the world's second-largest economy. From the legal perspective of economic development, the "Chinese Dream" and the "rule of law Dream" have shown the inherent strong foundation and the due historical responsibility of a civilized China. To let the rule of law demonstrate its value and strength in realizing the "Chinese Dream" of the great rejuvenation of the Chinese nation, we should expand a broader space in the field of rule of law culture and strive to make the confidence in the rule of law culture our spiritual symbol.

Participating in Global Governance and Contributing Chinese Wisdom in the Rule of Law

The report to the 19th National Congress of the Communist Party of China stated that "Socialism with Chinese characteristics has entered a new era, which means that the path, theory, system, and culture of socialism with Chinese characteristics have kept developing, blazing a new trail for other developing countries to achieve modernization. It offers a new option for other countries and nations who want to speed up their development while preserving their independence. It offers Chinese wisdom and a Chinese approach to solving the problems facing mankind." After 40 years of reform, development, and exploration, China has witnessed a series of transitions, including from "rule of law" to "rule of law", from "governing the country by law" to "comprehensively governing the country by law", from building a "rule of law" to building a "rule of law system", and from a "focus on the economy" to a "people-centered" approach. China has accumulated a series of valuable experiences in democratic and legal construction. The concept of the rule of law has become more mature, the idea of the rule of law has gradually taken root in people's hearts, the rule of law system is moving towards improvement, and a Chinese rule of law discourse system with logical strength in the rule of law concept, sound rule of law institutions, and rich rule of law practices has been formed. In the history of global governance, China has made numerous contributions to international rule of law. Examples such as the "Five Principles of Peaceful Coexistence", the "One Country, Two Systems" theory, and the "One Machine, Two Wings" international judicial theory fully demonstrate China's participation in building a new international order and its promotion of the development of international rule of law (Zhao, 2015). In the new era, the proposal of the Belt and Road Initiative and the establishment of the Asian Infrastructure Investment Bank showcase China's discourse refinement and innovative practices. They contribute to the improvement of the international rule of law and the transformation of the global governance model, greatly enhancing the international influence of China's legal discourse and also helping to further shape China's image as a country under the rule of law.

9.3 Responding to Globalization and Enhancing Chinese International Rule of Law Discourse Power

Foucault believes that discourse is a way for people to engage in struggles. The formation of a discourse system also means the formation of discourse power. Once discourse power is established, it brings about dominance, and dominance creates legitimacy. Critical Discourse Analysis (CDA) is obviously influenced by Foucault's ideas. Norman Fairclough, one of the founders of CDA, pointed out in his article "Critical Discourse Analysis" that "Discourse reflects power relations. CDA explains how social power relations are realized and exchanged in or through discourse" (Liu & Cui, 2010, p. 501). The dominance of any discourse is not automatically generated but is formed through dissemination, communication, and dialogue. In the new era, implementing the "strategy of promoting the rule of law globally" to enhance the internationalization level of Chinese rule of law discourse and convey Chinese rule of law discourse power to the world will surely enable an equal dialogue between the Eastern and Western rule of laws.

Therefore, if China wants to transform its development advantages into discourse advantages in the era of globalization and inject Chinese elements into the global competition of rule of law discourses, it must rely on a mature dissemination and promotion mechanism. It should present the theories and experiences of the rule of law with Chinese characteristics in an easily understandable and acceptable way, so as to effectively and rapidly spread them internationally. Undoubtedly, this is an important mission for Chinese rule of law discourse planning in the new era.

9.4 Chinese Rule of Law Discourse Planning

As a global platform for cooperation and exchange, the Belt and Road Initiative naturally involves legal topics such as the formulation of international relations rules and the handling of international disputes. As the initiator of the Belt and Road Initiative, the significance of China's international rule of law discourse is self-evident. Constructing a multi-dimensional and all-round international rule of law discourse system not only helps to create a favorable external environment for China's reform, development, and stability but also facilitates the management of affairs with countries along the Belt and Road.

9.4.1 Connotations of Chinese Rule of Law Discourse

Generally speaking, international rule of law discourse refers to the legal language behavior expressed by individuals or collectives, whether civilian or official, through top-down or bottom-up approaches, with the fundamental purpose of safeguarding a country's legal rights and interests, promoting the spirit of the rule of law, and disseminating legal culture. According to the nature of the discourse subject, international rule of law discourse can be divided into official national rule of law discourse and civilian rule of law discourse, both of which are committed to enhancing a sovereign state's international rule of law discourse power. The international rule of law discourse under the Belt and Road Initiative is a specific manifestation of China's international rule of law discourse and an important indicator for measuring Chinese international discourse power.

As an important part of Chinese international rule of law discourse, the international rule of law discourse under the Belt and Road Initiative refers to a series of legal language symbols and forms of expression used by China in information dissemination among countries along the Belt and Road, the interpretation of its governing legal concepts, and the handling of international affairs with these countries. Promoting the construction of the rule of law discourse system for the Belt and Road Initiative is an important guarantee for the smooth implementation of the initiative and also a good opportunity to enhance China's international discourse power. In his letter to the 2019 Chinese Rule of Law International Forum, General Secretary Xi Jinping also mentioned that China is willing to work with other countries to create a favorable legal environment, build a fair, reasonable, and transparent international economic and trade rule system, promote the high-quality development of the Belt and Road Initiative, and bring more benefits to the people of countries along the route.

9.4.2 Challenges and Difficulties Faced by the Rule of Law Discourse

Due to the varying legal discourses, diverse rule of law cultures, and distinct legal service models across different countries, the rule of law discourse under China's Belt and Road Initiative, whether disseminated through official government entities or civil society legal practitioners and researchers, will inevitably encounter various challenges and difficulties.

Weak Initiative of Rule of Law Discourse Subjects

Rule of law discourse agents determine the questions of "what to say, how to say it, and where to say it" (Feng, 2012, p. 2). As the spokespersons for Chinese rule of law discourse "going global", rule of law discourse agents are of vital importance in the rule of law construction of the Belt and Road Initiative. However, currently, the subjective initiative of China's international rule of law discourse agents under the Belt and Road Initiative is relatively weak. Especially, non-official rule of law discourse agents are at a loss regarding "what to say, how to say it, and where to say it". This, to a certain extent, undermines the credibility of Chinese rule of law discourse in the rule of law process within the Belt and Road region. With the in-depth advancement of the joint rule of law construction under the Belt and Road Initiative, cooperation and exchanges in the fields of national economy, technology, and service trade have become increasingly frequent. Meanwhile, international disputes involving foreign parties have also emerged one after another. Due to the lack of a mandatory dispute-resolution mechanism under the Belt and Road Initiative, rule of law discourse agents, such as the judicial and arbitration institutions of relevant countries, are unable to apply unified international laws when hearing cases of cross-border disputes related to the Belt and Road Initiative. This often leads to differences and controversies (Gu, 2016, p. 93). It is precisely at such times that rule of law discourse talents are urgently needed to offer their insights and wisdom. General Secretary Xi Jinping also mentioned in the China Rule of Law International Forum (2019) that deepening the construction of the rule of law discourse for the Belt and Road Initiative does not only involve the legislative, law-enforcement, and judicial departments of the participating countries. Instead, it requires a wide range of rule of law discourse agents, including legal scholars, lawyers, arbitrators, mediators, notaries, and corporate legal counsels, to actively and proactively participate in the construction of the rule of law discourse system for the Belt and Road Initiative.

Insufficient Follow-Up of the Rule of Law Discourse Translation Mechanism

Fundamentally speaking, rule of law discourse belongs to professional discourse, which is generally expressed by professional personnel such as legal practitioners or research scholars. The Belt and Road's international rule of law discourse has even higher professional requirements. It requires a proficient command of both domestic and international rule of law discourses and a deep understanding of the Belt and Road Initiative. The high-level professionalism it entails is obvious. However, this has also largely led to the disconnection between the Belt and Road's international rule of law discourse and the public discourse, especially among the audiences in the countries along the Belt and Road.

Currently, more than 140 countries and international organizations have joined the Belt and Road Initiative, and each country has its own language. Facing such a complex linguistic situation, the follow-up capacity of the Belt and Road's international rule of law discourse translation mechanism is significantly insufficient, failing to meet the requirements for Chinese rule of law discourse to "go global". There is a gap between the official rule of law discourse and the public discourse. The official rule of law discourse is not transparent to non-legal professionals, thus causing communication barriers. This phenomenon is already quite evident within China, let alone on the international stage under the Belt and Road Initiative. Neither the conversion mechanism between legal professional discourse and public discourse nor the translation and conversion mechanism for the Belt and Road's rule of law discourse has matured.

Weak Binding Force of International Rule of Law

The compatibility between Chinese rule of law discourse for the Belt and Road Initiative and that of the countries along the routes has not yet reached an ideal state. Moreover, the innovation in international rule of law concepts, rules, and mechanisms is also limited. The Belt and Road Initiative involves numerous countries. As the saying goes, "It's difficult to satisfy everyone's needs." Therefore, formulating internationally applicable rules that can be uniformly implemented poses a significant challenge to Chinese rule of law discourse. The advancement of the Belt and Road Initiative cannot be achieved without the guarantee of the rule of law, which encompasses both domestic and international rule of law (Liu, 2015, p. 16). However, the current issue lies in the fact that due to the lack of specific institutional arrangements and clear definitions of rights and obligations in the Belt and Road Initiative, it does not possess the legal force of a national offer. Even if bilateral or multilateral cooperation memorandums or cooperation plans are signed, specific projects still require well-developed agreement arrangements for implementation (Xiao & Zhang, 2017, p. 34). Traditional international cooperation is based on contractual negotiations, where the rights and obligations of each party are clearly defined and stable. In contrast, the Belt and Road Initiative is characterized by the establishment of mutual benefit, trust, and consensus through inter-governmental consultations among participating countries (Zhang, 2015a, p. 98). Therefore, transforming the Belt and Road Initiative from a unilateral proposal into a unified action by all parties and even a legally binding institutional arrangement is of utmost importance and also a major challenge in China's planning of the international rule of law discourse for the Belt and Road Initiative.

9.4.3 Research Framework of Chinese Rule of Law Discourse Planning

To construct an international rule of law discourse system for the Belt and Road Initiative and enhance China's international rule of law discourse ability, it is necessary to conduct strategic planning research from all aspects and at multiple levels. Based on the "5W" model proposed by communication scholar H. Lasswell (i.e., Who, Says What, In Which Channel, To Whom, With What Effect) and relevant language planning and language policy theories. It is believed that for the systematic construction of the strategic planning of the Belt and Road rule of law discourse, it is necessary to recognize its current specific problems and underlying causes. We should determine the main levels and specific planning contents of the Belt and Road rule of law discourse system planning from three levels: macro, meso, and micro, namely the main levels of status planning, corpus planning, acquisition planning, and communication planning.

Traditional rule of law discourse planning usually regards official groups such as the state and the government as the main subjects of international rule of law discourse. In contrast, modern language planning calls for the participation of multiple parties in the whole process of formulating, implementing, evaluating, and adjusting rule of law discourse planning. According to the classification of discourse subject identities by Wu and Gu (2019) and Dong (2015), the main subjects of the Belt and Road rule of law discourse should cover the national level, the industrial level, the academic level, and the media level. These four types of rule of law discourse subjects should work together in parallel, jointly targeting the audiences in the countries along the Belt and Road and promoting the "going-out" of the Belt and Road rule of law discourse.

At the National Level

The main subjects of the Belt and Road rule of law discourse mainly involve national leaders and government departments, representing the highest level of China's international rule of law discourse. Official rule of law discourse usually appears in major international speeches and important internationally-released documents, directly reflecting Chinese rule of law governance guidelines and rule of law diplomacy for the Belt and Road Initiative. Since the proposal of the Belt and Road Initiative in 2013 and the 18th National Congress of the Communist Party of China, national leaders have voiced their views in the local mainstream media during their visits to the countries along the routes. This not only accelerates the legalization process of the Belt and Road Initiative but also helps to enhance Chinese rule of law discourse power (Sun, 2019, p. 31). The role of government departments in the planning of the Belt and Road rule of law discourse is mainly reflected in aspects such as legislation, implementation, adjustment, and supervision. The national legislative body is responsible for language legislation, determining the status and value of various languages (mainly Chinese and English), allocating language uses and functions, and stipulating language usage scenarios. National functional departments (administrative and judicial institutions) jointly guide language planning in the legal field within the scope of their legal powers, manage the language life in the legal field. That is, they gain the in-depth understanding of the language life situation in the legal field, timely adjust national language policies within the rule of law to ensure they are in line with the actual language life in the legal field, and formulate and implement various detailed rules of national language policies in the legal field, thereby facilitating the more effective implementation of legislative laws and language policies in the legal context of the Belt and Road Initiative (Dong, 2015, p. 41).

At the Industrial Level

Generally speaking, the main industrial subjects of the rule of law discourse typically include law societies, law firms, corporate legal departments, and legal translation companies in relevant industrial fields. They are mainly responsible for conducting research and providing services on the rule of law discourse in the countries along the Belt and Road, and providing reasonable grounds for rule of law discourse legislation. Currently, one of the main problems in the discourse life within the legal field of the Belt and Road is that relevant institutions and associations have a weak awareness of foreign-related rule of law discourse and lack basic knowledge of linguistics. Overall, the number of lawyers and law firms specializing in foreign-related legal affairs of the Belt and Road in China is relatively small, and there is also the possibility of low-level professional competence among them. It is extremely urgent to enhance the discourse participation of the industrial group in the rule of law cooperation of the Belt and Road. Professor Han Dayuan, the Dean of the Law School of Renmin University of China, proposed that the legal guarantee and legal services for the Belt and Road should follow the principle of "Five Orientations and Three Avoidances", namely, systematization of theoretical systems, scientific decision-making, diversification of communication methods, specification of strategic goals, legalization of processes and implementation methods, and avoiding over-Sinicization, instrumentalization, and vulgarization (Li, 2017, p. 58). To achieve this goal and meet these requirements, the legal professional group represented by lawyers should, based on the functional positioning of their regions in the Belt and Road, build legal service platforms to make the rule of law discourse in the Belt and Road process penetrate into the hearts of the people. The expression of the rule of law discourse of the lawyer group needs further innovation to conform to the rule of law discourse in the countries along the Belt and Road and gain the recognition of the local people. Corporate legal departments should provide legal support for companies implementing the Belt and Road strategy, remove legal obstacles, and focus on enhancing the value-creation of legal services (Jiang, 2015, p. 2), actively providing legal services for enterprises to "go into" the countries along the Belt and Road. As a self-regulatory organization in the legal community, the law society should fully play the leading role of an industrial organization and establish a special research institution to study the rule of law discourse of the Belt and Road. Of course, the importance of translation activities cannot be ignored. More translators should be encouraged to engage in the translation of the Belt and Road rule of law discourse.

At the Academic Level

The formulation of the norms for the Belt and Road rule of law discourse is highly specialized and particular, involving numerous academic disciplines such as law, linguistics, and communication. Thus, it urgently requires strong academic support. The academic players in the Belt and Road rule of law discourse mainly include academic associations, university research institutions, students, and individual scholars, who jointly contribute their research capabilities to the dissemination of the Belt and Road rule of law discourse. It is worth noting that achieving academic breakthroughs in China's Belt and Road rule of law discourse planning is not only necessary for the development and improvement of its own discourse system but also a requirement for breaking through Western restrictions and making its voice heard on the international stage. Compared with the academic circles in Europe and America, domestic theoretical research on "interpreting international rule of law discourse academically" is still in its infancy, especially the research on the rule of law discourse under the Belt and Road Initiative is extremely scarce. Moreover, relying solely on domestic academic research is far from sufficient to form international academic public opinion on the Belt and Road rule of law discourse. It is also necessary to actively carry out international academic exchanges, and leverage the participation and promotion of foreign academic elites, adhering to the combination of openness and autonomy. On the one hand, various Chinese academic associations, research institutions, scholars, and individual students should take a global perspective based on the actual situation of the rule of law discourse under the Belt and Road Initiative, objectively and comprehensively analyze foreign academic research results on the rule of law discourse, and extract their essence.On the other hand, the research on the Belt and Road rule of law discourse should continuously explore its own excellent traditions and historical experiences of the rule of law discourse, summarize the unique concepts, wisdom, and methods of the Chinese rule of law discourse, and form academic achievements of the Belt and Road rule of law discourse with Chinese characteristics. This will enable China to conduct international academic exchange activities with a positive attitude of self-respect and self-confidence.

At the Media Level

As a crucial part of enhancing international rule of law discourse power, the Belt and Road rule of law discourse is first manifested in the voices from China. To avoid being voiceless on the international rule of law discourse stage, efforts are required not only at the national, governmental, industrial, and academic levels but also at the media level. To smoothly promote the Belt and Road rule of law discourse onto a broader international stage, we must first gain the right to speak in the media. Mainstream media at home and abroad serve as the fundamental means for China to communicate and interact with the world in the field of Belt and Road rule of law cooperation. They are also important channels for audiences in partner countries to understand China's Belt and Road Initiative. When it comes to the dissemination of the Belt and Road rule of law discourse, the media should meet three requirements: First, the reporting content must be objective and fair. Only fair and objective media reports can serve as the prerequisite for normal communication and exchanges between China and the international community. Only through reliable and objective accounts can the rule of law discourse within the Belt and Road Initiative actively guide the international rule of law discourse and public opinion, and provide the world with authentic information about the progress of the Belt and Road rule of law construction. Second, the language expression should be appropriate. The news media shoulder the important task of conveying information and concepts regarding Belt and Road rule of law cooperation. Therefore, media professionals should use media news language appropriately and reasonably to spread the real voices of the Belt and Road rule of law discourse to the outside world. This enables the world to understand the Belt and Road rule of law cooperation and recognize the embedded rule of law discourse. Third, the information dissemination should be effective. In the information age, media information should emphasize the timeliness of Belt and Road rule of law discourse reporting and the integration of information content. The goal is to achieve in-depth perspectives, wide-ranging views, and rapid dissemination. Additionally, the content, form, and strategies of rule of law discourse reporting should be continuously adjusted to give full play to the role and effectiveness of the media in promoting the Belt and Road rule of law discourse.

9.4.4 Contents of Chinese Rule of Law Discourse Planning

The planning of rule of law discourse content is a practical issue that involves multiple disciplines (at least including linguistics, law, literature, communication studies, education, and social sciences), and it is also one of the new frontiers in language competition and the dissemination of cultural soft power (Dong, 2015, p. 37). Western developed countries in Europe and America, which dominate the international rule of law discourse power, have always attached great importance to the planning and construction of their own rule of law discourse content. If the Belt and Road rule of law discourse is to truly "go global", it is necessary to comprehensively and multi-dimensionally plan the content of the Belt and Road rule of law discourse, and form a multi-level theoretical and practical research system involving individual researchers, academic groups, universities, research institutions, and national think-tanks. By drawing an analogy from the studies on language planning types by Haugen (1968), Cooper (1989), and Dong (2015), the content planning of the Belt and Road rule of law discourse can be divided into the following four aspects: status planning, corpus planning, acquisition planning, and spreading planning.

Status Planning

In essence, the status planning of the Belt and Road rule of law discourse is about determining the status and value of legal languages for the Belt and Road rule of law discourse, allocating the uses and functions of rule of law languages, and specifying the places where these languages are to be used. This can fundamentally address the confusion and difficulties of the subjects of the Belt and Road rule of law discourse regarding "what to say, how to say it, and where to say it". First of all, the primary concern in the status planning of the Belt and Road rule of law discourse is which language should serve as the legal language for China's Belt and Road Initiative and the legal validity of such language. Mandarin Chinese is, of course, the official language of China. However, considering the rich variety of languages along the Belt and Road routes, most of which are minority languages, and the fact that the "going-global" of the Belt and Road rule of law discourse cannot solely rely on foreign audiences learning Chinese to understand Chinese rule of law discourse, both Chinese and English, the world's lingua franca, can be jointly designated as the legal languages for China's Belt and Road rule of law discourse.

Corpus Planning

As the name implies, the corpus planning of the rule of law discourse under the Belt and Road Initiative refers to the transformation of the rule of law discourse used in the process of the Belt and Road rule of law construction. Its fundamental purpose is to promote the continuous standardization and improvement of the Belt and Road rule of law discourse. In essence, the rule of law discourse of each country can be analyzed from three aspects: "what to talk about", "in what capacity to talk", and "how to talk". Wen (2016) argues that Halliday (1994) proposed that language has three major functions: ideational, interpersonal, and textual. This is an ideology-neutral theory and can serve as an initial analytical framework for corpus planning. In addition, it is undoubtedly a more urgent task to conduct discourse analysis and rhetorical analysis on Chinese rule of law discourse texts and make comparative analyses with the rule of law texts of the countries involved; to construct a national capacity model and operating mechanism for Chinese rule of law discourse; to summarize strategic countermeasures for improving the efficiency of Chinese rule of law discourse ability and the operation of the rule of law discourse system; and to establish a narrative structure model and a rhetorical reasoning model for Chinese rule of law discourse, so as to form a connected and corresponding network with the rule of law discourse system.

Acquisition Planning

Legal education undertakes the task of supplying excellent legal talents for the country and determines the reserve of a country's rule of law forces. China's traditional legal education can no longer meet the needs of the Belt and Road rule of law discourse to "go global" under the new situation. It is necessary to reform the cultivation of Belt and Road rule of law discourse talents from an international perspective, taking into account its own characteristics (Chen, 2015a, p. 27). The acquisition planning of the Belt and Road rule of law discourse should focus on reforming the existing legal education model, breaking the closed-door teaching method that mainly focuses on domestic laws and has serious disciplinary boundaries, and cultivating more high-quality, compound, applied, and international legal talents for Belt and Road rule of law cooperation. In addition to legal talents, there is currently a serious shortage of talents proficient in the languages of the countries along the Belt and Road. According to the official data from *China Belt and Road Network*, as of the end of October 2019, China had signed 197 cooperation documents on jointly building the Belt and Road with 137 countries and 30 international organizations, covering all five continents and four oceans comprehensively. Naturally, the languages used in these countries are diverse, and it is almost impossible to achieve language consistency. Even when using the world's lingua franca, English, to translate Chinese rule of law discourse, it may encounter great difficulties. In reality, China's training programs for translation talents mainly focus on English, a major language, while the coverage of minor languages is relatively narrow, not to mention the compound minor-language translation talents proficient in legal knowledge. Whether from the perspective of globalization and ecological development or from the perspective of spreading Chinese rule of law culture, minor-language courses should be appropriately and reasonably arranged in the entire foreign-language education system; the foreign-language planning for minor languages should be strengthened to serve the Belt and Road countermeasures and construction (Shen, 2015, p. 9). Therefore, to further promote the process of Belt and Road rule of law cooperation, while continuously supplying English-speaking translation talents, we urgently need to strengthen the cultivation and education of Belt and Road minor-language translation talents.

Spreading Planning

First, in addition to relying on leaders' international oral exchanges and government rule of law reports, the "going global" of the Belt and Road's international rule of law discourse can also utilize multi-modal media carriers such as movies, TV shows, periodicals, music, fine arts, dance, drama, the Internet, and even virtual reality to comprehensively engage the audio-visual senses of the Belt and Road audience. Second, it is necessary to actively build and participate in international rule of law activities. From China's own stance and perspective, reasonable interpretations should be provided for international law concepts, international relations rules, and common legal issues in the rule of law of various countries, and key issues should be put forward. By actively engaging on the international rule of law stage, the discourse power on the rule of law and international influence can be enhanced (Cai, 2017, p. 4). Both official and non-official subjects of international rule of law discourse should give full play to their roles in public rule of law diplomacy in the Belt and Road international rule of law context and actively participate in the construction of China's international rule of law discourse system for the Belt and Road. In 2019, the Ministry of Justice of China took the lead in convening the inauguration ceremony and the first inter-ministerial joint meeting of the China-Shanghai Cooperation Organization Legal Service Commission, which safeguards the Belt and Road construction. From December 9th to 10th, at the World Lawyers Conference in Guangzhou, the Belt and Road Lawyers Alliance was announced to be established, which builds a new communication platform for lawyers from countries along the Belt and Road and effectively promotes China's image as a country under the rule of law. In the future, it is hoped that more such Belt and Road rule of law exchange activities can be built or participated in. Finally, translation activities are an inevitable path for the construction of the Belt and Road rule of law discourse system, as all foreign-related activities cannot do without translation. Only when the translation of rule of law discourse achieves the goals of accuracy and efficiency can the effectiveness of China's Belt and Road rule of law discourse be enhanced, and the acceptance and recognition of Chinese rule of law discourse by countries along the Belt and Road and the international community be improved. The quality and efficiency of the translation of the Belt and Road rule of law discourse should be continuously improved to achieve the best legal translation results. For example, the international translation of the Belt and Road has been adjusted from the initial "strategy" to the current "initiative", aiming to eliminate other countries' misunderstandings and misuses of its political connotations and better promote the rule of law discourse exchange activities between China and countries along the Belt and Road. In this regard, the international translation policy of the Belt and Road rule of law discourse should be planned comprehensively from multiple angles. The top-level design of the Belt and Road rule of law discourse translation policy should be carried out starting from cultivating legal translation talents, selecting translation content, formulating translation strategies, expanding translation dissemination channels, and establishing a translation effect evaluation mechanism.

9.5 Chinese Translation Policies

Policies are the guidelines of action formulated by a country or a political party to achieve a certain political line. A translation policy refers to the guiding principles and specific regulations made by a state or government agencies, as well as non-governmental civil groups or organizations under the guidance or influence of the state regarding translation activities. General Secretary Xi Jinping emphasized in an important speech during the 30th collective study session of the Political Bureau of the CPC Central Committee that it is necessary to accelerate the construction of China's discourse and narrative systems and the construction of China's international discourse system in the new era. To gain the initiative in the complex and ever-changing international situation and better serve the overall situation of China's reform, development, and stability is not only a proposition of the times but also the bounden duty of the international communication community. The Belt and Road Initiative has brought about changes and challenges to China's translation industry. "As long as translation activities exist, they are influenced by translation policies" (Teng, 2014, pp. 35–39). Translation policies play a role in regulating and guiding translation activities. The Belt and Road Initiative is a huge systematic project, and the cultural strategy is an integral part of this system. An active translation policy can promote a country's cultural and economic development, standardize, stimulate, and mobilize translation activities, and enhance a country's international discourse power.

9.5.1 *Definition and Research Status of Translation Policies*

The concept of translation policy was first proposed by Holmes in his 1972 paper "The Name and Nature of Translation Studies". Translation policy research aims to "provide reasonable suggestions to determine the status and role of translators, translation activities, and translated works in society, such as which works should be selected for translation in a specific socio-cultural context; what the socio-economic status of translators is and what status they should have; and what role translation should play in foreign language teaching" (Holmes, 1988/2000). Gideon Toury believes that translation policy refers to "the dominant factors in the selection of the types and texts of imported texts through translation in a specific language and culture at a specific time" (Toury, 2001, p. 58). British translation theorist Jeremy Munday argues that compared with the concept proposed by Holmes, "translation policy is now more related to the ideology that influences translation" (Munday, 2001, p. 13). Belgian scholar Reine Meylaerts focuses on the official-level translation policy and defines it as "a set of laws and regulations used to regulate translation activities in public fields such as education, legal affairs, political institutions, administration, and the media" (Meylaerts, 2011, p. 165).

In China, since the beginning of this century, the academic circle has started to emphasize the importance of translation policy research (Liu, 2003; Wang, 2012a). Some scholars have studied the influence of ideology, sponsorship, and institutionalized translation on translation activities (Wang, 2003a, 2003b, 2006; Ren & Gao, 2015). Since 2008, specialized research on translation policies has gradually increased. For example, Teng (2008, 2013) and Zheng (2013) studied the translation policies since 1919 and after the founding of the People's Republic of China; Huang and Zhu (2012), Yang (2013), and Wang (2013) respectively studied the translation policies during the late Qing Dynasty, the translation policies of the Westernization Group, and the translation policies during Zhang Zhidong's tenure as the governor of Hubei. In addition, some scholars have studied the situation and trends of the translation research funded by the National Social Science Foundation of China (Zhang, 2015b).

In recent years, against the background of the "Going Global" of Chinese culture, scholars have studied the translation strategies, translator identities, dissemination effects, and the influence on American poetics and culture of various Chinese texts such as Chinese classics, Tang and Song poems, and contemporary literature translated and published in the West (especially in the United States) (Song, 2014; Tan et al., 2012; Shang & Gao, 2014; Wei, 2010; Ma, 2013; Ji, 2015; Ou & Hu, 2008). In addition, Gong et al. (2015) studied the translation funding projects of the National Endowment for the Humanities in the United States and believed that the United States has achieved the goal of enhancing its national language and cultural strength by funding the translation of texts from all over the world.

Looking at the research at home and abroad, although scholars have made beneficial explorations in translation policy research from both theoretical and practical aspects, there is a lack of specialized and forward-looking research on the translation policies for the Belt and Road Initiative.

9.5.2 Prospective Considerations on the Research Content of Translation Policies

In Chinese history, translation policies have played an indispensable role in translation activities. From the climax of Buddhist scripture translation in the Tang Dynasty, the translation of scientific and technological works by foreign missionaries in cooperation with Chinese translators during the late Ming and early Qing Dynasties, to the establishment of the Tongwen Academy (Interpretation Bureau) and the Jiangnan Arsenal by the Westernization Group in the late Qing Dynasty, all these translation activities were the products of the government's policies at that time. After the founding of the People's Republic of China, translation activities also showed the characteristics of serving politics, economy, and culture. In the early days of the People's Republic, the "leaning to one side" foreign policy led to a boom in the translation of Soviet and Russian works. Meanwhile, the ideological confrontation determined the relative decline in the Chinese translation of British and American works, especially literary works. Since the reform and opening-up, China has witnessed a new wave of translation. In particular, a large number of Western works have been introduced through translation, which has further promoted China's modernization process. The Belt and Road Initiative is a far-sighted initiative, and the research on the content of translation policies under the cultural dissemination of the Belt and Road is bound to have a certain degree of foresight. The translation policies under the cultural spreading of the Belt and Road should, from a macro-perspective, include legislation to regulate the translation market (industry access, pricing of royalties, standardization of translated names, evaluation criteria for translation quality), translation academic research, etc.; from a micro-perspective, it includes the establishment of translation institutions, translation planning (selection of translation materials, determination of key languages, translation projects, translation models, cultivation of translation talents, establishment of translation funds, selection of translation awards), etc.

The Translation Market Needs to be Regulated by Legislation

Since the proposal of the Belt and Road Initiative, there have been several English expressions for the term "一带一路", such as "One Belt, One Road", "Belt and Road", and "Land and Maritime Silk Road Programs". In 2015, the National Development and Reform Commission, together with the Ministry of Foreign Affairs and the Ministry of Commerce, standardized the English translation of "一带一路". The abbreviation of "一带一路" is translated as "the Belt and Road", with the English abbreviation "B&R", and the term "倡议" is translated as "initiative" in the singular form. The standardization of the translation of "一带一路" by national institutions has reversed the phenomenon of mis-translation and random translation in the market. Strategically, it has established the authority of national institutions in organizing and managing translated names and maintained a good image for the country's cultural dissemination abroad; tactically, it has facilitated the better dissemination of the translated name of the "一带一路" in the international community and among the countries along the route, making it easier for readers and the general public in the target languages to accept.

Since such prudence and rigor are required for the establishment of a single translated name, the standardization of the entire translation market and the evaluation of translation quality are even more systematic projects that need to be elevated to a certain level and draw the attention of relevant departments. In 2012, at the National Symposium on Translation Work and the 30th Anniversary Commemoration Conference of the Translators Association of China, Huang Youyi, a member of the National Committee of the Chinese People's Political Consultative Conference and the executive vice-president of the Translators Association of China, called for "legislative protection and industry access regulations for the translation industry" (Huang, 2012). The standardization of the translation market includes the establishment and improvement of a series of systems such as industry access, royalty pricing, copyright protection for translated works, qualification review of translation companies, evaluation and standards for translation quality. Legislative regulation of the translation market not only provides a guarantee for improving the quality of translation services but also enhances the overall social status of translation.

"Strengthening translation legislation is a legal guarantee for enhancing the country's cultural soft power. At present, China's translation legislation lags far behind, and translation services are unable to effectively transform the connecting role of translation between knowledge and power into a political advantage for enhancing the country's cultural discourse" (Wang, 2012a). Under the Belt and Road Initiative, with the increase in foreign cultural exchange activities and translation business volume, establishing supporting systems to provide guarantee measures for the healthy development of the translation market is a rational demand that conforms to the laws of the market economy at a certain stage of translation development.

In-Depth Academic Research on Translation Is Needed

Since the Belt and Road Initiative was proposed in 2013, most of the academic research on translation targeting countries along the Belt and Road has been based on macro-level discussions, and in-depth micro-level research has not been carried out. There is a lack of sufficient understanding of the politics, economy, culture and many other aspects of the countries along the Belt and Road, as well as little knowledge of the national conditions and cultural dissemination methods of the target-language countries. In addition, there is a significant knowledge gap regarding the dissemination and reception of translated works by domestic authors in these regions. Much of this research remains dormant, representing a vast, untapped "goldmine" with immense market potential and research value.

Currently, many case studies on the "going-out" of literary works focus on developed countries in Europe and the United States. There is even a lack of the most basic data statistics on the translated works in "minor languages" for countries along the Belt and Road, not to mention the analysis of their dissemination and reception in the corresponding countries. As the practice of the Belt and Road Initiative deepens, translation academic research should shift from focusing on developed countries with strong cultural dissemination capabilities to the developing countries along the Belt and Road. How to better disseminate Chinese culture in the countries along the Belt and Road and tell Chinese stories well will also become the direct orientation of translation academic research. Relevant government departments and academic publishing institutions should launch more research projects and topics on Belt and Road translation, provide more financial support, conduct more thematic studies, enrich research results, and offer insights for the formulation of translation policies.

Translation Alliance and Overseas Cooperation Should Be Strengthened

Translation institutions play a crucial role in the entire translation activities. As Zhu (2014) pointed out, translation institutions function between the government and translators. They are not only the executors of translation policies but also the bridges connecting translators and the government, playing an indispensable role in relaying the public's concerns to the government and in the process of policy-making and implementation. In recent years, some scholars have recognized the necessity of establishing specialized translation institutions. Teng Mei believes that it is an urgent task to establish a National Translation Institute (Ying, 2014). Zhu Yongxin, the vice-chairperson of the Central Committee of the China Association for Promoting Democracy and the vice-president of the Chinese Education Society, proposed to quickly form a "national team" for translation (Zhu, 2014). He suggested establishing a "National Translation Institute" integrating translation and research functions, improving relevant systems, and incorporating translation work into the academic evaluation system to attract more talents to the translation cause.

In July 2014, the China Academy of Translation Studies was established in Beijing. Zhou Mingwei, the first president, stated that the establishment of the China Academy of Translation Studies is also an urgent need to better serve the national strategy, enhance international communication capabilities, and expand the international influence of Chinese culture. One of the main tasks of the academy is to integrate domestic and foreign translation talents, especially high-end translation resources in minor languages, and provide a platform for the exchange, cooperation, and career development of high-end minor-language talents" (Ying, 2014).

The Belt and Road Initiative calls for the establishment of targeted translation institutions. These institutions should not only provide a basis for relevant government departments and industry associations to formulate policies and development plans but also establish a high-end Chinese-to-foreign translation talent database to offer basic services for the "going-out" of Chinese culture and truly build a bridge for cultural exchanges between countries.

Relying solely on the China Academy of Translation Studies is insufficient. It is necessary to integrate existing resources and form an "alliance" for cultural translation and research on countries along the Belt and Road by combining the efforts of research centers in higher education institutions, publishing houses, cultural communication companies, media, and overseas "Confucius Institutes". This alliance should form a strong aggregating and radiating force to meet the needs of national cultural dissemination.

Currently, many universities have established research centers in line with the national strategic goals, such as the China-Arab Research Institute at Ningxia University, the Institute for the Construction of the Core Area of the twenty-first-Century Maritime Silk Road at Fuzhou University, the Arab Research Center and the China Belt and Road Strategy Research Institute at Beijing International Studies University, the English-Chinese-Portuguese Language Laboratory jointly established by Macao Polytechnic University and GTCOM, the Silk Road Language Service Collaborative Innovation Center at Xi'an International Studies University, the China International Discourse System Research Institute at Sichuan International Studies University, the China International Image Research Center at Shanghai Jiao Tong University, the China Diplomatic Discourse Research Center at Zhengzhou University, and the Belt and Road Language and Culture Communication Strategy Research Center at Nanjing University of Science and Technology (Huang, 2017b). Universities, through a "bottom-up" approach, actively explore and respond to the national "top-down" development goals. They can form an "alliance" for cultural dissemination along the Belt and Road, improve the alliance's charter, clarify rights and responsibilities, and hold regular academic conferences to serve the country's cultural dissemination.

The translation alliance targeting the Belt and Road Initiative should not only strengthen academic research but also enhance cooperation with countries along the route to promote the better dissemination of Chinese culture in these countries. The experiences of many countries have provided mature models for China. "The French Ministry of Culture allocates special funds to set up a 'Translation Prize Fund'. Each year, it invites about thirty outstanding translators from around the world to visit France for two months. They can bring their translation research or projects and have direct exchanges with relevant writers, publishers, or research experts... The French government also acts as a bridge, providing various assistance for exchanges between Chinese and French publishers, Chinese translators and French writers, and literary institutions" (Xu, 2001).

To ensure the more effective dissemination and acceptance of Chinese culture in countries along the Belt and Road, it is crucial to take into account the cultural environment of the target-language countries and the psychological acceptance of target-language readers. This requires leveraging the strength of Sinologists and translators in Belt and Road countries and seeking cooperation with translation and publishing institutions in these countries to better disseminate Chinese culture and Chinese stories and avoiding negative effects such as "narrow readership, narrow dissemination channels, and inadequate market research" (Geng, 2014). It is also worthy of attention that cultural dissemination should attach importance to cooperation between cross-border media, which has been almost ignored in previous translation research.

The communication influence of the Belt and Road Initiative depends on the media's dissemination channels, methods, and capabilities. Currently, the promotion of the Belt and Road Initiative mainly relies on domestic media for self-promotion. While relying on self-efforts, it is equally important to seek external support and cooperate fully with media in Belt and Road countries to identify appropriate dissemination channels and explore effective dissemination methods tailored to local conditions through various means such as print media, television, radio, the Internet, and social media. In seeking overseas cooperation, the government should not only provide financial and material support but also play the role of a bridge and a link.

Comprehensive Planning Is Required for the Cultivation of Translation Talents

The cultivation of translation talents for the Belt and Road Initiative falls within the scope of "education planning". The cultivation of minor-language translation talents necessitates a comprehensive consideration of the cooperation dynamics between China and countries along the Belt and Road. Starting from cooperation needs, exchange programs, and key languages, multiple approaches should be taken simultaneously: firstly, emphasizing training initiatives; secondly, prioritizing volunteer services; and thirdly, focusing on the establishment "minor-language" majors in universities and the formulation and implementation of talent cultivation programs. The training of "minor-language" translation talents can draw on the strength of non-governmental organizations. It is necessary not only to provide opportunities for foreign-language majors in domestic universities to receive "minor-language" training and education but also to attract international students and young scholars from countries along the Belt and Road to actively learn Chinese, so as to reserve translation talents. Valuing volunteer services means selecting outstanding student volunteers from majors such as minor-language and international education in Chinese as a foreign language in domestic universities to provide short-term Chinese teaching services in countries along the Belt and Road. Cooperation can be carried out between Confucius Institutes and middle schools in these countries to offer Chinese elective courses in middle schools and provide Chinese teaching services. This not only provides opportunities for college students to participate in national cultural dissemination and gain practical experience but also helps cultivate potential translation talents in countries along the Belt and Road through young people's dissemination of Chinese culture and values.

9.5.3 Significance of Research on Translation Policies

The people-to-people bond among the countries along the Belt and Road depends on the understanding, communication and integration of different cultures. Translation serves as an invisible bridge for cross-cultural exchanges. Under the Belt and Road Initiative, the translation and spreading of cultures are presented with unprecedented opportunities and challenges. Not only has the volume of translation work increased, but the countries targeted for translation also represent a diverse array of cultures, encompassing a wide range of languages. The content of translation has shifted from purely literary works to more application-oriented materials. In order to better promote Chinese culture, enabling it not only to "go global" but also to "go deep" in other countries, the formulation of translation policies at the national level is indispensable. As stated in *The Book of Rites: The Doctrine of the Mean*, "Forewarned is forearmed; to neglect planning is to court failure." Positive translation policies can standardize, stimulate and mobilize a country's translation activities, thus promoting the prosperity of the translation industry. It is a common political practice in the modern international community for governments to effectively supervise and guide translation behaviors and the translation industry through translation policies.

Unlike the strategy of promoting Chinese culture to European and American countries, there are still many unforeseen difficulties in promoting Chinese culture to the countries along the Belt and Road. Most of the Belt and Road countries are developing nations, and our in-depth understanding of these countries varies. Each country has different economic, social, and cultural needs, so the existing experience cannot necessarily be directly replicated and applied. Through forward-looking research on translation policies for the Belt and Road, on one hand, it is necessary to clarify the research fields and objects, boldly predict the potential challenges that Chinese culture may face when going global, summarize the experience and lessons, and propose methods and steps to solve the problems, so as to provide decision-making references for formulating scientific and reasonable translation policies.

On the other hand, promoting Chinese culture globally is a systematic project that involves not only translation activities but also cultural dissemination. It encompasses multiple stakeholders such as government agencies, industries, academic institutions, and media. Therefore, it is urgent to establish a comprehensive system for researching translation policies at the national policy level. This requires not only macro-level framework construction for the systematic research, integrating the multiple stakeholders and summarizing the potential problem areas in cultural translation and dissemination, but also in-depth micro-level refinement to clarify the specific responsibilities of each stakeholder and break down the "barriers" between different entities to achieve positive interaction and effective cooperation.

The formulation and implementation of translation policies are practical endeavors that should be based on social realities and fully consider a series of cultural factors in the target countries, including national conditions, public sentiment, customs, and rule of laws. As China's economic and trade exchanges with Belt and Road countries become increasingly frequent, cultural communication and integration will surely deepen, and translation activities targeting these countries will also become more diverse. In the future, we can collaborate with Sinologists, university scholars, and media institutions in Belt and Road countries to conduct in-depth micro-level research on the dissemination effect of Chinese culture in these countries. By employing more quantitative research methods, we can analyze the dissemination effect of translated Chinese cultural products in these countries, summarize the laws and experiences of cultural dissemination, and then feed this back into the formulation of translation policies. In this way, we can truly build a cultural bridge to promote people-to-people bonds between countries.

9.6 Chinese Translation Planning

Translation planning is an extension and manifestation of translation policies and the specific implementation of translation legislation. The theory of translation planning can provide a theoretical basis for the formulation of translation policies and regulations. Language planning is generally divided into "status planning, corpus planning, and prestige planning". Meanwhile, it is believed that translation planning encompasses discourse planning, status planning, education planning, and spreading planning.

"The international cultural strategic order refers to the relatively stable international cultural power relations regarding the right to speak, voice, and dominance of countries in global cultural affairs under certain international circumstances (Chen, 2015b, p. 7)." The power of discourse is the result of cultural strategic competition and game-playing among countries and groups of countries. Discourse planning aims to establish, consolidate, and strengthen China's cultural discourse power in the Belt and Road countries through translation activities. "Meeting the needs of foreigners and demonstrating our cultural confidence ultimately boils down to establishing China's international discourse power (Hu, 2011)."

Translation planning should be carried out through a series of planned and systematic activities, including translation material selection, key language selection, translation projects, translation models, and translation talent cultivation. When formulating translation policies, we should not only serve political purposes but also fully consider the national conditions, public sentiments, social cultures, and customs of the target countries. For the selection of translation materials for Belt and Road countries, we should give full play to international cooperation and market research, and determine the content of cultural dissemination based on the actual needs of readers in the target countries. The formulation of translation policies should not be carried out in isolation. We should know ourselves and our counterparts, truly achieve "people-to-people bond", and then "prescribe the right medicine".

"The first issue that a country's foreign language education policy needs to address is the selection of foreign languages (Zhang, 2012, p. 34)." The United States formulated the "Critical Languages Initiative" in 2006. The "critical languages" in translation planning refer to the relatively important official and non-common languages in Belt and Road countries. According to the statistics of Wang Hui and Wang Yalan, "Among the 65 countries along the Belt and Road, there are 53 official languages belonging to nine language families, with rich language resources and complex language situations (Wang &Wang, 2016)." Apart from English, French, Spanish, Russian, and Arabic, the number of talents proficient in other "minor languages" is very limited. Current translation activities cannot cover all 53 official languages, nor is it necessary to do so. We need to identify "critical languages" and highlight the key points.

The implementation of translation projects can effectively promote translation activities and facilitate cross-cultural communication. "The state has launched many translation-related projects, such as the 'Translation and Publication Project of Chinese Cultural Works', the 'China Book International Promotion Plan' and the 'Classical China International Publishing Project' led by the National Press and Publication Administration and the State Council Information Office, the 'National Social Science Foundation Project for the Translation of Chinese Academic Works Abroad', the 'Dubbing Project for Film and Television Works', and the 'Silk Road Film and Television Bridge Project' led by the Publicity Department of the CPC Central Committee." Among them, the 'Silk Road Film and Television Bridge Project' is directly related to the Belt and Road Initiative. In addition, projects such as the 'Standardization Project for the Translation of Chinese Political Discourse Abroad', the 'Dissemination Project of Chinese Ideological and Cultural Terms', and the 'China Keywords' project are also in progress (Huang, 2017a)."

Translation models involve technical issues such as translator selection and translation methods. Without excellent translators to translate works into foreign languages, the communication and influence of these works in foreign countries will be affected. In the process of spreading Chinese culture, involving foreign writers, translators, and publishing institutions can also promote better spreading of works in the target countries.

9.6.1 *Content of Chinese Translation Planning for the Belt and Road Initiative*

Under the Belt and Road Initiative, translation serves as a bridge for Chinese culture to "go global". Translation activities involve multiple entities such as the state, the government, translation agencies, publishers, translators, and the media, thus necessitating strategic planning. Translation planning is not only a linguistic act but also a cultural one, mainly encompassing four aspects: discourse planning, status planning, education planning, and spreading planning.

Discourse Planning

Cultural discourse power reflects a country's soft power and comprehensive national strength. The display of cultural discourse power on the international stage cannot be achieved without the intermediary role of translation. The countries along the Belt and Road feature diverse cultural traditions, religious beliefs, rule of laws, and social customs, presenting significant differences from China's cultural system. "As the 'voice' of cultural discourse power, the success of translation culture and research not only symbolizes a country's cultural communication and dissemination capabilities but also concerns its political and cultural stances, as well as its influence and say on the international stage" (Xu & Wang, 2017, pp. 77–78). The introduction of foreign cultures and the dissemination of Chinese culture overseas are two different approaches. The former aims at learning and exchange, while the latter is more about expanding influence and reversing China's relatively "weak" influence in countries along the Belt and Road to gain a certain degree of "discourse power".

As a cultural exchange activity, the fundamental value of translation lies in enabling literary and cultural works to "transcend" into the target language's discourse system through translated versions, gaining understanding and acceptance from readers, and fostering a sense of cultural identity and inclusivity. Under the goal of cultural "going global", discourse planning in translation planning includes the research of discourse systems, the selection and determination of core values, core cultures (or key cultures) and their carriers (such as literature, film, television, and art), as well as language planning. The research of discourse systems and country-specific studies require the integration of multi-faceted forces, even the involvement of overseas scholars and relevant academic research forces.

"Core culture" refers to the classic works of thought, culture, literature, film, television, and art that best represent the core values of Chinese culture. By promoting these as the brand representatives of Chinese culture, China can gain a certain influence in international communication and hold a certain discourse power in world culture. Language is the carrier of culture and the external manifestation of cultural expression. The core of discourse planning in translation planning lies in the establishment of "critical languages", which determine the audience, targets, and scope of influence for Chinese culture to "go global".

Status Planning

The core of translation status planning is to legislate for translation. It aims to regulate the translation market through laws and regulations, enhance the social status of translation, and safeguard the quality and reputation of translation services. Currently, there is a social consensus on translation legislation, which has even attracted a certain level of media attention. Many scholars have written articles proposing to standardize, supervise, and manage the translation market through legislation, improve translation quality, strengthen the qualification of translation practitioners, and establish a translation access system (Guo, 2010, p. 36; Huang, 2011, p. 30; Xie, 2011). Translation is an important means of cultural communication and spreading in the era of globalization. Strengthening translation legislation serves as a legal guarantee for enhancing a country's cultural soft power (Wang, 2012b, p. 60). Some have introduced the legislative practices of the German translation industry to provide references for China's translation legislation (Jiang et al., 2012, pp. 49–50).

The project report titled "Formulation of Policies for the Development of the Language Service Industry and Service Trade", commissioned by the Ministry of Commerce from the Translators Association of China in 2013, was rated as an excellent research project by the Ministry of Commerce. It clearly proposed legislation for translation (China Translators Association Website, 2013).

From a "society-institution" perspective, interdisciplinary investigations have been carried out to theoretically elaborate on the necessity, feasibility, and operability of language service legislation (Zhao & Kou, 2017, p. 4). In 2015, the China Academy of Translation Studies commissioned China Accreditation Test for Translators and Interpreters to conduct a "Research Project on Translation Legislation". The "Feasibility Research Report on Translation Legislation" has been approved by the experts of the China Academy of Translation Studies (www.catticenter.com, 2016). In addition to legislative regulation of the translation market, translation status planning also includes increasing translation royalties, incorporating translation into the academic evaluation system, and setting up national-level or government-level awards for translation.

Education Planning

The "going global" of culture and the translation of literary and cultural works hinge on the availability of outstanding translators. Therefore, cultivating outstanding translation talents is the focus of translation education planning. There are relatively few studies on the cultivation of minor-language translation professionals. Most of the existing studies use "foreign language education" and "foreign language disciplines" as keywords. For example, scholars have explored discipline development strategies from aspects such as discipline planning, cross-cultural talent cultivation, international academic discourse power, quality of translated products, overseas resource construction, teacher professional development, and expansion of cultural dissemination channels. These studies provide certain insights for further promoting the development of foreign language disciplines in China, facilitating the overseas promotion of culture, and enhancing cultural soft power (Dai & Wang, 2015, p. 1). The provision and teaching of minor languages in the foreign language education system are often overshadowed by English. Whether from the perspective of globalization, ecological balance, or the dissemination of Chinese culture, minor-language courses should be reasonably arranged in the entire foreign-language education system. Based on the strategic transformation tasks of national foreign-language ability construction in four aspects: strategic orientation, ability requirements, resource types, and resource quality, suggestions have been put forward to strengthen foreign-language planning and formulate countermeasures and construction plans to support the Belt and Road Initiative (Shen, 2015, p. 9).

Foreign-language teaching is not equivalent to translation teaching, and foreign-language talents are not necessarily translation talents. Learning a foreign language does not guarantee the ability to become a translator. The content of translation education planning includes systematic indicators such as market research, professional setup, talent cultivation, faculty development, teaching material development, curriculum construction, and quality standards and evaluation for talent cultivation.

Spreading Planning

Whether Chinese culture can be well-disseminated abroad largely depends on the communication channels and the acceptance psychology of the audience. The field of cultural communication has increasingly attracted the attention of scholars. The "going global" of culture cannot solely rely on Chinese people who learn foreign languages for translation. The selection of Chinese and foreign translators and the cooperation with foreign publishing institutions have gradually received more attention. For example, Xie (2013) directly proposed that it might be advisable to invite foreign assistance when translating and introducing literary works. Wang & Xie (2013, p. 22) argued that for the successful "going global" of Chinese literature and culture, various factors such as the authors, translators, and sponsors must be comprehensively considered.

Huang Youyi pointed out that since the volume of translated and published works is large, foreigners should be employed in various forms for translation or polishing. Regardless of the form, whether self- sourced or publisher-facilitated partnerships, a manuscript must be jointly worked on by a Chinese and a foreigner before publication (Jia, 2017, p. 112). Hu (2013, p. 21) believed that a misunderstanding in the "going global" of culture is self-unilateralism, that is, ignoring or underestimating other communication forces. Geng (2014, p. 77), taking the "Panda Series" as a case study to examine its acceptance process in the American cultural system, found that the series had "a narrow readership, limited readership channels, and insufficient market research". He then proposed that government-sponsored translation and introduction should recognize the laws of foreign translation and introduction of literature, and summarize experiences and lessons. Zhou Mingwei, Director of the China Foreign Languages Publishing Administration, pointed out in his speech at the inauguration ceremony of China Academy of Translation Studies that "in the practice of 'Chinese-to-foreign' translation, the translation of literary works will rely more on the role of foreign translation experts. Their ability to re-create in the process of literary translation is is unparalleled by our own efforts" (Zhou, 2014, p. 6). Translators are the spokespersons of cultural communication. They are both the subject and the medium of communication. The spreading planning of translation includes not only the communication subject (the selection of foreign translators and cooperation with foreign publishing institutions) but also the communication purposes, contents, media, thinking, targets, structures, channels, audience, effect, and environment. The spreading planning of translation requires comprehensive and overall consideration, thus featuring comprehensiveness and holistic perspective.

9.6.2 Research Framework for Chinese Translation Planning

It is believed that to systematically construct a research framework for China's translation planning that adapts to the Belt and Road Initiative, it is necessary to combine the characteristics of the Belt and Road construction. With the goal of meeting the need of "people-people bonds", and based on four dimensions of planning, namely discourse planning, status planning, education planning, and spreading planning, the main levels and specific language-related problem areas of the Belt and Road translation planning research should be determined from three levels: macro, meso, and micro levels.

Main Participants

Translation planning is an extension and manifestation of translation policies and the specific implementation of translation legislation. The theory of translation planning can provide a theoretical basis for the formulation of translation policies and regulations. The formulation and implementation of any major plan involve the cooperation of multiple parties, including government departments, non-governmental organizations, social forces, and individuals. Li (2013, p. 86) argues that the basic operating mechanism of domain-specific language planning should be that the industry's competent departments "take charge", the state's functional departments provide guidance, and expert teams offer academic support. Dong (2015, p. 41) divides the main levels of language planning in the field of Chinese law into three levels: the national level, the industry level, and the academic level. A strategy for cultural "going global" is incomplete without considering communication channels and methods, and it also depends on the full cooperation of the media. The main body of translation planning consists of four levels: the national level, the industry level, the academic level, and the media level.

"For thousands of years, it has been a common cultural-political practice in the international community for governments to exercise effective supervision and guidance over translation activities through translation policies (Teng, 2013, p. 4)." State functional departments are responsible for formulating the overall strategies and plans for the cultural "going-global" initiative, enacting laws and regulations related to translation, and ensuring the authority of these laws and regulations. Meanwhile, government functional departments serve as a communication link. They integrate translation resources, connect translation institutions and organizations, establish cooperation mechanisms between Chinese and foreign translation industries and media, and build a bridge for communication.

The translation industry has a wide scope, encompassing translation associations, translation companies, and publishing institutions. Industry guilds are mainly responsible for conducting market research on translation in countries along the Belt and Road, providing reasonable grounds for legislation, and drafting relevant laws and regulations. They are also in charge of core tasks such as selecting critical languages for countries along the Belt and Road, planning, selecting, and publishing literary and cultural works, and determining translators and publishing institutions. Moreover, they integrate high-end translation talents and provide basic services for translation. "Translation institutions operate between the government and translators. They are not only the executors of translation policies but also the bridges connecting translators and the government, playing an indispensable role in the process of transmitting policies from top-down and in policy formulation and implementation (Teng, 2013, p. 115)."

Translation research associations, Belt and Road research institutions established in universities, translation scholars, as well as doctoral students, postgraduate students, and some undergraduate students are all components of the academic level. Currently, many universities are serving the national cultural strategy by establishing Belt and Road research centers. For example, there are the China-Arab Research Institute at Ningxia University, the Institute for the Construction of the Core Area of the twenty-first-Century Maritime Silk Road at Fuzhou University, the Arab Research Center at Beijing International Studies University, the China Belt and Road Strategy Research Institute, the "Chinese-English-Portuguese Language Laboratory" jointly established by Macao Polytechnic University and GTCOM, the "Silk Road Language Service Collaborative Innovation Center" at Xi'an International Studies University, and the "Research Center for the Belt and Road Language and Culture Communication Strategy" at Nanjing University of Science and Technology. The establishment of these Belt and Road research centers in universities, with the combined efforts of scholars, doctoral students, and postgraduate students, provides intellectual support for the formulation of translation plans and policies from an academic perspective.

In terms of the structure of communication, the media includes not only domestic media but also foreign media. Through Sino-foreign cooperation, domestic media jointly explore effective communication forms with local media in countries along the Belt and Road. In terms of communication media, books, newspapers, radio, television, the Internet, etc., are all effective means of cultural "going global". The content of communication should focus on China's core values and core culture while also taking into account the actual cultural needs and acceptance psychology of the target-language countries. National government agencies should play the role of a bridge in the communication and cooperation between Chinese and foreign translators and between different media.

Problem Domains

Language serves as a link for connectivity among countries along the Belt and Road, and translation acts as a bridge for cultural exchanges between nations. With the process of globalization and China's rapid development, translation services are gradually going international.

Firstly, as the Belt and Road Initiative is being steadily advanced, China and the countries along the route are gradually engaging in closer communication and cooperation. This will directly place translation services under the "spotlight". The translation industry will face new opportunities and challenges, and the demand for translation services will be greater and more extensive than ever before.

Secondly, the Belt and Road Initiative demands a diverse range of translation languages. As China's comprehensive national strength in society, economy, culture, etc., continues to grow and its international status rises, China needs to actively adapt to these changes, participate in international cooperation and competition, and expand its overseas interests. The previous strategy dominated by "bringing in" must be transformed into one of "going global". As Shen (2015, p. 10) put it, "Chinese culture should 'go global', spread China's voice, tell China's stories well, and build an international discourse system that integrates Chinese and foreign elements to serve as a 'bridge' for China to connect with the world in the new Belt and Road pattern." Statistics show that there are 65 countries along the Belt and Road, involving 53 official languages belonging to nine major language families (Wang & Wang, 2016, p. 13). The rich language resources, complex language situations, and diverse language-service needs in the countries along the Belt and Road pose higher requirements for translation.

Thirdly, the international cultural dissemination is extending from simple literary translation to applied fields. According to Li (2011), "The key areas of the cultural industry should include cultural creativity, film and television production, publishing and distribution, printing and reproduction, advertising, performing arts and entertainment, cultural exhibitions, digital content, and animation industries." In the past, due to the single-dimensional development of culture, the "going out" of culture mainly relied on literary translation. With the diversification of the cultural industry, the connotation and extension of cultural dissemination have expanded, and the requirements for translation content in cultural dissemination have become more diverse.

Fourthly, machine translation is presented with new opportunities. With the development and application of translation software, questions like "Will the translation industry be replaced by artificial intelligence in the future?" have become widespread. As technology continues to innovate, articles that are pessimistic about the future of translation are prevalent. It must be recognized that machines can indeed handle low-level, repetitive, and translation tasks in some specific fields. However, in high-level, high-quality, and creative humanistic translation, such as literary and cultural translation, machines can never replace human translators. Since readers always have high demands for translation quality, the cultivation of advanced translation talents will never become obsolete.

Basic Principles

The implementation of any major project relies on meticulous planning, and all plans should adhere to certain principles. Guided by a set of concepts and ideas, specific planning tasks can be accomplished. The principles of translation planning serve as the criteria and starting points for ensuring scientific decision-making and reasonable planning. The main participants in the planning are not only the formulators of the plan but also the main force in its implementation.

Scientific and reasonable translation planning and translation policies must be based on comprehensive and thorough research. Currently, there is a lack of basic information about the countries along the Belt and Road. The understanding of their infrastructure construction, political systems, and cultural characteristics is rather limited. As Chu and Chai (2015, p. 55) pointed out, "Whether in Southeast Asia or Central Asia, many are Islamic countries. Some of them are relatively conservative and have numerous cultural taboos unfamiliar to Chinese enterprises." Compared with the knowledge of the cultural characteristics of European and American countries, the understanding of the cultures of the Belt and Road countries is still rather scarce. "A great deal of information can only be obtained through on-the-spot and down-to-earth research. This requires us, on the one hand, to strengthen country-specific studies and dispatch more researchers to gather data locally. On the other hand, we should promptly collect and integrate the information obtained by private sectors going abroad" (Chu, 2015a). Translation planning involves many aspects, such as the construction of core cultures and values, the setting of translation projects, the selection of cultural and literary classics, the choice of translation languages, and the cultivation of minor-language talents. It requires a comprehensive understanding of the needs of target-language countries, as well as domestic economic, trade, and political cooperation with them. Without solid research, scientific decision-making is unattainable. During the research process, the main participants in translation planning, especially industry associations, translation agencies, and academic research centers in universities, should play an active role. They should conduct on-site inspections in the Belt and Road countries instead of making plans behind closed doors and being divorced from reality".

The complexity and diversity of political, economic, and cultural differences among countries along the Belt and Road necessitate targeted translation planning that avoids blindness and proposes categorized strategies for rational planning. The needs of different regions and countries vary. In the cooperation fields with the Belt and Road countries, such as infrastructure construction, trade, tourism, communication, and traditional Chinese medicine, there are different focuses. Due to ethnic feuds, interest conflicts, cultural frictions, and religious barriers, there are five major risks in the Belt and Road regions, namely, "security risks, political risks, economic risks, legal risks, and social risks" (Chu & Chai, 2015, p. 51). Facing this complex situation, the "going global" of Chinese culture requires precise positioning, tailoring content and strategies to the actual needs of countries along the route, and fully considering cultural differences, political diversity, national security, and the complexity of the public opinion environment. Finally, targeted, reasonable, and well-directed translation plans should be formulated. The formulation of translation plans cannot be mature and perfect at once. It always needs to go through the process of practice-inspection-revision. Whether a plan is reasonable and can achieve effective goals can only be tested by practice, and it should be further revised and improved in practice. The "going global" of Chinese culture should not rely on a one-size-fits-all approach but should be implemented through pilot projects, gradually expanding from point to area to enhance the radiating power and influence of Chinese culture.

Under the Belt and Road Initiative, the "going global" of culture also involves reconstructing China's cultural strategic order in countries along the route. "The international cultural strategic order is the result of cultural strategic competition and strategic games between countries and country groups (Hu, 2011, p. 36)." Due to the complexity of cultural strength and influence among the countries along the route, China's current cultural dissemination in these countries is still in a "weak position." In the context of globalization, the dissemination, penetration, communication, and integration of different national cultures, as well as the contention for discourse power, exhibit both coexistence and strong competitiveness. Therefore, the formulation of translation plans needs to reflect certain competitive strategies.

The goal of telling China's story well under the Belt and Road Initiative is to enhance understanding of China among countries along the route and to increase their recognition and acceptance of Chinese culture and values. However, many countries still have misunderstandings about China, and some even view the Belt and Road Initiative as a form of "conquest" over them. "I asked local students in Kazakhstan: Why do you have such a strong opinion about China? Currently, newspapers in Kazakhstan are discussing how long it would take for China to conquer Kazakhstan. Their conclusion is: China can conquer Kazakhstan in 42 minutes, as stated in the newspapers (Chu, 2015b)." The essence of "going global" of culture is to enhance the recognition of Chinese values among countries along the route. The prerequisite for "people-to-people bonds" is to strengthen mutual understanding, which necessitates equal dialogue and communication.

"The implementation of any policy cannot be achieved without the cooperation and participation of the entire society. These prescriptive requirements not only need top-down national guidance but also bottom-up acceptance and participation from the public (Luo, 2015, p. 95)." The translation planning involves four levels of stakeholders. They are both participants in formulating the plan and specific executors, and they need to be proactive and engage in full-scale participation. Moreover, the legislative standardization of the translation market not only requires the participation of non-governmental organizations in research but also the implementation and operation of laws and regulations are based on a general consensus reached by the whole society. "In fact, the role of statutory law is not omnipotent in any society." "Even if the government enacts laws, these laws and regulations cannot immediately enter the activities of all actors and play an actual regulatory role just because they are promulgated (Su, 1996, p. 102)." "The coordination and cooperation of all aspects of society are also indispensable. Moral ideals, science and culture, and legal education are important aspects,constituting what is termed 'comprehensive governance' (ibid.:120)." To ensure that the translation planning progresses towards the established goals, extensive social consensus needs to be reached at all levels. Only with a comprehensive and rational understanding of translation policies and plans can a favorable social environment be created for the implementation of translation planning. The promulgation of laws and regulations should also stimulate the enthusiasm and initiative of all stakeholders, enabling the translation planning to be implemented more effectively. The top-down promotion by the state also requires bottom-up interaction and cooperation from the non-governmental sectors.

9.7 Conclusion

The current international situation is undergoing profound changes, and human civilization development is confronted with numerous challenges. China is now situated within the strategic context of the great rejuvenation of the Chinese nation and the once-in-a-century global changes. Under the leadership of the Communist Party of China, the Chinese people have blazed a new path of rule of law modernization with Chinese characteristics. To help the international community understand the Chinese path and the Chinese governance model, and to transform China from a "major translation country" to a "powerful translation country", translation plays a strategic supporting role in the construction of the country's international rule of law discourse capacity, which is essential for meeting the needs of human civilization development and promoting exchanges between Chinese and foreign rule of law civilizations.

In response to the new circumstances and requirements, it is essential to adhere to the guidance of Xi Jinping Thought on the Rule of Law, leverage global cooperation and exchange platforms such as the Belt and Road Initiative, and prioritize enhancing the country's international rule of law discourse capacity. With unwavering determination and perseverance, translation should be harnessed to propel the great rejuvenation of the Chinese nation and amplify the international influence of Chinese legal culture.

Firstly, it is crucial to strengthen the planning of rule of law discourse and construct a rule of law discourse system with Chinese characteristics. To present a true, multidimensional, and comprehensive image of China to the world, an international discourse and narrative system that bridges Chinese and foreign perspectives is indispensable, with translation playing a pivotal role in bridging differences in values and linguistic cultures between China and other countries. Efforts should be made to enhance the translation and interpretation of Chinese rule of law ideological theories, its rule of law paths and systems, and its policy proposals on global rule of law governance, creating more internationally disseminated public products like "Key Terms of Chinese Rule of Law". Timely research and publication of standardized translations for crucial rule of law terms and sensitive rule of law discourse should be conducted to firmly grasp the primary right of definition and the final interpretative authority in the international dissemination of Chinese rule of law discourse. By fully leveraging linguistic advantages to engage in international communication, it is essential to extensively promote the Chinese concepts and propositions of the new path of rule of law modernization with Chinese characteristics, striving for understanding and recognition from the international community and thereby elevating China's international legal discourse power.

Secondly, formulate reasonable translation policies. A country's international discourse capacity does not merely refer to the ability of language conversion, nor is it simply the ability of an individual or an institution. Instead, it is a concentrated manifestation of a country's overall capacity in the field of translation. It is a comprehensive capacity to construct international rule of law discourses, conduct rule of law cultural dissemination, and shape the country's rule of law image through translation activities. The formulation of national translation policies covers various fields such as the construction of translation talent teams, the establishment of international discourse systems, the layout of crucial language construction, the research and development and application of translation technologies, the organization and coordination of major translation projects, and the management and service of the translation industry. It also involves all aspects including the government, the market, and the industry. It serves as an important guarantee and support for a country's language capacity building and cultural soft power.

Thirdly, strengthen translation planning and enhance the fundamental role of translation in Chinese rule of law discourse dissemination system. With the continuous enhancement of China's comprehensive national strength and international influence, the international community has an unprecedented expectation for China's voice and solutions. The role of translation in discourse transformation and international communication has become even more prominent. The international communication of Chinese rule of law discourses should be oriented towards bridging the gap between China and the rest of the world. The international communication of Chinese rule of law discourse should aim to bridge Chinese and foreign perspectives, contributing significantly to enhancing international communication capabilities and shaping trustworthy, respectable, and friendly image of a country under the rule of law through rigorous logic, precise expression, and vivid international discourse.

In conclusion, the situation determines the tasks, and the mission guides the future. In the new era, China must adhere to Xi Jinping Thought on the Rule of Law as the guide. Centering on the strategic needs of national initiatives such as the Belt and Road Initiative and the "going global" of culture, China should strengthen top-level design, pool the strength of all parties, adhere to upholding the correct orientation while making innovations, highlight key tasks, and strive to create a new situation for the international communication of Chinese rule of law discourses. This will contribute significantly to promoting the global spreading of Chinese rule of law culture and making greater contributions to building a community with a shared future for mankind.

References

Cai, M. (2017). On China's legal discourse power and its construction. *Legal Review, 26*, 1–4.

Chen, J. (2015a). Seize the opportunity of the "Belt and Road" to enhance international rule of law discourse power. *People's Rule of Law, 11*, 5.

Chen, Z. (2015b). *An introduction to language planning*. The Commercial Press.

China Translators Association Website. (2013). *The research project "Formulation of policies for the development of the language service industry and service trade" was rated as "excellent" by the Ministry of Commerce*. http://tac-online.org.cn/ch/tran/2013-12/19/content_6554185.htm

Chu, Y. (2015a). *The "Belt and Road" strategy must take "people" as the decisive factor*. http://views.ce.cn/view/ent/201502/02/t20150202_4489472.shtml.

Chu, Y. (2015b). *What the local people along the "Belt and Road" care about is what the Chinese really want*. http://pit.ifeng.com/a/20151027/46014429_0.shtml

Chu, Y., & Chai, P. (2015). Plan ahead for the five major risks of the "Belt and Road". *Financial Viewpoint (Wealth), 6*, 52–55.

Cooper, R. L. (1989). *Language planning and social change*. Cambridge University Press.

Dai, W., & Wang, X. (2015). The development strategy of China's foreign language and literature discipline under the background of "culture going global". *Journal of PLA University of Foreign Languages, 4*, 1–11, 159.

Dong, X. (2015). Research on language planning in the legal field: Problems and methods. *Foreign Language Teaching: Theory and Practice, 4*, 37–43.

Dong, X. (2018, June 26). Legal translation contributes Chinese wisdom to global governance. *China Social Sciences Journal,* 003.

Dong, X. (2021). Rule of law discourse planning: A new task of language planning in the legal field in the new era. *Journal of Lüliang University, 11*(5), 17–21.

Du, J., Zhang, F., & Yuan, L. (2004). Problems and solutions in English translation of Chinese laws and regulations. *Chinese Translators Journal, 25*(3), 72–76.

Feng, W. (2012, December 21). The situation and improvement of legal discourse. *People's Court Daily*.

Feng, Y. (2019, December 6). The rule of law is an important support for the country's governance system and governance capacity. *Guangming Daily*.

Geng, Q. (2014). An exploration of the effects of the government-led translation and introduction model for Chinese literature going global. *Chinese Comparative Literature, 1*, 66–77.

Gong, X., Qin, J., & Shen, Q. (2015). An analysis of the translation-related project grants of the US National Endowment for the Humanities since 1980. *Foreign Language Teaching and Research, 1*, 119–129.

Gu, H. (2016). Research on Chinese rule of law in the co-construction of the "Belt and Road". *Journal of Hunan University of Finance and Economics, 02*, 92–104.

Guo, X. (2010). The development situation, problems and countermeasures of China's language service industry. *Chinese Translators Journal, 6*, 34–37.

Haugen, E. (1968). Language planning in modern Norway. In J. Fishman (Ed.), *Readings in the sociology of languages*. Mouton de Gruyter.

Holmes, J. (1988/2000). The name and nature of translation studies. In L. Venuti (Ed.), *The translation studies reader*. Routledge.

Hu, H. (2011). Several issues in the current development of China's cultural strategy. *Hundred Schools in Arts, 6*, 36–43.

Huang, L., & Zhu, Z. (2012). Discussions on translation policies in the late Qing dynasty. *Chinese Translators Journal, 3*, 26–33.

Huang, Y. (2011). Promote translation legislation to promote the healthy development of the translation industry. *Chinese Translators Journal, 3*, 29–30.

Huang, Y. (2012, December 6). *The translation industry urgently needs legislative protection and industry access regulations*. http://news.china.com.cn/txt/2012-12/06/content_27333484.htm

Huang, Y. (2017a, March 10). *Suggestions for translating major Party and government documents in advance and releasing Chinese and foreign language versions simultaneously*. http://www.china.com.cn/fangtan/2017-03/10/content_40437337.htm

Huang, Y. (2017b, April 27). *The "Belt and Road" and Chinese translation*. http://www.yeeworld.com/article/info/aid/10512.html

Ji, S. (2015). Chinese translators and the "entry into the United States" of Li Qingzhao's ci poems: English translation and inspiration. *Journal of Huaibei Normal University (Philosophy and Social Sciences Edition), 2*, 94–98.

Jia, H. (2017). Research on the promotion path of the external translation of Chinese cultural classics. *Foreign Language Research, 4*, 110–114.

Jiang, A. (2015). Experts and scholars discuss the rule of law thinking and legal services for the "Belt and Road". *China Justice, 01*, 17.

Jiang, L., Wang, H., & Yan, L. (2012). The path of translation industry legislation in China: Lessons from Germany. *Chinese Translators Journal, 4*, 49–52.

Li, H. (2017). Legal experts and lawyers share insights: How judicial cooperation safeguards the "Belt and Road". *China Lawyer, 6*, 60.

Li, X. (2011, November 21). Promote the cultural industry to become a pillar industry of the national economy. *Economic Daily*.

Li, Y. (2013). On domain-based language planning. *Journal of Huazhong Normal University (Humanities and Social Sciences), 3*, 86–92.

Li, Y. (2018). New situations in language planning research. *Language Resources and Intelligence*, (2).

Li, Y., & Wang, C. (2019). On functional classification of languages. *Contemporary Linguistics, 21*(1), 1–22.

Liao, M. (2008). *A study on the standardization of legal language*. Law Press.

Liu, J. (2015). The legalization of the "Belt and Road" construction and the responsibilities of the people's courts. *People's Rule of Law, 11*, 18–20.

Liu, M. (2003). *Translation teaching: Practice and theory*. China Translation and Publishing Corporation.

Liu, R., & Cui, G. (2010). *Selected readings of modern linguistics classics* (Vol. 2). Foreign Language Teaching and Research Press.

Luo, L. (2015). On the translation policy as a national cultural strategy. *Shandong Foreign Language Teaching Journal, 2*, 91–97.

Ma, H. (2013). The current situation and problems of the translation of modern and contemporary Chinese literature in the English-speaking world. *Chinese Translators Journal, 1*, 64–69.

Meylaerts, R. (2011). Translation policy. In Y. Gambier & L. van Doorslaer (Eds.), *Handbook of translation studies* (Vol. 2). John Benjamins Publishing.

Munday, J. (2001). *Introducing translation studies*. Routledge.

Qu, W. (2012). Reflections on the problems and causes of Chinese legal terms translation and the standardization of translated legal terms in recent years. *Chinese Translators Journal, 33*(6), 68–75.

Qu, W. (Ed.). (2018). *Legal translation studies*. Shanghai People's Publishing House.

Ou, H., & Hu, A. (2008). Text travel and classic construction-The canonization of Han Shan's poems in American translated literature. *Chinese Translators Journal, 3*, 20–25.

Ren, D., & Gao, Y. (2015). Translation institutionalization and institutionalized translation. *Chinese Translators Journal, 1*, 18–23, 126.

Ruiz, R. (1984). Orientations in language planning. *NABE: The Journal for the National Association for Bilingual Education, 8*(2), 15–34.

Shang, H., & Gao, R. (2014). A review of the research on the art of war in the United States in the past century. *Journal of Binzhou University, 5*, 58–66.

Shen, Q. (2019). *China's foreign language planning from the perspective of global governance*. Foreign Language Teaching and Research Press.

Song, X. (2014). On the "deep translation" tendency in classical Chinese translation-taking three English translations of the Doctrine of the mean in the early 21st century as examples. *Foreign Language Research, 6*, 939–948.

Su, L. (1996). *Rule of law and its native resources*. China University of Political Science and Law.

Sun, J. (2019). The shaping and promotion path of China's international discourse power-taking China's diplomatic practice since the 18th National Congress of the Communist Party of China as an example. *World Economics and Politics, 03*, 21–45 + 158.

Tan, X., Ames, R. T., & Hall, D. L. (2012). The translation of the Doctrine of the mean and American pragmatism. *Chinese Translators Journal, 4*, 75–79.

Teng, M. (2008). *A preliminary study on China's translation policy issues since 1919*. Fudan University.

Teng, M. (2013). *Research on China's translation policy*. China Renmin University Press.

Teng, M. (2014). Research on translation policy and its reference significance for contemporary China. *Shanghai Journal of Translators, 1*, 35–39.

Toury, G. (2001). *Descriptive translation studies and beyond*. Shanghai Foreign Language Education Press.

Wang, D. (2003a). An invisible hand-on the manipulation of ideology on translation practice. *Chinese Translators Journal, 5*, 16–23.

Wang, H., & Wang, Y. (2016). Language situations in countries along the "Belt and Road". *Language Strategy Research, 2*, 13–19.

Wang, K. (2012a). *Research on foreign language education abroad*. Foreign Language Teaching and Research Press.

Wang, L. (2012b). Legal guarantee for a culturally powerful country: Thoughts on strengthening China's translation legislation. *Chinese Translators Journal, 6*, 60–63.

Wang, Y. (2003b). Ideology and the history of Chinese translation literature in the 20th century (1899-1979). *Chinese Translators Journal, 5*, 11–15.

Wang, Y. (2006). The issue of sponsorship in Chinese translation. *Chinese Translators Journal, 3*, 15–20.

Wang, Y. 2013. Research on the translation policy during Zhang Zhidong's tenure in Hubei (1889–1907).: Centre for Translation Studies, The Chinese University of Hong Kong.

Wang, Z., & Xie, T. (2013). Chinese culture and literature going global: Problems and essence. *Academic Monthly, 2*, 21–27.

Wei, J. (2010). The translation ethics of Burton Watson's English translation of the book of songs. *Journal of Dalian Maritime University (Social Science Edition), 3*, 96–100.

Wen, Q. (2016). National discourse research-a new field serving national strategies. *China Foreign Language, 06*, 1–3.

Wu, Y., & Gu, Y. (2019). The connotation and planning of the country's foreign discourse strategy. *Applied Linguistics, 4*, 44–53.

Xiao, J., & Zhang, X. (2017). The "Belt and Road" and international rule of law: Opportunities, new issues and interaction strategies. *Theoretical Exploration, 03*, 32–37.

Xie, T. (2011, June 21). *It's time to legislate for translation*. http://www.chinanews.com/cul/2011/06-21/3127055.shtml

Xie, T. (2013). *January 10*. It's advisable to invite foreign experts to translate literary works.

Xu, J. 2001. Characteristics of the introduction and translation of French literature in the 20th century in China. Contemporary Foreign Literature, 2: 80–89.

Xu, J. & Wang, Q. 2017. An analysis of the current situation of legal translation research based on corpora: Problems and countermeasures. Foreign Language Research, 1: 73–79.

Yang, W. (2013). *On the translation policy of the westernization group in the late Qing dynasty and the translation activities of the Imperial polytechnic institute*. Sichuan International Studies University.

Zhang, W. (2015a). An investigation of the current situation of translation research in China-based on the statistics and analysis of the National Social Science Foundation projects (2000–2013). *Foreign Language Teaching and Research, 1*, 106–118.

Zhang, Y. (2015b). How to understand the grand strategic design of the "Belt and Road". *World Affairs, 2*, 25–31.

Zhang, Z. (2012). China's "key languages". In R. Zhao (Ed.), *Foreign languages and foreign language policies from the perspective of National Strategies*. Peking University Press.

Zhang, Q., & Zhang, F. (Eds.). (2019). *Language and law studies (2019.1)*. China University of Political Science and Law Press.

Zhao, J. 2015, May 13. The interaction and enlightenment between international rule of law and domestic rule of law. *Guangming Daily*.

Zhao, J., & Kou, Y. (2017). An investigation and analysis of the current situation of legislation in China's language service industry. *China Foreign Language, 1*, 4–10.

Zheng, Y. (2013). *The relationship between national policies and the external translation of Chinese literature-Taking Chinese Literature (1951–2000) as an example*. Sichuan International Studies University.

Zhou, M. 2014. Build an international-oriented translation talent team to promote Chinese culture going global. Chinese Translators Journal, *5*, 5–6.

Zhu, Y. (2014, May 28). We need a "national team" for translation. *China Youth Daily*.

Zhu, Z. (2017). Accelerate the construction of a Chinese-characteristic legal discourse system. *China University Teaching, 05*, 27.

Chapter 10
The Enhancement of the Spreading Ability of Chinese Rule of Law Discourse

10.1 Introduction

Currently, the global governance system is undergoing profound changes. Globalization has not only reshaped the international political landscape but also accelerated the interaction and collision among the legal systems of different countries, and triggered fierce competition for international discourse power. Since the founding of the People's Republic of China, the course of Chinese rule of law construction has not only been a process of exploration, deepening and international spreading of Chinese rule of law practice system but also a process of enlightenment, expansion and construction of international rule of law discourse power for Chinese rule of law discourse system. Against the backdrop of the profound changes unseen in a century, the international spreading of Chinese rule of law discourse is not only a strategic necessity for enhancing the country's soft power but also an important practice in constructing a new model of international rule of law cooperation. Leveraging the Belt and Road Initiative as a platform, China is promoting a shift in rule of law cooperation from "unilateral output" to "bilateral mutual construction". The rule of law thoughts conveyed in Chinese rule of law discourse not only lay a solid foundation of rules for the Belt and Road construction but also reshape the discourse coordinate system of global governance in the mutual learning of civilizations. This spreading strategy, which combines subjectivity and inclusiveness, is the underlying logic of the construction of Chinese rule of law soft power in the new era. To tell the story of Chinese rule of law well and firmly grasp the discourse power in Chinese rule of law construction, it is imperative not only to construct a rule of law discourse system with "Chinese characteristics, Chinese style, and Chinese grandeur" but also strengthen the spreading of rule of law discourse. "Only through effective spreading can excellent culture give full play to its influence and appeal and be transformed into the country's 'soft power'" (Pan, 2013). As an embodiment of excellent legal culture, rule of law discourse also needs

X. Dong, M. Zhang, *Chinese Rule of Law Discourse System*, Understanding China, https://doi.org/10.1007/978-981-95-6260-2_10

to be effectively spread to fully exert its influence. Effective spreading of rule of law discourse is a necessary prerequisite and important guarantee for realizing the functions and values of rule of law discourse. For China, which is approaching the center of the world stage, strengthening the construction of rule of law discourse spreading and telling the story of Chinese rule of law well is a major task at present.

10.2 Significance of International Spreading of Chinese Rule of Law Discourse

President Xi Jinping emphasized, "It is imperative to vigorously enhance the capacity for international communication, strengthen the construction of discourse systems, and focus on creating new concepts, categories, and expressions that bridge China and the outside world, thereby increasing our discourse power on the international stage" (Yin, 2024). Strengthening the international spreading of Chinese rule of law discourse is a crucial measure to enhance China's international influence in the rule of law field and promote the development of global rule of law civilization, holding significant importance both theoretically and practically.

At the theoretical level, the international spreading of Chinese rule of law discourse contributes to the construction of a legal theory system with Chinese characteristics, enriches the international rule of law discourse system, and fosters innovation in international relations theory. By spreading Chinese rule of law concepts, practices, and achievements to the international community, it promotes the innovation and development of Chinese legal theory, aligning it more closely with China's national conditions and the demands of the times. For instance, Xi Jinping Thought on the Rule of Law, as the core content of Chinese rule of law discourse, not only showcases China's achievements in rule of law construction to the world through its international spreading but also provides new theoretical resources for the development of global rule of law civilization (Zhang & Chen, 2024(1): 54–57). In international relations, rule of law discourse serves as a vital form of soft power, influencing interactions and cooperation among nations. For a long time, the West has dominated the international rule of law discourse system, to some extent, shaping the cognitive framework of the international community regarding the rule of law. The spreading of Chinese rule of law discourse can break this entrenched dominant pattern, offering a different perspective and approach from Western rule of law discourse, thereby enriching the diverse theories of international law. By spreading Chinese rule of law discourse, new perspectives can be provided for international relations theory, emphasizing the importance of the rule of law in international relations and promoting a shift in international relations theory from traditional power politics to rule of law-based politics (Zhang & Sun, 2023(5): 17–32).

At the practical level, the international spreading of Chinese rule of law discourse aids in enhancing China's international discourse power, serving national development strategies, promoting foreign-related rule of law construction, and facilitating international rule of law exchanges and cooperation. With the continuous enhancement of China's comprehensive national strength and a significant rise in its international status, the international community's attention to and expectations for Chinese rule of law system have also increased, providing a rare historical opportunity for the international spreading of Chinese rule of law discourse. By showcasing China's achievements, concepts, and experiences in rule of law construction to the international community, it can promote exchanges and cooperation between Chinese rule of law system and those of other countries worldwide, thereby enhancing China's international discourse power. Through rule of law dialogues with countries around the world, China can absorb and learn from beneficial international rule of law experiences while introducing its rule of law concepts and practices to the international community, fostering the development of global rule of law civilization. Chinese rule of law system serves national development strategies, necessitating active participation in the transformation of global governance. This requires enhancing China's discourse power and influence in international affairs through the international spreading of rule of law discourse. For example, in the context of the Belt and Road Initiative, proactive spreading of Chinese rule of law discourse can lay a solid legal foundation for participating countries, effectively promoting international cooperation and fully stimulating regional economic development vitality.

In the new era, as China strides towards the center of the world stage and achieves remarkable accomplishments in its rule of law construction, ranging from scientifically sound legislation to fair and efficient law enforcement and judicial practices, and the gradual strengthening of the public's belief in the rule of law, a rule of law system with Chinese characteristics has been established. How to enhance the capacity for international spreading of Chinese rule of law discourse, effectively communicate these achievements to the international community, shape a positive and proactive image of Chinese rule of law system, and elevate the international influence of Chinese rule of law discourse has become an urgent and important issue to address.

10.3 Planning the Spreading Strategy with "One Break and One Establishment"

"One break" means to break the Western world's stereotyped and misinterpreted perception of Chinese legal culture. In the field of translating Chinese legal culture, especially in the translation and spreading of ancient cultural classics, Western professional Sinologists have long dominated, while Chinese scholars entered this field much later. Therefore, breaking the Western scholars' monopoly on the translation and spreading of Chinese rule of law culture and firmly grasping the initiative in the translation and introduction of Chinese rule of law civilization can help improve the cultural misunderstandings and misinterpretations that occur during the translation process by foreign translators. It can objectively restore the true features of Chinese rule of law civilization, promote the international community's acceptance and recognition of Chinese rule of law civilization, and lay a solid ideological foundation for creating a favorable external environment for the great rejuvenation of the Chinese nation. Meanwhile, it is conducive to reversing the international community's one-sided and stereotyped impression of Chinese rule of law civilization, eliminating the long-accumulated institutional prejudices, actively spreading the core values of Chinese rule of law civilization, and promoting equal exchanges between Chinese rule of law civilization and other rule of law civilizations.

"One establishment" refers to innovating the discourse presentation mode for the external spreading of Chinese rule of law civilization and enhancing the ability of external rule of law discourse. General Secretary Xi Jinping (2019) pointed out that "Chinese culture belongs not only to history but also to the present, and it is not only national but also global." To tell the story of Chinese rule of law well and ensure that the world hears, clearly perceives, and comprehensively understands Chinese rule of law voice, the following steps should be taken: Firstly, promote the exchange and mutual learning between outstanding Chinese legal culture and other ethnic cultures to highlight the civilized connotations and global significance of the Chinese-style modernization of the rule of law. Secondly, carry forward the essence of outstanding traditional Chinese culture, and encourage cultural products that embody Chinese values, spirit, and wisdom to go global. Showcase the common values of all humanity contained in outstanding traditional Chinese legal culture, and shape a more trustworthy, amiable, and respectable image of Chinese rule of law. Thirdly, innovate the rule of law discourse system, make good use of new media technologies, and promote the global, regional, and targeted expression of Chinese rule of law civilization and Chinese rule of law stories, continuously improve the effectiveness and appeal of the international spreading of Chinese legal culture. Fourthly, build new platforms for international cooperation, deepen international cultural exchanges, and promote both domestic rule of law and foreign-related rule of law in a coordinated manner, enabling the world to understand the new path of Chinese-style modernization of the rule of law.

10.4 Constructing a Spreading System by Strengthening Top-Level Design

The international dissemination of Chinese rule of law discourse is a systematic project involving basic elements such as spreading subjects, contents, and media. These elements form an organic and unified whole. They coordinate with each other around the achievement of the goal of international dissemination of Chinese rule of law discourse and jointly play their roles. General Secretary Xi Jinping (2021) pointed out when presiding over the 30th collective study session of the Political Bureau of the 19th CPC Central Committee that "we must strengthen top-level design and research layout, construct a strategic spreading system with distinct Chinese characteristics, and strive to enhance international spreading influence and the appeal of Chinese culture".

Firstly, it is essential to delve deeply into Chinese legal culture. General Secretary Xi Jinping stated that "we should better promote the spread of Chinese culture abroad, use culture to convey ideas, spread voices, and influence people, and present to the world more excellent cultural works that embody Chinese characteristics, spirit, and wisdom". To strengthen the capacity building of Chinese rule of law discourse and enhance the spreading power and influence of Chinese rule of law civilization, in-depth exploration of Chinese legal culture should be carried out in terms of spreading content. Chinese culture has a long history, and outstanding traditional Chinese legal culture is an important source of its growth. Chinese civilization is extensive and profound, and Chinese legal civilization is an important part of it. On June 2, 2023, General Secretary Xi Jinping pointed out at the Symposium on Cultural Inheritance and Development that "there are many important elements in outstanding traditional Chinese culture, which together shape the prominent characteristics of Chinese civilization". These prominent characteristics include outstanding continuity, innovation, unity, inclusiveness, and peacefulness. In the new era and on the new journey, to continuously enhance the country's cultural soft power and the influence of Chinese culture, it is imperative to uphold our cultural confidence, adhere to the position of Chinese culture, strive to extract and display the spiritual symbols of outstanding traditional Chinese legal culture, and actively promote the spread of Chinese legal civilization abroad.

Secondly, it is imperative to construct a spreading system for rule of law discourse with Chinese Characteristics. In the new era, while China has significantly enhanced its international discourse power and influence, it also confronts new circumstances and tasks. The overall situation where Western countries dominate international public opinion remains unchanged. Only by constructing a strategic spreading system with distinct Chinese characteristics can China effectively coordinate resources and forces, give full play to the collective effect, and strive to enhance international spreading influence, the appeal of Chinese legal culture, the affinity of China's image, the persuasiveness of Chinese rule of law discourse, and the guiding power of international public opinion. Constructing a strategic spreading system with distinct Chinese characteristics is a systematic project that requires systematic thinking and overall planning. Firstly, the international spreading of Chinese legal civilization not only requires the strong promotion of official media but also the active participation of non-official forces. The coordinated cooperation among spreading subjects can effectively improve the effect of the international spreading of Chinese rule of law civilization. Currently, the participation of non-official forces in the international spreading of Chinese legal civilization needs to be further improved. Therefore, in the process of continuously promoting the international spreading of Chinese rule of law civilization, on the basis of giving full play to the role of national mainstream media and other forces, China should further enhance the awareness of non-official spreading subjects such as the public and cultural enterprises in spreading Chinese rule of law civilization, give full play to the advantages of different spreading subjects, increase the integration of different spreading subjects, and pool the strength of multiple subjects for the international spreading of Chinese rule of law civilization. Secondly, it is crucial to forge a media cluster with international influence. Particularly by creating world-class new-type mainstream media with strong leadership, spreading power, and influence. By adopting precise spreading methods tailored to different audiences, China can promote the global, regional, and targeted expression of Chinese stories and voices, and enhance the affinity and effectiveness of international spreading. Thirdly, it is important to give better play to the role of high-level experts, and leverage important international conferences, forums, and mainstream foreign media as platforms and channels to voice our opinions. Emphasis should be placed on harnessing the role of overseas Chinese, Chinese-funded enterprises overseas, and international friends in international spreading. It is imperative to employ the strategies and art of international public opinion struggle, make more friends, unite and win over the majority, seize the initiative in international public opinion, and consciously safeguard the dignity and image of the Party and the country. Fourthly, China should make good use of international spreading platforms. When inspecting China Central Television, General Secretary Xi Jinping emphasized that "we should make good use of international dissemination platforms to objectively, truthfully, and vividly report on China's economic and social development, spread Chinese culture, and tell Chinese stories well". Thirdly, establish a talent team support mechanism to meet the needs of international spreading of Chinese civilization in the new era. A high-quality spreading talent team serves as the intellectual support for enhancing the international spreading power and influence of Chinese rule of law civilization. In the construction of the talent team for the international spreading of Chinese rule of law civilization, on the one hand, it is essential to improve their professional competence and strengthen practical training. On the other hand, a talent incentive mechanism should be established to effectively stimulate the innovative vitality of talents engaged in the international spreading of Chinese civilization, strengthen the capacity for national legal translation, and promote the sustainable development of the talent team responsible for the international spreading of Chinese rule of law civilization. Fourthly, establish and improve an evaluation and feedback mechanism for the international spreading effect of Chinese rule of law civilization. Conducting objective and scientific evaluation and feedback on the international spreading effect of Chinese civilization helps to promptly identify the problems and deficiencies in the spreading process, adjust and optimize spreading strategies in a timely manner, and enhance China's international rule of law discourse ability.

10.5 Enriching Spreading Theories through In-Depth Academic Research

To tell the story of Chinese rule of law civilization well, showcase its long-standing history and humanistic heritage, and enable the world to understand China, the Chinese people, and the Chinese nation, the key lies in clarifying fundamental issues such as the spiritual essence, contemporary value, and global significance of Chinese rule of law civilization, so as to arouse emotional resonance among the audience. In-depth academic research on Chinese rule of law civilization can provide strong theoretical support for this.

First of all, China should strengthen cultural confidence. Through multi-disciplinary, multi-perspective, and all-round academic research on Chinese rule of law discourse, China can provide spreading materials with strong explanatory power for the international spreading of Chinese rule of law civilization and continuously enrich the content of its international spreading. On the one hand, China needs to summarize the experience and wisdom of Chinese rule of law civilization, refine the Chinese legal principles of outstanding traditional Chinese legal culture, deeply interpret the spiritual essence of Chinese civilization, and extract the spiritual symbols and cultural essence that can represent Chinese legal civilization. In this way, China can provide spreading materials with distinct Chinese characteristics and styles for the international spreading of Chinese rule of law civilization. On the other hand, through academic research, China should dig deep into the value elements with world-wide significance contained in Chinese rule of law civilization. The modernization of the rule of law in China has created a new form of human rule of law civilization. Peace and development are among the Chinese characteristics of the modernization of the rule of law in China. Promoting the construction of a community with a shared future for mankind is an essential requirement of the modernization of the rule of law in China. The common values of all mankind are the theoretical cornerstone for building a community with a shared future for mankind and also the value requirement throughout the entire process of the modernization of the rule of law in China. In the face of the era's question of "What's wrong with the world and what should we do?", it is imperative to vigorously promote the common values of all mankind, strive to create new concepts, new categories, and new expressions that integrate Chinese and foreign cultures, provide support for the rule of law discourse in promoting the international spreading of Chinese rule of law civilization, and contribute Chinese wisdom and Chinese solutions to global legal governance.

Secondly, strengthen the construction of Chinese rule of law think tanks. The rule of law is a country's core competitiveness. As the world enters a period of turbulence and transformation, international discourse competition is increasingly manifested as competition over systems, rules, and laws. It is crucial to strengthen the construction of the foreign-related legal system, improve the efficiency of foreign-related law enforcement and justice, and resolutely safeguard national sovereignty, security, and development interests. In the process of cultural exchanges, academic exchanges play a unique and valuable role in promoting cultural exchanges. It is necessary to build a number of high-level and leading Chinese rule of law think-tanks, present high-level academic exchange results to the international academic community, and engage in dialogue with it, so as to deepen the international spreading of Chinese rule of law civilization.

In addition, we should be good at leveraging the spreading approach of setting international topics and proactively set topics related to the spreading of Chinese rule of law discourse. "The setting of international topics is not only a direct manifestation of the strength of international discourse power but also an important way to compete for international discourse power" (Zhang, 2012). As a large country with a vast territory, a large number of ethnic groups, complex national conditions, and a population of over 1.4 billion, China has blazed a socialist path of the rule of law with Chinese characteristics. Practice has proven that this path has strong advantages in achieving economic development, political integrity, cultural prosperity, social justice, and ecological well-being. It can be said that China has abundant topic materials for setting international topics in the field of rule of law construction. Therefore, China should have the confidence to "go global", actively participate in international exchanges on rule of law construction, and proactively set relevant international topics to guide the international community to pay attention to the socialist rule of law discourse with Chinese characteristics. Of course, "the proposal of international topics fundamentally stems from the perception of international discourse needs by the academic community and think-tanks" (Zhang, 2012). We should be good at combining the development situation of the international community with the requirements for spreading the socialist rule of law discourse with Chinese characteristics to put forward international topics related to rule of law construction that can attract the attention of the international community.

Furthermore, to enhance the spreading ability of Chinese rule of law discourse, it is necessary to further strengthen the research on the communication science of rule of law discourse. As a product of rule of law culture, the spreading of rule of law discourse belongs to cross-cultural communication. The research on cross-cultural communication originated in the United States in the late 1940s, which was the result of the change in the global pattern after World War II and the global expansion of Western countries led by the United States. The academic community in China did not start research in this area until the 1980s. At present, China's research on cross cultural communication "is still in its initial stage" (Sun, 2015). As a result, the relevant research on the communication science of Chinese rule of law discourse is relatively weak and has not been able to provide strong academic support for the spreading of rule of law discourse. For example, in the study of the audience in communication science, in the era of the geometric growth of information explosion, it has a significant impact on the communication effect. "Only original, distinctive, and attractive communication content is valuable to the audience" (Zhang & Zhou, 2006). Currently, the spreading of the socialist rule of law discourse with Chinese characteristics lacks an audience-oriented awareness and has deficiencies in targeting the audience. Its spreading methods still mainly remain at the level of "paternalistic" political propaganda, lacking the transformation of spreading methods and strategies from the perspective of the audience. With the continuous development of communication technology, especially the rise of new Internet media, the spreading methods and patterns of rule of law discourse are undergoing radical changes. Therefore, traditional media and spreading methods need to be upgraded according to the new situation. Therefore, it is of great significance to strengthen the research on the communication science of Chinese rule of law discourse. At present, research should be problem-oriented to substantially solve the problems in the process of rule of law discourse spreading, such as the social interaction and recognition of rule of law discourse, the research on the cognitive system and psychology of rule of law discourse, and the adaptability and spreading ability of rule of law discourse. By strengthening the research on the communication science of Chinese rule of law discourse, an academic research foundation can be laid for the effective spreading of rule of law discourse.

10.6 Innovating Spreading Channels by Building an Omnimedia Matrix

Whether the international spreading of Chinese rule of law civilization can be carried out in a form that foreign audiences are willing to accept and easily understand directly affects the effectiveness of the international dissemination of Chinese rule of law discourse. Currently, the continuous emergence of emerging technologies has brought about profound changes in international spreading platforms. Facing the significant changes in media technology, the public opinion ecosystem, and the media landscape, strengthening international communication capabilities requires seizing the new opportunities brought by the development of advanced information technologies. It is necessary to accelerate the layout of new-type spreading platforms, actively use information technologies such as 5G in news spreading practices, continuously improve the spreading efficiency of media content, and form a multi-channel and precise international spreading system. Firstly, it is crucial to correctly recognize the tool attributes of social media and big-data algorithms, actively develop the applications of technologies such as 5G, artificial intelligence, big data, and cloud computing in international spreading, expand the platforms, channels, and terminals for international spreading discourse, and build an integrated matrix for omnimedia international spreading discourse. By presenting the content of Chinese civilization in a multi-modal way, and enriching the presentation forms of Chinese civilization, more foreign audiences can understand and recognize Chinese rule of law civilization in a way that they are willing to accept and easily understand. Secondly, it is necessary to accelerate the construction of mobile-end spreading platforms, innovate diversified information release forms such as short videos, micro-videos, cloud live-broadcasts, and voice broadcasts. We should encourage more international friends to share "the rule of law in China as I see it" to better showcase the profound Chinese legal culture to the world. Thirdly, it is imperative to study and master the development trends of spreading platforms, promote the all- round iterative upgrading of spreading strategies, and create more immersive and interactive news products that audiences love. Through new forms, means, and channels, the spreading power and influence of Chinese rule of law discourse can be further enhanced. Fourthly, it is vital to strengthen the core role and value-leading awareness of China's mainstream flagship media for international spreading. Establishing a deeply integrated linkage mechanism, accurately positioning the target audience of international spreading discourse, providing omnimedia products that better meet the needs of overseas regional audiences can facilitate a localized expression of Chinese voices. Fifthly, enriching the omnimedia product forms of international spreading discourse and providing intelligent, mobile, and personalized product forms that conform to the characteristics of social media can innovate China's international rule of law discourse system through omnimedia construction and effectively enhance the effectiveness of international spreading.

In conclusion, under the current development trends of international spreading towards mobility, socialization, and visualization, exploring the application of emerging technologies such as big data and artificial intelligence in the innovation of the presentation forms of Chinese rule of law discourse in international spreading has become an inevitable requirement for enhancing the international spreading power and influence of Chinese rule of law discourse.

10.7 Cultivating a Talent Team for Spreading Chinese Rule of Law Discourse

Enhancing the professional level of rule of law discourse means that those who tell the story not only need to have a solid empirical foundation in the legal field but also possess knowledge beyond the law. The cultivation of rule of law talents is an important part of the systematic project of comprehensively governing the country by law. The theoretical foundation of the rule of law in China lies in making efforts in theory and education (Xi, 2020: 174–175). It is necessary to build a research team with a solid theoretical foundation, clear research directions, rich academic qualities, and a distinct Chinese stance. This team should always serve the strategic needs of the country and society, respond to the forefront of domestic and international practices, and realize its academic value in the process of thinking and providing suggestions for the cause of the country, the nation, and the people. A research team with high-level, high-quality, and high-responsiveness capabilities should be established.

First, the construction of the talent team should always adhere to the national stance as the starting point. In the process of building the research team, it is always emphasized that there should be a sense of subjectivity, presenting "China in concepts", "China within theories", "China in writings", and "China in the media". This requires all members of the legal community to pay attention to Chinese practices, care about China's present and future. All practical topics discussed should revolve around China's development, and all suggestions provided should focus on China's future.

Second, the construction of the talent team should focus on the forefront of practice. When considering questions related to the discourse of foreign-related rule of law, it is necessary to pay attention to the world pattern and the overall environment that China faces in the international community, and explore the responses brought about by China's stance and actions in the international community. Therefore, the summary and induction of theories must be firmly based on the forefront of practice, rather than a process that goes from books to books, from theories to theories, and from textual explanations to textual explanations.

Third, in the process of building the talent team, it is necessary to promote the cultivation of rule of law talents with theoretical discussions as the key. Regarding the practical experiences and lessons accumulated by the West and China in foreign-related rule of law, especially in aspects such as economy, environment, human rights, and the use of force, it is necessary to provide academic explanations and elaborations, and finally incorporate them into teaching materials and other teaching contents, transforming them into long-term and continuous talent-cultivation content, thus promoting the systematic and disciplinary construction of theories. That is, to summarize the experiences formed in practice, use the laws summarized from them as basic theoretical assertions, and on the basis of these assertions, conduct cross-era, cross-regional, and cross-cultural comparisons with peers from different regions, and finally accumulate them into a disciplinary system.

Fourth, the construction of the talent team should emphasize the discourse system as the anchor point. The expression of the rule of law discourse in China should take socialist rule of law with Chinese characteristics and foreign-related rule of law as the research fields, aiming to condense, think about, and build the discourse system of Chinese-characteristic rule of law and foreign-related rule of law. Therefore, the observation, sorting, and refinement of practice aim at conducting reflective discussions and critical analyses of the existing discourse, then refining it into theories, activating theories into discourse, and transforming knowledge into discourse, while paying attention to the spreading characteristics of rule of law discourse, so as to serve the improvement of the country's international image and overall reputation.

10.8 Conclusion

In the era when the profound transformation of the global governance system is intertwined with the once-in-a -century changes, the construction of the international spreading capacity of Chinese rule of law discourse has become the core strategic fulcrum for enhancing the country's soft power and building a new model of international rule of law cooperation. This chapter systematically explains the theoretical connotations, practical paths, and institutional guarantees of the international spreading of Chinese rule of law discourse, and constructs a complete six-dimensional collaborative analytical framework of "significance—ideas—system—theory—approach—talent", providing theoretical guidance and a practical blueprint for enhancing the international spreading capacity of Chinese rule of law discourse in the new era.

From the perspective of strategic significance, the international spreading of Chinese rule of law discourse has profound theoretical innovation value and practical empowerment effects. In the theoretical dimension, through the spreading of Chinese rule of law concepts, practical achievements, and institutional innovations, it promotes the construction of the theoretical system of Chinese-characteristic jurisprudence and the reconstruction of the international rule of law discourse system, breaks the long-standing Western-dominated international rule of law cognitive framework, and provides a new perspective for the transformation of international relations theory from power politics to rule of law politics. As the core carrier of the discourse, Xi Jinping Thought on the Rule of Law not only demonstrates the institutional achievements of Chinese rule of law construction but also contributes original theoretical resources to the development of global rule of law civilization. In the practical dimension, the spreading of rule of law discourse promotes the formation of international rule of law influence commensurate with China's comprehensive national strength by enhancing international discourse power, serving the country's development strategy, and promoting the construction of foreign-related rule of law. Especially in the construction of the Belt and Road Initiative, China consolidates the rule-based foundation through rule of law cooperation, realizes cultural exchanges through a two-way interactive communication strategy, reshapes the global governance discourse coordinate system, and demonstrates a soft-power construction logic that combines subjectivity and inclusiveness.

In terms of spreading strategies, the dialectical thinking of "One break and one establishment" forms the methodological basis. "One break" aims to break through the Western dominance on the misinterpretation of Chinese legal culture. By strengthening the dominant position of Chinese scholars in the translation of legal classics, it objectively restores the true features of Chinese rule of law civilization, eliminates institutional prejudices, and promotes equal dialogue. "One establishment" focuses on the innovation of the way of discourse expression. Through the empowerment of new media technologies, it realizes global, regional, and segmented expressions, integrates outstanding traditional Chinese legal culture with the common values of all mankind, and shapes a trustworthy, respectable and friendly image of Chinese rule of law. This combination of breaking and establishing not only responds to the structural challenges of the Western-dominated international communication but also reflects an open attitude of cultural exchanges.

The construction of the communication system emphasizes the systematic nature of top-level design. By deeply exploring the content production of Chinese legal culture, extracting spiritual symbols that reflect Chinese spirit and wisdom, creating a media cluster with international influence, and building a multi-subject collaborative communication network. Official media and non-governmental forces work together. High-level experts voice their opinions through international conferences and mainstream foreign media platforms, and overseas Chinese, Chinese-funded enterprises and other groups form a communication synergy. At the same time, a spreading effect evaluation and feedback mechanism is established to form a closed-loop management system of "communication—evaluation—optimization" to ensure the dynamic adaptability of communication strategies.

Academic research provides in-depth theoretical support for communication. Through interdisciplinary research, it explores the spiritual essence and contemporary value of Chinese rule of law civilization, extracts legal elements of world significance, and constructs a new concept system that bridges China and the rest of the world. The construction of rule of law think tanks strengthens the ability to set agendas, actively proposes international issues that reflect China's practical experience in rule of law construction, and guides the international community to pay attention to the path of Chinese-style modernization of the rule of law. Communication studies focus on cutting-edge issues such as audience psychology, social interaction, and cognitive systems, solve practical problems such as insufficient communication effectiveness and outdated methods, and promote the dual innovation of communication theory and technology.

The innovation of communication channels relies on the digital transformation of the all-media matrix. The in-depth application of technologies such as 5G, artificial intelligence, and big data promotes the innovation of communication platforms, forming a multi-modal, immersive, and interactive all-media communication ecosystem. The construction of mobile platforms strengthens new content forms such as short videos, micro-videos, and cloud live-broadcasts to achieve precise and localized expressions. Mainstream media play a core leading role, and through in-depth integration mechanisms, they build a regional and segmented all-media product system to enhance the affinity and persuasiveness of international communication.

The construction of the talent team is the fundamental guarantee for capacity improvement. Through a four-dimensional mechanism guided by national stance, focused on the forefront of practice, deepened by theoretical discussions, and anchored by the discourse system, it cultivates compound talents with both legal professional qualities and cross-cultural communication abilities. The research team emphasizes the sense of subjectivity, refines theoretical propositions around Chinese practice, and transforms practical experience into disciplinary and discourse systems. The incentive mechanism and translation ability building are promoted simultaneously to ensure the sustainable development and innovation ability of the talent team.

In summary, enhancing the international spreading capacity of Chinese rule of law discourse is a systematic project that requires a synergistic effect in six dimensions: significance recognition, strategy innovation, system construction, theoretical deepening, channel innovation, and talent cultivation. Through the "one break and one establishment" approach, it breaks the Western discourse dominance and constructs a communication system with Chinese characteristics; relies on academic research to deepen theoretical supply and innovate all-media communication forms; and finally achieves sustainable improvement of spreading capacity through a high-quality talent team. This path not only reflects the summary and refinement of China's practical experience in rule of law construction but also demonstrates a sense of responsibility for the development of global rule of law civilization, contributing Chinese wisdom and solutions to the construction of a community with a shared future for mankind. In the new era of digital and global integration, the improvement of Chinese rule of law discourse communication capacity will continuously promote the progress of international rule of law civilization, realize a strategic transformation from a rule-follower to a rule-maker, and finally engrave a distinct Chinese mark in the history of human rule of law civilization.

References

Pan, Y. (2013). Eliminating the "weakness" of soft power and spreading the vision of the "Chinese Dream": On the strategies for enhancing cultural communication ability in soft power construction. *Ethnic Art Studies, 6*, 15–20.

Sun, C. (2015). *Inter-cultural communication*. Peking University Press.

Xi, J. (2019, May 16). Deepen exchanges and mutual learning among civilizations and build an Asian community with a shared future. *People's Daily*.

Xi, J. (2020). *On upholding comprehensive law-based governance*. Central Literature Publishing House.

Xi, J. (2021, June 1). Strengthen and improve international communication work to present a true, multidimensional and comprehensive China. *People's Daily*.

Yin, L. (2024, August 22). Tell Chinese stories to the world and comprehensively improve the effectiveness of international communication (Targeted advice). *People's Daily*.

Zhang, Z. (2012). Enhancing academic discourse power and constructing China's discourse system. *Red Flag Manuscript*, 13.

Zhang, F., & Chen, Z. (2024). New thinking on the international communication of Chinese rule of law discourse in the new era. *International Communication, 1*, 54–57.

Zhang, F., & Sun, B. (2023). Legal translation: Past, present and future. *Journal of Beijing International Studies University, 5*, 17–32.

Zhang, M., & Zhou, Z. (2006). Build an irreplaceable communication ability. *Media, 9*, 12–14.

Index

X. Dong, M. Zhang, *Chinese Rule of Law Discourse System*, Understanding China, https://doi.org/10.1007/978-981-95-6260-2

MIX
Papier aus verantwortungsvollen Quellen
Paper from responsible sources
FSC® C105338

If you have any concerns about our products,
you can contact us on
ProductSafety@springernature.com

In case Publisher is established outside the EU,
the EU authorized representative is:
Springer Nature Customer Service Center GmbH
Europaplatz 3, 69115 Heidelberg, Germany

Printed by Libri Plureos GmbH
in Hamburg, Germany